D0202883

WESTERN CIVILIZATION

WESTERN CIVILIZATION

A Critical Guide
to Documentary Films

NEIL M. HEYMAN

GREENWOOD PRESS
Westport, Connecticut • London

Library of Congress Cataloging-in-Publication Data

Heyman, Neil M.
    Western civilization : a critical guide to documentary films /
    Neil M. Heyman
       p.   cm.
    Includes bibliographical references (p.   ) and index.
    ISBN 0–313–28438–5 (alk. paper)
    1. Civilization, Western—Film catalogs. 2. Documentary films—
    Reviews. I. Title.
    CB245.H45 1996
    909′.09812—dc20   95–35676

British Library Cataloguing in Publication Data is available.

Library of Congress Catalog Card Number: 95–35676
ISBN: 0–313–28438–5

First published in 1996

Greenwood Press, 88 Post Road West, Westport, CT 06881
An imprint of Greenwood Publishing Group, Inc.

Printed in the United States of America

The paper used in this book complies with the
Permanent Paper Standard issued by the National
Information Standards Organization (Z39.48–1984).

10 9 8 7 6 5 4 3 2 1

To my parents

CONTENTS

ACKNOWLEDGMENTS

I wish to offer my thanks to many individuals who aided me in this project. Danette Boots and Larry Lewis of the Audio-Visual Section, Department of Media Services, the San Diego County Office of Education, were cordial and helpful during my many visits. The staff of the Media Technology Services, San Diego State University, provided me with a wealth of assistance. I owe a particular debt of gratitude to three individuals there. Beda Johnson, now retired, provided crucial guidance in locating and ordering films at the early stages of this project. Jim Edwards has worked diligently and cheerfully to help me deal with projectors, video players, and a host of other issues. Rachel Litonjua-Witt has earned more thanks than I can readily express by her extraordinary competence with computers and her willingness to share that competence with me.

Two of my colleagues in the Department of History, San Diego State University, provided advice and encouragement. Professor Joanne Ferraro graciously shared her immense knowledge of early modern European history with me. Professor Paul Vanderwood has encouraged my interest in film for many years. He provided help in more ways than I can possibly enumerate. In addition, I wish to thank my editor, Cynthia Harris for her help and advice over a period of years.

I received exemplary service in ordering films from the audio-visual centers at Indiana University and Penn State University. Kent Ireland at Films for the Humanities & Sciences, Princeton, New Jersey, was gracious in providing examination copies of films for my use.

Finally, as always, my thanks go to Brenda, Mark, and David. My wife and my two sons have been supportive friends and companions in this long endeavor.

INTRODUCTION

The purpose of this book is to present useful and critical reviews of a significant number of historical documentaries. The reviews are intended primarily to aid instructors teaching courses in the History of Western Civilization. But they should also prove of assistance for those teaching in more specialized areas of European history.

The number of films available for rental from major film collections, either those affiliated with universities or those offered by free standing commercial organizations, is vast. The one hundred seventy-three films offered here were selected with several factors in mind.

These are films likely to attract the eye of an instructor teaching Western Civilization or related courses. Most of them are available at reasonable cost from at least one major rental organization, and many can be purchased outright at reasonable cost. I have found the vast majority of the films available for rental from audio-visual collections at the following institutions: Indiana University, Iowa State University, Kent State University, the University of Minnesota, and Penn State University.

The selection of films began with several widely used series that have been available for a long period of time. Kenneth Clark's <u>Civilization</u> series in thirteen episodes is the outstanding example. All episodes of this kind of production have been reviewed. Beyond such serial works, I have added individual titles that loom large in film catalogues. Some come from areas that are widely covered in documentary film; others come from areas where there are few titles. In each case, a primary criterion has been the likelihood an instructor would consider using such a film to aid his students' understanding of a given topic. Some of the films are too recent to be listed in current catalogues; these have been chosen because of their inherent interest and the great likelihood they will become available for rental in the immediate future. A few films of significant quality, e.g., <u>Good-bye Billy: America Goes to War, 1917-1918</u>, are not widely available. They are worth seeking out in local university and commercial collections.

This book seeks to make it possible to obtain the films reviewed with a minimum of difficulty. A review of film catalogues from the most important university and commercial rental collections makes it evident that information on the same film can vary considerably from one catalogue to another. The listing of each film in this volume starts with what the author has found to be the most characteristic listing of the film's title.There follows in parentheses an indication of the series, if any, of which the particular film is a part. The listing for each film gives an indication of its length.This must be considered approximate: not only are catalogue listings themselves approximate, they also vary from one catalogue to the other. Similarly, a date is given to indicate the copyright or release date of the film;here too catalogues provide variant information. Finally, the listing for each film gives either the producer or the distributor. The name in this category is given primarily for the purpose of readily identifying the film, and I have chosen the most characteristic and helpful designation.

The essential source for finding films is Educational Film & Video Locator, 4th edition (New York: R.R. Bowker, 1990). Also useful are The Video Source Book, 16th edition (Detroit: Gale Research, Inc., 1994), and Bowker's Complete Video Directory, 1992 (New Providence, N.J.: R.R. Bowker, 1992).

The individual reviews reflect the author's view of what an ideal documentary should be and what it should seek to accomplish. I believe that the ideal film should be clear and succinct. The attention span of present-day viewers is conditioned by television, by the films they see in commercial theaters, and, increasingly, by their use of computers. Leisurely and rambling films appropriate and effective in decades past are not likely to continue to be effective.

I believe that the ideal documentary film should use visual means-- whether work of art, archive film footage, visits to important historical locales, interviews with historical authorities or interviews with eyewitness participants in events--to show students aspects of historical events that cannot be presented verbally by even the most eloquent lecturer. I believe the ideal film should be accessible to students in a course without extensive introduction. I furthermore believe that an ideal documentary should remind students that there are differing interpretations of historical events. In its highest ideal a documentary film should serve to stimulate an active and useful discussion about historical issues.

To make the reviews as useful and accessible as possible, they follow a general format designed to present crucial information in a clear and consistent manner. Each review begins with a summary, or, better said, a summary judgement about its subject matter and quality. This comes in the form of a brief statement followed by a letter grade. There follows a discussion of the techniques and tools the film makers have employed and the basic theme--or themes--the film presents.

The bulk of the ensuing review discusses the film in terms of its organization. Since some films are most valuable when shown in part rather than in their entirety, most reviews have been arranged to indicate what topics are taken up in what order, how they are presented, and what the overall architecture of each film is. This is to allow instructors to present relevant portions of films they would not choose to show in their entirety.

Most reviews contain a specific statement of the film's strong and weak points. The omission of a discussion of strong points in a film will often follow directly upon a highly critical review. Less frequently, the omission of a discussion of weak points indicates the high esteem that a film evokes. Many reviews contain specific indications of how a film can be integrated into a course on Western Civilization, including some suggestions for drawing discussion materials from specific films.

The book employs the following set of general standards for evaluating films and assigning them a letter grade:

A - excellent film; highly useful for class; impressive historical qualities

B - good film; useful for class; significant historical qualities

C - mediocre film; limited possibility at best for use in class; likely to require extensive introduction; useful in presenting such factors as the physical setting of historical events

D - inferior film; contains major cinematic or historical flaws; avoid using this for class

Such grades reflect the following general questions with which I have approached all films:

To what extent does this film serve to illustrate an important historical topic, to heighten our understanding of it, and to stimulate discussion? Is the information it contains accurate?

To what extent does the film incorporate useful cinematic qualities: good photography, pacing, clarity?

To what extent does the film help a student to understand the physical setting in which events took place or to recapture the emotional atmosphere of a given time?

To what extent does the film require extensive commentary or introduction in order to be useful?

To what extent is the length of the film (and the "yield"/hour of information it provides) appropriate?

I have in many cases varied the pure letter grade in order to present a more nuanced judgement. The plus sign (+) indicates that the film in question is substantially superior to the specific standards indicated. Thus a film evaluated with a "B +" is more than merely good, useful, and reflective of good historical qualities, although it does not merit the grade of "A." Similarly, a minus (-) indicates that a film falls somewhat below the standard indicated by a specific letter grade, without, however, dropping to the next level.

The letter grades are intended as a useful shorthand for rapid evaluation, and several caveats are in order. The text of the review is intended to justify and explain such a blunt and direct letter-style judgement. It is also, however, designed to show how even films that are adjudged flawed as a whole can be used in part with considerable success.

In general, a grade of "B" or above indicates my overall enthusiasm for a given film. Also in general, a grade of "B -" or less reflects my judgement that a film should be used with caution or avoided entirely. Certainly that is the case with films that fall in the "D" category as individual reviews make clear.

The factual accuracy of most films is generally very good. Thus, it has not seemed necessary to make specific mention of this issue unless a particular film is deficient in this area.

WESTERN
CIVILIZATION

PRE-HISTORY

The Harvest of the Seasons
(The Ascent of Man series)

52 minutes   color
1974   BBC-TV

Summary: A lucid, slow paced description of human evolution from the stage of nomadic herdsmen to the era of settled agriculture

Grade: B

The film is an extended discussion by scientist Jacob Bronowski. Visits to important locales in the history of human development play a major part in this account. There are as well as several recently filmed sequences in Iran and Afghanistan showing how the practices of early nomadic communities continue to exist in the late twentieth century. Slow motion footage shows the growth of forms of plant life, and there are scenes illustrating twentieth-century warfare. The basic theme of the film is the way in which human groups made the spectacular leap from the life of nomadic herdsmen to become members of settled agricultural communities.

At the film's start, narrator Jacob Bronowski notes that the story of man's evolution from the close of the era of food gathering to the present covers a span of only twelve thousand years. Thus, by approximately 10,000 B.C., man had begun to domesticate animals and was on the verge of cultivating plants in a system of settled agriculture.

The first half of the film takes up an examination of the Bakhtiari nomads of Iran in the 1970s. Unlike the Lapps in Lower Than the Angels (q.v.), the Bakhtiari control their flocks of sheep and goats and direct them to fresh pasture throughout the year. Scenes of the nomads' winter and spring migration show the heroic mountain and river crossings they perform to maintain their herds. There follows a discussion of early agriculture in the Fertile Crescent of the Middle East: it includes a technical consideration of the development of crops like red wheat and scenes of Jericho, a typical community that developed in the early stage of agricultural settlement.

The second half of the film centers on the role that various animals played as mankind settled in farming villages. Draft animals promoted the growth of village life, but Bronowski emphasizes the wartime potential of the horse. A visit to brutal Buz Kashi mounted games in modern Afghanistan, in which hundreds of riders fight for possession of the body of a dead calf, shows a living relic of martial, mounted cultures like those of the Mongols of the thirteenth century. The film then presents scenes of World War II tank combat. Bronowski discusses how war as an organized institution arose from the conflict between desert nomads and settled farm communities with the latter's harvest surplus as a prize to be taken or defended.

The Harvest of the Seasons features fine photography and it is clear in describing this fundamental leap in the early development of human communities. Nonetheless, it is marred by a slow pace and an overly technical discussion of issues such as the evolution of crops.

Lower Than the Angels
(The Ascent of Man series)

52 minutes   color
1974   BBC-TV

Summary: A lucid and imaginative although slow paced examination of pre-historic man and his cultural evolution

Grade: B +

The film is an extended discussion by scientist Jacob Bronowski. He illustrates his presentation with historical artifacts, and there are demonstrations of human capabilities such as those shown by an infant and an athlete in today's world. There are also views of important locales in the history of early human development, and a visit to the Lapps of northern Scandinavia who still live much as our prehistoric ancestors did. The basic theme of the film is the ability of even pre-historic man to adjust to various environments and, with the help of his physical and mental capacities, to change those environments.

The film begins with Jacob Bronowski visiting the California coast. There the grunion run at the time of the full moon serves to illustrate the adaptive behavior of lower animals. Bronowski sets the theme of the entire The

Ascent of Man series by noting that such animals merely fit their individual environments. Man, with his reasoning ability and toughness, can fit into numerous environments and can also change his environment.

The first half of the film features a visit to the valley of the Omo River in Ethiopia, where scholars believe man first appeared and began his evolution. Bronowski discusses the skull of a child, five or six years old at its death. The skull has survived for two million years, and he shows how it demonstrates the appearance and capacities of early man. There follows an examination of the special characteristics of modern humans produced by evolution: a child of fourteen months stands, illustrating the human ability to walk upright; a pole vaulter's feat demonstrates the ability to plan and direct physical action in advance.

In the second half of the film Bronowski uses computer displays to show the evolution of the human head. Scenes of wildlife in present-day Africa serve a backdrop for a discussion of man's evolution into a hunter. According to Bronowski, this encouraged the organization of communities as well as the necessity to migrate to find a steady supply of animals to eat.

The film closes with two striking episodes. In the first Bronowski shows the Lapps, who continue to live in the extreme northern regions of Scandinavia. Their practice of following the migration of reindeer herds is a rare carry-over to the present of the lifestyle of early man. Secondly, Bronowski shows the cave paintings of Altamira, Spain. These animal images, twenty thousand years old, indicate to Bronowski that early man had developed the capacity to look ahead to future tasks and future dangers.

Lower Than the Angels features an imaginative and authoritative narration accompanied by a series of striking visual images. Bronowski is both clear and forceful in showing how early humans displayed and developed the capabilities that distinguished them from the animal world. The film proceeds, however, at a leisurely pace that makes it difficult to sustain a viewer's interest for its full length.

A People Is Born
(Heritage: Civilization and the Jews series)

60 minutes   color
1984   WNET

Summary: A lucid, well-organized, and brilliantly photographed treatment of the Ancient Middle East, the origins of the Jewish people, and the emergence of monotheism

Grade: B +

The film employs narrator Abba Eban, maps, models of ancient buildings, actors reading from the Bible and other important historical documents, and contemporary views of historical locales. One theme of the film is the diversity of the set of cultures and societies that stretched from the Nile Delta to Mesopotamia in the three millennia before the birth of Christ. The second theme is the story of how the Jewish people was formed, how they were distinguished from their neighbors, and how they accepted the concept of a single God under whose law they agreed to live.

The film begins by noting that, among the traditions of the Western World, the Jews and their beliefs form the only unbroken thread that stretches back for five thousand years. The narrator of the entire series, Abba Eban, describes the Jewish people and how the Jewish belief in a single god constituted a great leap for the human mind. He notes that this concept would eventually be shared by most of the world's religions.

The first half of the film describes the civilizations of the Ancient Middle East: Mesopotamia where cities first developed, the Canaanite settlements along the Red Sea, and Ancient Egypt with its prosperous and stable system of agriculture. Statues, figurines, and wall paintings show the religious traditions of these regions. Such works of art feature numerous gods who often represented the different forces of nature.

The treatment of Ancient Egypt leads to a discussion of the great building program of Pharaoh Ramses II. His employment of forced foreign labor for his projects, along with Egypt's military campaigns in Canaan against the Hittites, combined to bring Canaanites as exiles to Egypt. The liberation of those Canaanites from slavery and exile appears to mark the historical origins of the Jewish people.

The second half of the film traces the story of the Jews through their acceptance of God's law at Mount Sinai, and on to their union with economically depressed elements of the population that had remained in Canaan. It discusses the evolution of the Jewish community, from a loose federation of villages to a kingdom and then an empire under Saul, David, and Solomon.

The empire and its accompanying social tensions led to the corruption of Jewish life, a decline punished by conquest and exile to Babylon. The film concludes by discussing how Jewish scholars in Babylon composed the Torah, the first five books of the Bible, out of the ideas and stories passed down by Jewish tradition. For the Jews the Bible broadened the concept of monotheism into a belief that all mankind lived under a single god. Moreover, God ruled, not through whim, but through a moral law that mankind was obliged to know and obey.

Since the film serves as an introduction to the entire series, its first few minutes include a personal introduction by Aba Eban and extensive views of today's Jews in various cultural settings. It is brilliantly photographed, featuring remarkable aerial views of regions like the Sinai desert. Scenes of the present Middle East, including commercial traffic on the Nile and the life of Arab villagers, give a vivid illustration of how life may have been lived in ancient times. The narration is clear and accessible, even when dealing with the complex story of the early evolution of the Jewish people.

The first portion of the film can be used as a general introduction to the Ancient Middle East. The second half would be an ideal accompaniment to a consideration of the Mosaic Code.

The Power of the Word
(Heritage: Civilization and the Jews series)

60 minutes   color
1984   WNET

Summary: A complex examination of the evolution of the Jewish people and Judaism from the Babylonian Exile of the sixth century B.C. to the destruction of the Temple by the Romans in 70 A.D.; it stresses the interaction of the Jews with Greek and Roman civilization

Grade: B

The film employs narrator Abba Eban, maps, models of ancient buildings, actors reading from the Bible and other important historical documents, and contemporary views of historical locales and their inhabitants. One main theme of the film is the development of Jewish law, as embodied in the Torah, in Babylonian exile, and the way it subsequently helped preserve Jewish identity. A second theme is the relationship between Greek and Jewish traditions of learning, and the more painful relationship between Roman imperialism and unsuccessful Jewish rebellion.

The first third of the film begins by examining the Jewish experience in Babylonian exile. Narrator Abba Eban stresses the way in which Jewish laws and traditions were codified there in the form of the Torah. These Jews in exile also came to see their God as the universal God of all mankind.

Next Eban recounts the story of the Jews upon their return from Babylon, after being released from exile by the Persian king. The film continues to stress the way in which the written law provided a clear standard against which the individual could measure his personal conduct.

The remaining two-thirds of The Power of the Word begins by analyzing the complex relationship between the Jews and Greek civilization. The narration indicates how profoundly Jews in much of the Mediterranean world were influenced by the Greek language and Greek culture. This tie led to the vast Jewish presence in the Hellenistic center of Alexandria in Egypt, the Maccabee rebellion against Greek influence in Palestine, and the impact of Greek logic on the scholars of the Pharisee movement.

There follows an extended consideration of the Jewish experience from 100 B.C. onward in the Roman province of Judea. The film presents a picture of Judea as the site of vast construction under the Jewish puppet ruler Herod and the scene of political turbulence and ensuing Roman repression. Against the background of unrest and emerging Jewish leaders, the figure of Jesus appears is presented as one of numerous individuals whom the Romans executed as political troublemakers.

This account closes with the rebellion of 66 A.D. and its suppression, followed by the destruction of Jerusalem and dispersion of the Jews. The film's final point, however, is that even in the midst of this catastrophe Jewish life went on. Academies of scholars following the tradition of the Pharisees preserved Jewish scholarship and trained the first rabbis. Meanwhile, the creation of Jewish communities in exile (the Diaspora) meant that the Jewish message of a single god and single moral code could be transmitted to the rest of the world.

The film features spectacular photography ranging from scenes of the ruins of Babylon to the mountain fortresses like Masada that provided the base for Jewish resistance to outside conquest. It presents a unusual and valuable view of Greece and Rome from the outside, as seen by another Mediterranean people with a vastly different identity. Present-day scenes of Jewish daily customs and worship vividly indicate the singular identity of the Jewish population of the ancient world.

Its major weakness is the range and occasional complexity of the narration it tries to present. The profusion of Jewish groups and different tendencies within Judaism is unlikely to be clear or useful to most students.

The film's most valuable application may be as a counterpoint to the usual discussion of Greece and Rome. Students can be encouraged to consider the film as a discussion of how Greek values and Roman power affected other parts of the ancient world.

ANCIENT GREECE

Aristotle's Ethics, Book 1: The Theory of Happiness
(Humanities, Classical Greece series)

29 minutes   color
1962   Encyclopedia Britannica Educational Corporation

Summary: A lecture by philosopher Mortimer Adler on one of the key works of ancient philosophy; although static and verbose, the film illustrates the nature of ancient Greek thought

Grade: C -

      Much of the film consists of Adler speaking to the camera. However, there are animated episodes (using the images of Greek vase painting from the fifth century B.C.), and occasional shots of the Greek landscape. The chief theme of the film is the subtle and profound meaning Aristotle gives to the word "happiness."   Adler explores how the ancient philosopher deals with the important question of what makes a human life good and worth living.

      Adler begins by contrasting the two Athenian philosophers, Aristotle and Socrates. The latter had no interest in nature and willingly chose death over exile from his native Athens. Aristotle, on the other hand, devoted much of his efforts to thinking about the physical world; when threatened with violence, he quickly left the city.

      Adler explores Aristotle's view that happiness is attainable by humans only at the end of a life devoted to the long-term pleasures of work, achievement, and cooperation with others. He makes the important point that such views from Ancient Greece have come down to us through the classical education received by founders of the United States such as Thomas Jefferson.

Thus, in the Declaration of Independence, Jefferson follows Aristotle in counting "the pursuit of happiness" as one of mankind's "inalienable rights."

The film illustrates a crucial textbook generalization that often goes unexplained to students: the seminal role that Ancient Greece played in defining the issues and drawing the guidelines for the entirety of Western thought. Students will benefit from an introduction stressing how large Ancient Greece looms as a source of Western ideas. It will be helpful to note how other, more familiar concepts such as man's reasonable nature and the right to participate in government are links between our society and that of Ancient Greece. Unfortunately, the stodgy presentation, including the pompous style of the speaker, and the intricate nature of the ideas detract from the film's value.

Athens: The Golden Age
(Humanities, Classical Greece series)

30 minutes   color
1962   Encyclopedia Britannica Educational Corporation

Summary: A lucid but extremely elementary and unimaginative introduction to the achievements the Athenian city-state of the fifth century B.C.

Grade: C +

The film is an illustrated lecture by Professor Charles Kahn of Columbia University. Professor Kahn accompanies his discussion with views of surviving Greek buildings, friezes, and paintings. There are readings from Greek authors like Thucydides, a segment performed from the Orestaia and samples of the music of the time.

Kahn starts with a summary of the achievements of fifth century Athens that have come down as a legacy to the present day: in theater, philosophy, art, and government. There follows an examination of Greek sculpture, and the curiosity toward human nature that it reflected, as well as the picture of daily life shown in the paintings on Greek pottery.

The second half of the film consists largely of a dramatized segment from the Orestaia. It shows how the Greek concept of justice, as distinct from individual vengeance, developed. Finally, the film examines the Parthenon and describes the annual Panathenaea procession in which the entire population of the city mounted the Acropolis to visit the shrine of Athena.

The film indicates clearly the main features of the Athenian city-state and its culture. The segment on fifth-century pottery painting is particularly rich in illustrating the life of the time. Unfortunately, the narration by Professor Kahn is flat and uninspired, and much of the film does no more than to show him lecturing.   The elementary character of his presentation makes this documentary more appropriate for a level below that of a college course in Western Civilization. The dramatic segment from the Orestaia is poorly acted and unlikely to impress viewers with the key point it wishes to make. A superior alternative to this film is Greece: The Golden Age (q.v.).

Black Athena

52 minutes	color
1990	Bandung File, Channel 4

Summary: A brilliantly constructed and beautifully filmed treatment of the scholarly controversy aroused by the work of Martin Bernal over the possible African and Near Eastern origins of Greek civilization; a rare demonstration on film of the nature of scholarly inquiry and debate

Grade: A

The film centers on numerous interviews with Bernal, his supporters, and his critics, with a lively give and take among these authorities. There are views of Greek and non-Greek works of art, visits to important locales involved in the controversy, photographs, maps, and even a segment of rap music. The key theme is Bernal's view that our understanding of Greek history has been distorted since the end of the eighteenth century by Eurocentric and racist views. His work in areas such as linguistics leads him to stress the links between the Greeks and the civilizations of Egypt and the (Semitic) Phoenicians. A second theme is the way in which Bernal now stands midway between more traditional scholars of the Greek world and extreme proponents of Afrocentrism like Leonard Jeffries.

The film begins by noting the controversy stirred up by the publication of the first volume of Bernal's Black Athena in 1987 and the imminent appearance of the second volume. Against a background of tourists visiting the Acropolis, the narrator asks if we have reconstructed the Greek past to suit our own preconceptions.

Bernal describes the challenge his view presents to traditional scholarship concerning the Greek world. He notes that for the past two hundred years, European scholars have sought to show that Greek civilization and its products like democracy, science, and modern philosophy, originated and thrived only in Europe. Moreover, Greece itself allegedly grew only from European roots.

During the remainder of the film, Bernal and his critics such as Richard Jenkyns at Oxford vigorously disagree over aspects of his views. Bernal receives conventional academic support from a number of scholars, but his strongest endorsement comes in scenes in which Leonard Jeffries teaches a Black Studies class at the City College of New York. Jeffries insists, however, that Bernal's immersion in white culture limits his understanding of the fact that Egypt itself was a product of black Africa.

Some issues that the discussion raises include whether or not nineteenth-century scholarship on Greece was anti-Black and anti-Semitic , whether Bernal as a scholar with credentials in Near East studies is convincing in discussing Ancient Greece, whether Greek myths and writers such as Herodotus can be understood as providing evidence to support Bernal. A broader question is whether or not a society like Ancient Greece can suddenly produce an age of genius on its own, or whether that can happen only by cross fertilization with an outside culture.

Black Athena is lucid and stimulating in presenting the history of our understanding of Greece. It demonstrates how scholarly inquiry takes place and the often contentious way in which historians and other scholars draw different conclusions from the evidence available to them. The range of interviewees and the clarity with which they present their views is superlative. Moreover, despite the film's emphasis on ideas, it features striking views of both Greece and Egypt.

Students can be asked to consider who has the stronger case, as presented in the film, and what other evidence they think scholars need in order to resolve the controversy the film presents. They can also consider what other topics might cause historians to disagree so strongly, e.g., the origins of the Renaissance, the impact of World War II.

The Cave

10 minutes color
1973   Churchill Films

Summary: A brief but lucid and entertaining cartoon presenting the famous parable from Plato's Republic on the nature of reality and the responsibility of the philosopher

Grade: B -

The film consists of a cartoon accompanied by Orson Welles's narration. The basic theme of the film is the difficulty the average person has in understanding the true nature of the world around him. The individual with a liberated mind, i.e., the philosopher, is obligated to enlighten those who remain in the dark, even at the risk of becoming the target of their violent response.

At first, the cartoon shows individuals in a dungeon. Facing a wall, with chained bodies and immobilized heads, they can see only the shadows of real objects that have been placed behind them. A prisoner is released and brought into the sunlight. He is then dazzled and disoriented by the light and contact with real objects. But he moves on to understand reality, and to disdain the limited and inaccurate understanding of the world he had when he was still a prisoner. The parable shows that he has the duty to return to enlighten his former companions in the dungeon.

This presentation of a key idea of the ancient world is distinguished by its imagination and charm. Unfortunately, the film does not tie these ideas to the life of Socrates or the Greeks' roles as the pioneers of modern thought. The film's brevity makes it valuable as an introduction to its themes. Moreover, students can be asked how individuals with a radically new understanding of the world, from Galileo to Voltaire to Karl Marx have been treated by their societies.

The Classical Age
(The Greeks: A Journey through Space and Time series)

52 minutes   color
1980   BBC-TV

Summary: A diffuse, poorly paced, but occasionally interesting survey of Greek civilization from the Persian Wars at the start of the fifth century B.C. to the time of Plato

Grade: B -

The film uses two narrators, Christopher Burstall and Professor Kenneth Dover of Oxford, art and architecture of the time, maps, dramatized scenes from the Greek past, and views of contemporary Greek life. The basic theme of the film is the continuing link between the main features of Greek civilization and the present-day culture of the Western world.

The Classical Age film begins with a series of images from Greek life including actors playing the roles of Socrates and Thucydides. There follows a panoramic description of Greek geography and the history of Greece through the Persian Wars and the growing conflict between Athens and Sparta.

Under the guidance of classical scholar Kenneth Dover, the film then examines the crucial Athenian invasion of Sicily during the Peloponnesian War. Dover enlivens this portion of the film by an on the spot discussion of the siege of Syracuse harbor. He continues with an incisive examination of Thucydides, the participant in the Peloponnesian War who became the great historian of that event. Next Dover considers Plato's philosophy, illustrating the topic with a dramatic rendition of Socrates's trial for treason.

The last third of the film swings wildly from the rediscovery of the culture of Ancient Greece during the Italian Renaissance to a discussion of Athenian democracy. Dover reminds the viewer of the slave-based Athenian economy with a visit to one of the silver mines helped to provide the resources that enriched Athens. The film closes with another look at the writings of Thucydides, presented in a long dramatization showing Athenian leaders debating the fate of the captured city of Mytilene.

The first third of the film is lucid and accessible in surveying the Greek achievement. Even the duller and more badly organized later sections occasionally come alive. Nonetheless, most of the film lacks a coherent structure. The dramatizations are excessively lengthy, and the main points of Dover's discussions are buried in his own verbosity.

The Classical Ideal
(Art of the Western World series)

60 minutes   color
1989   WNET

Summary: A lucid examination of Ancient Greece, Rome, and early Christianity, and their significance for the present time; the film's concentration on the artistic developments of the time leads to extensive excursions into the technicalities of architecture

Grade: B

The Classical Ideal uses a narrator, the art of the time, scenes from the present, and mini-lectures by academic specialists in the ancient world.   The main theme of the film is how the civilization of the ancient Mediterranean world served as the starting point for Western art and culture. While noting the flaws of these societies, the film stresses the contrasting achievements of Greece and Rome.   Greece is presented as the home of western respect for the individual, where the growth of democracy and realistic artistic depictions of the individual coincided in time. Rome is seen as the heir and preserving agent of Greek culture, but also as a more potent state whose wealth and ambition was expressed in immense engineering and architectural achievements.

The film begins by exploring the theme set down by the poet Shelley: "We are all Greeks." It presents a panorama of scenes from European painting, views of European gardens, and visits to such classical American buildings as Thomas Jefferson's Monticello. The narrator notes the way in which members of Western society have constantly referred back to idealized image of the ancient world.

The first half of the film considers Ancient Greece and the Hellenistic era. The narrator notes that the Greek ideals of harmony, order, and freedom must be considered side by side with Greek slavery, imperialism, and sometimes murderous internal politics.   But the chief thread of this account is the development of a society that increasingly cherished the individual and his capacities. Its gods appeared in human form, beautiful male nudes were the basis for its statuary, its great buildings like the Parthenon were constructed to human scale. The section concludes by sketching the expansion of the Greek world under Alexander the Great, as well as the emotionally heightened art of the Hellenistic era.

The second half of the film presents the story of Rome, expanding from a small hill town in central Italy to become an empire. The narrator notes that Rome passed to our age the rich legacy of Greek culture, Christian belief, its own principles of government, as well as its huge engineering and architectural monuments. The buildings of Rome, including the spectacular Sanctuary of Fortune and the better known Coliseum and Pantheon, display both Roman wealth and technical expertise.

The arrival of Christianity and the way it blended with Roman civilization can be seen in the Christian imagery on the burial sarcophagus of a Roman official, converted to the new religion on his death bed. The Classical Ideal concludes by sketching the future synthesis of Classic, German, and Christian elements that will soon produce the civilization of the Early Middle Ages. The significant shift from Roman to Christian ideals, it notes, is the move from external achievement to moral fulfillment and personal salvation. Rome provided the former, but only Christianity offered citizens of the ancient world the latter.

The film is beautifully photographed, well-paced, and features a clear chronological narration. The contrast between Greece and Rome appears vividly by comparing the Greek Parthenon with the Roman Pantheon. Regrettably, the film gives only a skeletal discussion of the key events in the history of the ancient world. Even the brilliantly effective sarcophagus scene is not clearly located in time. Moreover, the brief lectures by academic experts on the art of the period vary in quality, some veering toward an excessive concentration on the technicalities of artistic development.

Students can be asked to consider precisely how the artistic and cultural legacy of Greek was transmitted to Rome: by soldiers, by travelers, by students? They can also be asked to speculate on why an influential Roman of the imperial period might be attracted to Christianity. The vast resources of Rome shown in this film can be compared with the resources of thirteenth-century Europe as seen in Cathedral (q.v.).

Greece: The Golden Age

29 minutes   color
1965   NBC

Summary: A crisply paced and vivid examination of Greece, stressing the role of Athens during the fifth century B.C.

Grade: A -

The film uses surviving works of art, visits to historical scenes such as the Plain of Marathon and the Temple of Apollo at Delphi, readings from the works of ancient authors, as well as a segment of Oedipus Rex presented by actors in the ancient amphitheater at Epidauras. The film encourages the viewer to look at key sites as the ancient Greeks did, e.g., by climbing up the ancient path to the Acropolis. The main theme of the film is the emergence of Greece as a brief, thriving civilization that has provided us with a rich legacy in art, literature, politics, and philosophy.

The film begins with a brief summary of Greek history from the Mycenaen age (1500-1150 B.C.) to the Greek defeat of Persia at the Battle of Marathon in 480 B.C. Next comes a consideration of the achievements of Greece in the years that followed, e.g. the Olympic Games, Greek sculpture. The remainder of the first half of the film focuses on the Acropolis, the hill at the center of Athens, and its great architectural monument, the Parthenon.

The second half takes up Greek religion. As in the visit to the Acropolis, the camera's eye takes the viewer along the path a Greek would have followed, this time in visiting the oracle at Delphi. The narration notes that we are the heirs of the Greeks in drama as well as in the visual arts. This point is illustrated in a brief scene from Sophocles's Oedipus Rex performed in the original Greek.

The film ends with a discussion of the fall of Greek civilization. The centerpiece of this segment is a reading of the funeral address given by Pericles over the Athenian dead in the first stages of the Peloponnesian war against Sparta. That speech contained the ideal of the Athenian citizen with his belief in democracy, equality, knowledge, and patriotism. There follows a brief sketch of the death of Socrates following Athens' defeat in the war.

Greece: The Golden Age features an eloquent and well constructed narration that presents the key achievements of fifth-century Greek civilization. The works of art are coordinated with the text in superlative fashion, and the readings from Greek authors are both lucid and powerful. The film's most significant flaw is its failure to mention the failings of the Greek city-state such as slavery, the subordinate role of women, and the lack of rights for those born outside any given community. Similarly, the focus on Athens partly distorts reality, notably in omitting consideration of the far different characteristics exhibited by Sparta.

Students will find it useful to consider how real the images of Greek art such as statues and friezes look to their own eyes. They can also be encouraged to discuss the film's omissions and whether or not the film ends up by presenting too positive a picture of Greece in this era.

The Greek Beginning
(The Greeks: A Journey through Space and Time series)

52 minutes   color
1980   BBC-TV

Summary: A sporadically interesting but poorly organized survey of Greek history and civilization that covers the period through the Peloponnesian War

Grade: C +

The film uses two narrators, Christopher Burstall and Professor Kenneth Dover of Oxford, maps, art and architecture of the time, dramatized scenes from the Greek past, and views of contemporary Greek life. The basic theme of the film is the continuing link between the main features of Greek civilization and the present-day culture of the Western world.

The film begins with a panorama of scenes from Greek civilization including surviving statues and buildings as well as present-day views of the Greek religious center at Delphi. Narrator Christopher Burstall describes his own fascination with the Greek world. With the aid of maps and scenes from key locales like Mycenae, he sketches Greek history from the migration of the Greeks' ancestors from Central Europe around 2000 B.C. down to the triumphs of Athens in the fifth century B.C. Burstall introduces Sir Oxford Professor Kenneth Dover who will serve as the scholarly expert and second narrator for the series. The film then jumps to a consideration of the Peloponnesian War and Dover's favorite Greek writer, the historian Thucydides. An actor reads from Thucydides's works, and present day scenes of the Sicilian port of Syracuse show where some of the great encounters of the war took place.

The second half of the film jumps backward in time to look at the Greeks' defeat of the Persian Empire at the start of the fifth century B.C. An actor playing the pioneer historian Herodotus presents his view of the war, while Burstall and Dover discuss the key naval encounter at Salamis from a small boat at that important historical locale. There are also present-day views of the battle fields at Marathon and Plataea.

The last portion of the film races through the last years of Greek history, noting how the Greek city-states were overrun from the outside, first by Philip of Macedon, then by the Romans. The Greek Beginning stresses the crucial question how ancient Greek civilization has helped to shape our own world. Its first half is a useful, lucid, and coherent introduction to Greek history. Even the disorganized second portion has memorable moments such as the discussion of the Battle of Salamis from a boat on the scene. On the whole, however, the film is diffuse and unchronological in a way that makes its historical yield notably low.

Greek Lyric Poetry
(Humanities series)

30 minutes   color
1962   Encyclopedia Britannica Educational Corporation

Summary: In examining an important Greek art form, the film focuses on questions of literary technique to the exclusion of broader questions about the direction and nature of classical Greek culture

Grade   D

The film is primarily a lecture delivered by Professor David Grene of the University of Chicago. It includes his recitation of several poems in the original Greek, as well as written English translations of the texts. Grene considers such literary elements as the musical quality of Greek lyric verse, the role of metaphor, and the way in which this poetry reflects individual emotions.
Grene examines works by Heraclitus, Sappho, Simonides, Pindar, and Aeschylus. The film concludes with a dramatized excerpt from Aeschylus. Unfortunately, there is only a tenuous connection at best between a historical consideration of Ancient Greece and its culture and the issues raised by the film. The film is static and unengaging.

Greek Sculpture

25 minutes   color
1961   McGraw-Hill Films

Summary: An examination of the evolution of a key feature of Greek visual art over a period of nearly two thousand years, stressing the techniques used by sculptors and the way in which sculpture reflected changes in Greek culture

Grade: C +

The film features a narration by actor Leo Genn, numerous examples of Greek sculpture, and scenes of sculptor Henry Moore illustrating the techniques used by his predecessors in Ancient Greece. One theme is the visual power of this Greek art form. Another theme is the growing realism and visible humanity in the later examples of Greek sculpture as a reflection an increasing individualism in Greek culture.
The film tells the same story twice. First, a narration, interrupted by scenes showing the hands of sculptor Henry Moore at work, describes Greek art

evolving from the small, stiff statues contained in graves in the Cycladic period (3000-1500 B.C.) to the vital masterpieces of Athens in the fifth century. The final quarter of the film recapitulates the story in silence, using a series of statues to remind the viewer of the transformation in statuary that has taken place between 3000 B.C. and 300 B.C.

The film provides a clear picture of how Greek sculpture changed over time, and it suggests that such artistic changes must be understood against the background of cultural and intellectual evolution in the Greek community. The individual works of art are photographed with skill. At the same time, the film gives only a sketchy outline of key events affecting Greek civilization. The narration contains no indication of important political changes and gives only brief discussion of Greek religion. At several points, as for example when it describes how Greek "sculpture spoke to men and gods," the narration becomes hopelessly murky.

The Greeks: In Search of Meaning
(Western Civilization: Majesty and Madness series)

26 minutes   color
1971   Learning Corporation of America

Summary: A crisp, clear, but verbose presentation of Greek civilization in the golden age of fifth-century Athens centering on the teachings of Socrates

Grade: B

The film employs a narrator, selections from several Greek plays, and views of Greek sculpture. But the bulk of the film consists of scenes in which actors play the roles of the teacher Socrates and several of his students. The basic theme of the film is the Greek fascination with man's nature, the value of human reason, and Socrates's dedication to free inquiry.

The film begins by showing the teacher Socrates with a small group of students considering such issues as the value of wisdom. Describing the scene, the narrator notes that Athens in the fifth century B.C. saw the rise of reason as a tool for investigating the world and cherished the freedom of the mind.

Following the titles, the narrator describes Athenian democracy's achievements and imperfections. Showing the Greeks' intense interest in political values, Socrates and his student Criton consider the value of democracy and the danger to society of uncontrolled liberty.

The film continues with a lengthy selection from Sophocles's Antigone to show how Greeks wrestled with the equally difficult issue of human law and its conflict with the demands morality places on the individual. A second extensive dramatic excerpt, this time from the comedy Lysistrata, shows how the playwright Aristophanes criticized the Peloponnesian War between Athens and Sparta by depicting Athenian women in revolt against their city's male dominated government.

The film moves to a close by showing Socrates and his students facing his death sentence in an Athens defeated in the war by Sparta. Socrates dies serenely, declaring his satisfaction in having obeyed divine orders to practice his craft as philosopher and social critic. The narrator concludes the film by noting how a victorious Rome conquered Greece and spread Greek ideas, making them a part of our present-day intellectual legacy.

The Greeks is lucid and well-acted. It presents, in effective form, many of the most significant cultural themes of Greece in its golden age. Nonetheless, the film is dominated to a fault by conversation among the actors playing Socrates and his students. This talky quality and the lengthy dramatic excerpts deprive the film of any visual impact.

The narrator notes how the problems of Ancient Greece, notwithstanding its obvious distance from present-day Western society, are similar to our own. Students can be asked to consider the truth of such a contention.

Heinrich Schliemann: The Rediscovery of Troy

26 minutes   color
1990   Films for the Humanities & Sciences

Summary: An entertaining but unfocused account of the life of the German businessman and pioneer archeologist and his passionate search for the treasures of ancient Greek civilization

Grade: C -

The film employs a narrator, portraits and photographs, maps, visits to historical locales of importance in Schliemann's life and excavations, as well as some of the artifacts he found and brought back to Germany. The basic theme of the film is the story of a young German at the start of nineteenth century who developed and fulfilled a passionate desire to find the city immortalized in Homer's Iliad. Other themes include the way in which the rough techniques used by Schliemann caused damage to the structures he excavated and the destruction and disappearance of much of what Schliemann found during the course of World War II .

The film begins by showing the tomb in present-day Athens where Schliemann and his Greek wife are buried. It then follows the story of Schliemann's boyhood and business career, showing present scenes of the Mecklenburg villages where he grew up, was educated, and started to work.

The second half of the film follows the story of Schliemann's second career. A millionaire as a result of business dealings in Russia and America, he turned to archeology with spectacular success. Schliemann found the site of ancient Troy, then excavated the treasures of Mycenae on the Greek mainland, and then returned to work again at Troy. The film concludes in late twentieth-century Berlin. The director of the museum in which Schliemann's finds were held until World War II describes the loss of many of the objects Schliemann brought to light at the close of the Second World War.

The film introduces an important figure in the study of Ancient Greece in the person of this remarkable businessman, linguist, and early archeologist. Unfortunately, the account wavers between a consideration of Schliemann's life and the discoveries he made. It fails to delve into either topic in a consistent and informative way. The treatment of Schliemann's childhood replete with visits to his home and the church where his father was a pastor is a lengthy and cumbersome segment at the start of the film. In the end the film tells us only a fragment of what a history student would want to know about nineteenth-century German life, the early efforts of archaeologists, or the relics of the world of Ancient Greece.

Heroes and Men
(The Greeks: A Journey through Space and Time series)

52 minutes   color
1980   BBC-TV

Summary: A muddled and poorly paced discussion of Greek culture stressing the epics of Homer and the plays of Aeschylus

Grade: C -

The film uses two narrators, Christopher Burstall and Professor Kenneth Dover of Oxford, works of art and architecture of the time, maps, and dramatized scenes from the works of Homer and Aeschylus. There is also a set of scenes from the recent English schoolboy production, Helen Come Home, a spoof of the Iliad. The basic theme of the film is how the rich tradition of Greek literature, founded by Homer and augmented by the dramatists of the fifth century B.C., continues to influence the culture of our day.

The film begins with a panorama of works of art from the Greek past and a visit to the Parthenon. The first half of the film features Kenneth Dover's discussion of Homer's Odyssey and Iliad and a consideration of Greek religion. The second half of the film stresses the dramatic achievements of Aeschylus, with extensive scenes enacted from the Orestaia.

Notwithstanding its clear purpose, <u>Heroes and Men</u> is marred by incoherent execution. The main interpretative points Dover tries to make are hard to discern, and whatever structure the film has is repeatedly disrupted by marginal elements such as the scenes from <u>Helen Come Home</u>.

<u>Minds of Men</u>
(<u>The Greeks: A Journey through Space and Time</u> series)

52 minutes   color
1980   BBC-TV

Summary: A diffuse and poorly paced examination of Greek culture stressing the Greek role as pioneers of Western scientific thought

Grade: C

The film uses two narrators, Christopher Burstall and Professor Kenneth Dover of Oxford, maps, art and architecture of the time, dramatized scenes from the Greek past, and an excerpt from <u>The Clouds</u> by Aristophanes. The basic theme of the film is the continuing link between the main features of Greek civilization and the present-day culture of the Western world.

The film begins with an actor playing the role of Anaximander, pondering the nature of the physical world. The theme of early Greek scientific achievement disappears, however, as the film moves into a consideration of the writing of Thucydides on the Peloponnesian War. There follows a discussion of the unifying force of the Greek language and religion in tying together this politically diverse people.

The film drifts into issues such as Homer's view of the gods and the speculation of Anaximander on the evolution of life forms. A segment from <u>The Clouds</u> shows the humorous side of Greek culture as Aristophanes satirizes the devoted scientists of his day. The second half of the films dispenses with any pretense at structure, jumping from a dramatization of Socrates at work in teaching the young to Herodotus speculating about the course of history.

As in other episodes of this series, the film raises important issues only to leave the viewer confused and frustrated by a shapeless, overlong, and verbose production.

<u>The Power of the Word</u>
(<u>Heritage: Civilization and the Jews</u> series)

See review under PRE-HISTORY

ANCIENT ROME

Buried Cities: Pompeii and Herculaneum

13 minutes   color
1962   International Film Bureau

Summary: An informative, although uninspired view of the physical world and lifestyle of the ancient Romans as seen in two cities buried by the eruption of Mount Vesuvius in 79 A.D.

Grade: B -

The film consists of a narration accompanied by extensive scenes from the recently excavated sites of two Roman cities located near present-day Naples. The basic theme of the film is how the eruption of Mount Vesuvius in 79 A.D. has given us access to two well-preserved Roman communities.

The film begins with street scenes from modern Naples as the narrator notes that this city rests near an active volcano. Views of the smoking crater of Mount Vesuvius lead to description of how that volcano erupted with devastating force at the close of the first century A.D.

The remainder of the film consists of an extended visit to excavated portions of Pompeii, which was largely buried by lava from the volcano, and to the smaller community of Herculaneum, which was completely covered as a result of the eruption. Eerie scenes preserved from the past include public monuments, religious shrines, and amphitheaters, along with bakeries, election graffii, and private homes.

Despite a stodgy narration and film footage obviously dating back to the 1950s, the film gives a clear picture of many physical features of Roman life. Even the flat tone of the narrator does not detract from the emotional impact of visiting these haunted ruins. The brevity of the film makes it easy to incorporate into a classroom discussion of Roman lifestyles.

The Classical Ideal
(Art of the Western World series)

See review under ANCIENT GREECE

Emperor and Slave: The Philosophy of Roman Stoicism
(Humanities, Classical Civilization series)

28 minutes   color
1965   Encyclopedia Britannica Educational Corporation

Summary: A presentation of the important Roman idea of Stoicism discussed by philosopher Mortimer Adler; more skillfully made and entertaining than the parallel work on Greek thought in Aristotle's Ethics (q.v.) the film has a low yield of significant information concerning Rome relative to its length and complexity

Grade: C -

Emperor and Slave is in part a lecture by Professor Adler, but much of its length consists of dramatized readings by actors playing two great Roman philosophers, the emperor Marcus Aurelius and the slave Epictetus. Each of them, believers in Stoicism, discusses its concepts. Cinematic techniques include the static device of putting printed excerpts of philosophical writing on the screen with voice-overs, but there are also good scenes of Roman buildings and roads as well as memorable views of Hadrian's country villa.

The basic theme of the film is an exposition of the concepts of Stoicism, an unofficial but influential philosophy in Ancient Rome. An accompanying theme is the way in which Stoicism exemplifies the numerous elements which modern society has inherited from the Roman era.

The film begins with engrossing scenes of Hadrian's villa as Adler introduces the two protagonists of the story. The early portion of the film also sketches the Roman achievement in engineering, law, and government. It notes how in the latter two fields the Romans took original Greek concepts and put them into the form of impressive practical institutions.

There follows a set of scenes in which the Emperor Marcus Aurelius, the slave Epictetus, and the teacher Mortimer Adler discuss Stoicism. They note its stress on the individual's need to control his desires, to use his will in determining how to respond to actions from the outside world, to be self-reliant, and to do one's duty. It is our reason, Stoicism tells us, that separates us from the beasts around us, and our use of reason keeps us from being beasts ourselves.

In the closing minutes of the film Adler attempts to tie this philosophy, which aims at shaping the individual, to the Roman achievement in law and government. He describes how Marcus Aurelius found in Stoicism an argument for the unity of mankind. He tries specifically to link stoicism to declarations by the newly formed United Nations on human equality.

The film is relatively fast paced and the good acting of its two characters helps to present Stoicism's ideas forcefully. Some students may find the tenets of Stoicism interesting as guidelines for living. Few students, however, are likely to find any justification in the film for Adler's contention that Stoicism was a significant element in the history of Rome. Moreover, the effort to link Stoicism, as articulated by Marcus Aurelius, with present day concepts of universal links among all peoples or the brotherhood of all men is singularly unclear. In all, the film scarcely offers enough of an insight into Roman civilization to justify its length.

Life in Ancient Rome

16 minutes   color
1964   Encyclopedia Britannica Educational Corporation

Summary: A brisk but simplistic overview of Roman life during the reign of the Emperor Trajan; touching on the basic themes of Roman history, the film is marred by poor photography and a wide-ranging and bland narration

Grade: C +

The film uses a narrator, numerous scenes taken from the movie The Fall of the Roman Empire, a briefly shown cartoon map, and present-day views of Roman ruins. Focusing on the city of Rome, the basic theme of Life in Ancient Rome is the contrast between the splendor of Rome in the year 106 A.D. and the underlying weaknesses of the system.

The film covers a multitude of topics in rapid fire fashion. Beginning with scenes showing the return of a victorious Roman army from the Balkans, it shifts quickly to a map illustrating the extent of the Roman Empire and then moves to consider such topics as the role of the emperor, the lifestyles of the wealthy, public assistance for the Roman population, and the nature of Roman slavery. In equally cursory fashion, there are brief discussions of the decline in traditional religion, the role of the public baths, and Rome's architectural and engineering feats.

Life of Ancient Rome manages to touch upon and illustrate most of the key issues of Roman life at a particular moment--the year 106 A.D.--during the imperial period. Nonetheless, the film's brevity makes anything more than a brief enumeration of those issues impossible. The photography, whether of crowd scenes or of individual Romans in their daily activities, is mediocre at best. The narration is equally flat and uninteresting.

The Power of the Word
(Heritage: Civilization and the Jews series)

See review under PRE-HISTORY

The Roman World

22 minutes   color
1963   International Film Bureau

Summary: A beautifully photographed, crisply edited examination of Roman civilization stressing the geographical extent of the Roman Empire as seen in surviving architectural monuments; the narration is directed at an audience below the college level

Grade: B

        The film features a narrator, maps, and scale models, but the centerpiece is a series of film visits to present-day locales from Scotland to the Middle East where there are extensive Roman ruins. The basic theme is the way in which a visitor to modern Europe, North Africa, and the Middle East can explore the extent of the Roman Empire in the contemporary world: surviving roads, aqueducts, temples, and fortresses.
        The Roman World begins with a brief description of the Roman era, showing models of the city of Rome, excavations of smaller Roman towns, and surviving buildings and monuments within Rome. The bulk of the film takes the viewer over the full extent of the Roman world. At the first the tour follows the Roman road system, much of which still exists, to the eastern sea coast and the Alpine valleys of Italy, to France and western Germany, and on to Spain, Britain, and finally the Danube valley.
        The second half ranges farther afield. Noting Rome's links by caravan with India and China and much of Africa, the film makers use aerial views to show the shape of Roman roads of North Africa, and descend to earth to look at the ruins of Leptis Magna (in present-day Libya), the surviving aqueduct of the city of Carthage (in present-day Tunisia), and Hadrian's Temple on the Nile.
        From the ruins of the walls that once surrounded Constantinople (now Istanbul), the film moves to the outward limits of the Roman Empire: Damascus

and especially the oasis of Palmyra in the Syrian desert, where the much of the old Roman trading center still exists.

The film's ability to show the extent of the Empire and, through examining existing ruins, to show the ambition and building prowess of the Romans is noteworthy. Nonetheless, the narration proceeds at an elementary level in sharp contrast to the sophistication of the photography and the overall structure of the film. The chipper tone of the narrator sometimes makes a striking contrast with the eerie splendor of the surviving Roman structures the film shows.

The Spirit of Rome
(Humanities, Classical Civilization series)

30 minutes   color
1964   Encyclopedia Britannica Educational Corporation

Summary: A rich, vivid, and imaginative examination of Roman civilization emphasizing the period from the founding of the city through the reign of the Emperor Augustus

Grade: B +

The film uses the surviving architecture and art of Ancient Rome, dramatic scenes by George Bernard Shaw and William Shakespeare, and selections from Roman and later European literature. Animated maps are also employed to show the expansion of Rome from a minor city to an empire stretched over three continents. A key theme of the film is the transformation of Rome: from a somber community whose citizens gloried in their patriotism and self-sacrifice to an expanding state facing the pressures of wealth and luxury on the one hand, and ambitious political entrepreneurs on the other. The film also considers Rome's dual role as military conqueror and law-giver to many of its neighboring societies.

The film begins with a flourish, showing the submerged ruins of once thriving Roman cities in Asia Minor. Other scenes of surviving Roman statuary and columns combine with the words of sixteenth-century poet Edmund Spenser to illustrate the fascination Rome had for Europeans of a later era. This first segment of the film includes a scene from Shaw's Caesar and Cleopatra, in which a loquacious Caesar discusses Rome's military strength and its relationship to its growing empire.

There follows a consideration of the dual achievements of Greece and Rome centered on the analysis of G.W.F. Hegel: Greece represented the youth and joy of a creative society, Rome the somber strength of a great state. The remainder of the first half of the film gives a synopsis of Roman history from the legendary founding of Rome to the first century B.C.

The second half of the film examines the transition to an imperial system. The works of Sallust and Cicero as well as memorable portrait busts from this era show the troubled feelings of Romans during this painful shift in the basis ft the state. The main character in the transition, Julius Caesar's ambitious and ruthless nephew Octavius, the future emperor Augustus, appears in various forms: in a scene from Shakespeare's Julius Caesar, in the writings of Plutarch, in his own words, and in the art of the time. The film ends with a brief consideration of the emperors after Augustus ranging from the demented Caligula to the warrior-philosopher, Marcus Aurelius.

The Spirit of Rome is consistently colorful and engrossing. It manages to be both lucid but imaginatively structured: the dramatic underwater prelude leads easily, for example, into a consideration of Rome's continuing influence. The literary selections appear in a forceful manner and make their points with great effect, as in the example of Hegel's distinction between the Greek and Roman achievement. The overall chronology of Roman history is also readily available for the viewer. The dramatic scenes from Shaw and Shakespeare feature skilled acting.

On the other hand, some historians will contest the film's emphatic view that, in the realm of culture, Rome was little more than the wealthy conqueror who swept up the treasurers of a superior Greece. Its treatment of the "bad emperors" such as Caligula is cursory, and the discussion of Marcus Aurelius ends in a jarring and abrupt fashion.

Students can be asked to put themselves in the position of a Roman citizen during the era of Julius or Augustus Caesar and asked the most pressing question: how does an individual respond to such a dramatic lurch away from an established political order?

CHRISTIANITY AND JUDAISM

The Christian Empire
(The Christians series)

39 minutes   color
1976   Granada

Summary: A slow moving, occasionally opaque examination of the development of Eastern Orthodox Christianity and monasticism in the eastern Mediterranean after 300 A.D.

Grade: C +

The film uses a narrator, maps, works of art and buildings of the time, and visits to contemporary sites of Christian devotion such as the monastic communities of central Greece and Ethiopia. One basic theme of the film is the development in Eastern Orthodox Christianity of a link between church and state resulting in the supremacy of political leaders over religious organization. A second theme is the emergence within eastern Christianity of a tradition of hermits and austere monastic communities.

The Christian Empire begins by noting the intimate ties between church and state in Eastern Orthodox Europe. The first major portion of the film illustrates this tie in the development of the Byzantine Empire after 300 A.D. It shows that here Christianity first emerged as a state religion. Views of the churches of Ravenna in Italy demonstrate how works of art indicated the subordination of the Church to political leaders. In contrast the story of Bishop Ambrose of Milan, who chastised the Emperor Theodosius, shows the rival tradition in Western Europe of a church critical of political leaders.

The remainder of the first half of the film focuses on the emerging problem of heresy. Divisive issues like the nature of the Trinity combined with the vast geographic extent of the Roman Empire to make complete unity of religious belief impossible. Byzantine emperors, worried that religious disunity would promote political disunity, promoted the creation of a body of orthodox views to which all would have to adhere.

The second half of the film jumps to Moscow to discuss how Eastern Orthodoxy reached Russia at the close of the tenth century. It then leaps back to the fourth century A.D. to consider why individuals like St. Anthony chose to seek religious consolation in a hermit's life in the Egyptian desert. The film concludes with extensive views of austere monastic communities, which date from these first centuries of Christianity. They can be found in Ethiopia and central Greece.

The film deals with topics that historical documentaries seldom examine: the origins and development of the Byzantine Empire and the emergence of Eastern Orthodox Christianity. Taking the viewer from Greece to Russia, Egypt, and Ethiopia, it emphasizes the vast geographic extent of a Christian tradition that extends back to Byzantium. But The Christian Empire is marred by muddled chronology. It treats a number of issues in murky fashion: the debate over nature of the Trinity, the way in which Christian religious leaders stepped into a new political role after the Turks conquered Constantinople, the historic relation between church and state in Russia. The political division of the Roman Empire under Constantine is crucial in the development of an Eastern Orthodox form of Christianity, but the film makes no mention of it. A number of topics are treated with confusing brevity: the fall of Constantinople to the Turks, the relationship of the Patriarch of Russia to political authority before and after the Communist Revolution of 1917. The section on Ethiopian monasticism is particularly slow moving.

A Peculiar People
(The Christians series)

41 minutes   color
1976   Granada

Summary: A lucid and informative survey of the development of the Christian religion from its origins to the conversion of the Roman Emperor Constantine at the start of the fourth century

Grade: B

The film employs a narrator, maps, actors reading passages from key works of the time, and contemporary views of important historic locales. The basic theme of the film is the novelty and attraction of the Christian message: namely, God as a human being who suffered and died a gruesome death. A second theme is the immense energy and effectiveness that St. Paul brought to the role of a missionary spreading the new faith.

The film begins with an extensive prelude stressing the size and diversity of today's Christian population. It notes as well as the great influence Christianity has had the formation of the modern world. Scenes from Christian communities as far removed from one another as Ethiopia, Luxembourg, and Mexico provide a preview of future episodes in the series.

The first half of the film describes the desert community along the eastern shore of the Mediterranean in which the new religion took shape. It features present-day views of the Sea of Galilee, the site of the Sermon on the Mount, and shows people living in the style of their ancestors two thousand years ago. The narration, accompanied by paintings of important New Testament scenes, retells the story of Jesus's adult life. It notes the era's political factors: the reputation of Galilee among Roman authorities as a center for terrorist activities, and the Roman authorities' practice of executing any agitator they found emerging there.

The film makes the important point that other religions, such as Judaism, featured a distant and awesome God. Thus, Christianity with its view of God as a human being, near at hand, and destined for a barbarous, degrading death, was unique. A Peculiar People illustrates the Resurrection with a remarkable present-day ceremony. In it the Greek Orthodox Patriarch of Jerusalem enters the Holy Sepulchre and emerges with flaming torches symbolizing the renewed life of Jesus.

The second half of the film focuses on the career of Saul of Tarsus, soon to be renamed Paul. Present-day scenes of ultra-Orthodox Jews vividly show the community in which Saul had his origins. Scenes of Damascus show the streets in which he encountered the Christian community he intended to obliterate.

Quotations from Paul's writings illustrate the power of his message. Maps indicate his vast travels and the energy he brought to its dissemination the word of Jesus. The film goes on to show Rome, the imperial center where both Paul and Peter were made martyrs to the new faith. Evidence of Christian communities in Pompeii (destroyed by a volcanic eruption in 79 A.D.) show how rapidly Christianity spread to the Italian peninsula.

The film concludes by noting the vast range of religious beliefs Roman authorities collected from their empire, e.g., the cult of Priapus, mystery cults, the religions of Mithra and Sol. In 313 A.D., it probably seemed that Emperor Constantine, in adopting Christianity in the midst of his struggle for the throne, was merely choosing one of these exotic faiths.

The film effectively indicates both the novelty of early Christian belief and the speed with which it spread. Contemporary views ranging from the terrain of Palestine to the Roman catacombs brings cliched episodes to life. The narration makes it easy to understand why Roman authorities would view the new faith, with its communion ceremony hinting at the practice of cannibalism, with considerable alarm.

The film's principal weakness is the prolonged introduction, which also serves as an introduction to the entire series. It detracts from the force and pace of the overall narration.

A Peculiar People could be shown in conjunction with The Shaping of Traditions which takes an alternate approach. It stresses the extended period in which Christianity can be considered one among many Jewish sects.

The Shaping of Traditions
(Heritage: Civilization and the Jews series)

60 minutes   color
1984   WNET

Summary: An examination of the history of the Jews from the peak of the Roman Empire to the early Middle Ages emphasizing the Jewish role in the basic developments in Western Civilization and Islam over this period

Grade: B -

The film employs narrator Abba Eban, maps, models of ancient buildings, actors reading from important historical documents, and contemporary views of historical locales and their present-day inhabitants. One theme of the film is the vast religious upheaval of the time that transformed the Mediterranean and European world hitherto dominated by the Roman Empire. This upheaval included the foundation of Christianity and Islam, as well as the continuing role of Judaism. A second theme is the set of changes brought about among Jews in this era. These included the crushing of Jewish rebellions in Roman Judea and the destruction of the Jewish temple at Jerusalem, the emergence of a Jewish faith preserved by teachers known as rabbis, and the concentration of the world's Jews in the Islamic world.

The Shaping of Traditions begins by describing the Mediterranean world of the first century A.D. The power of the Roman Empire dominated the times, and Jews were already scattered in a wide ranging "diaspora." A visit to a two thousand year-old synagogue in Tunisia shows the form of worship practiced at that time. The film goes on to describe the spread of both conventional Judaism and its offshoot Christianity in the Roman world. Key events in the process were St. Paul's success in opening Christianity to non-Jews and the first destruction of the temple at Jerusalem in 70 A.D. Viewing Christianity from a Jewish perspective, the narration describes the bitter quarrels between the two religions over whether or not the Messiah had come and whether or not Jewish law and daily ritual should be preserved.

The remainder of the first half of the film takes up the second and final destruction of the temple at Jerusalem in 135 A.D. and the compilation of Jewish writings into the Mishna, which linked together Jews in the Diaspora. It also considers the turmoil in the Roman world during the third century.

The second half of the film traces the rise of Christianity as the official religion of the Roman Empire, the split of the Empire, and the rising authority of the papacy as the religious authority in the West. The film concludes with a consideration of the spread of Islam and the new role Jews now undertook as merchants linking the Moslem and Christian worlds.

The film offers a lucid description of the decline of the Roman Empire, and its transformation into two halves: a brilliant state centered at Byzantium and a more primitive system, racked by barbarian invasions, in the West. The photography is often spectacular, featuring eerie scenes of Roman ruins in the desert and the excavated remnants of synagogues from the ancient world. The aerial views of the Holy Land are equally gripping. The film makes the important point that Christianity was an offshoot of Judaism that only gradually achieved its separate identity.

Unfortunately The Shaping of Traditions shifts its focus continuously and abruptly. Thus it moves from the larger events influencing the Mediterranean world to the narrower perspective of changes within the Jewish community. Moreover, the vast extent of the Diaspora makes it difficult to consider many aspects of the Jewish experience.

Students can be asked to use the Jews as an example of how the vast events overturning so much of the Mediterranean world affected one relatively powerless group within this area.

EARLY MIDDLE AGES

The Birth of Europe
(The Christians series)

42 minutes   color
1976   Granada

Summary: A complex, detailed, but occasionally gripping account of Western Europe from the collapse of the Roman Empire in the fifth century to the start of the High Middle Ages six hundred years later

Grade: B

      The film employs a narrator, maps, the art, buildings, and monuments of the time, and present-day views of key historical locales. One theme of the film is the way in which western Christianity survived during the dark ages in both Ireland and Italy, centers from which Christian influence went on to spread. A second theme is the role of Charlemagne in establishing and expanding a vast empire, linked to the Catholic church, in Western and Central Europe.

      The Birth of Europe begins with a menacing torchlight parade. It is a preview of the barbarian invasions that would torment Western Europe for more than six centuries. The power of the Roman Empire is shown by visits to Hadrian's Wall in northern England and the Roman imperial capital at Trier in western Germany. The narrator notes how that Empire came to be seen by Christians as a key factor in God's plan for the spread of their religion.

      A visit to the islands off the coast of western Ireland shows where the hardy remnants of the Catholic church survived the barbarian invasion. From here Irish missionaries like St. Columbine helped restore Christianity in England and Western Europe, penetrating as far as Italy. At the same time Italian missionaries moved northward. A later surge of missionary activity centered around the Englishman, St. Boniface, who took the gospel to Holland and Germany.

The second half of the film shows how Charlemagne used forcible conversion to carry the Christian religion across the Rhine. Charlemagne's military power and ambitions to convert the heathen can be seen in the surviving Baptistery he built near the modern Dutch city of Nijmegen. Allied with the papacy and crowned Holy Roman Emperor, Charlemagne used this structure and the vast Byzantine-style church he built stands in the German city of Aachen to demonstrate his power and ambition.

The film reaches a climax in describing the Viking raids from Scandinavia that devastated Western Europe after Charlemagne's death. The torchlight parade in the first scene of the film turns out to be the yearly performance of a Viking fire ceremony still held in the Shetland Islands. Each winter it commemorates the coming of the Norse raiders. The influence of Christianity on the Vikings appears in scenes of churches established in Scandinavia as the Norsemen were brought into the Christian fold.

The film concludes with a description of the network of monasteries that stretched across Western Europe by the eleventh century. Their links to Rome provided the pope with a framework to influence political leaders everywhere.

The film is lucid and vivid in describing such factors as the survival of the Irish church and the coming of the Vikings. Students will benefit in particular from the film's account of Christian missionaries and the conversion of Northern Europe, an important but often neglected topic. The commemoration of the Viking raid and a half pagan half Christian ceremony still performed in Luxembourg are engrossing.

Unfortunately, the narration suffers from excessive detail or a lack of clarity at several points, notably in describing the origins of Catholicism in England and in tracing missionary activity into Scandinavia. The final segment, discussing the monasteries and pope's growing authority in Western Europe, presents a crucial issue obscured by excessive haste.

The Birth of the Middle Ages
(Europe in the Middle Ages series)

42 minutes   color
1989   Films for the Humanities

Summary: An inaccurate and incoherent effort to examine aspects of medieval history; painful to watch and impossible to decipher, it is a model of everything a documentary should strive to avoid

Grade: D

The Birth of the Middle Ages employs a narrator, extensive scenes from present-day societies that ostensibly resemble Europe in the Middle Ages, examples of medieval architecture and art, pageants, and visits to locales important in medieval history.   The sole identifiable theme of the film is the continuing presence of institutions like those of medieval Europe in present day Africa.

The film begins with an extensive consideration of the tribal society of Cameroon. Containing such features as class of mounted warriors, it supposedly resembles feudal European society.   There are also views of present day India and Japan where the film claims to find survivals of institutions resembling those of medieval Europe.

This introductory section occupies almost one third of the film's length. Thereafter, the narration shifts abruptly to a discussion of the Early Middle Ages illustrated by scenes from pageants in Italian cities such as Pisa commemorating events from the medieval past.

The film jumps repeatedly from topics in the Late Middle Ages to events following the collapse of Rome. It ends with a mystifying discussion of the work of Cyril and Methodius in converting the Eastern Slavs.

The Birth of the Middle Ages has nothing to recommend it. It should be noted in particular that in its discussion of modern Africa inaccurate and misleading: it suggests the absolute monarch in Cameroon is somehow a modern replica of the vastly different kinds of monarchs of medieval Europe.

Charlemagne: Holy Barbarian
(Western Civilization: Majesty and Madness series)

26 minutes   color
1969   Learning Corporation of America

Summary: A vivid and well-constructed dramatization of two key events in the life of Emperor Charlemagne: his brutal effort to subordinate and to convert the German tribes of Saxony to Christianity, and his coronation in 800 by the pope

Grade: B +

The film uses a narrator who gives the historical background and describes the events shown. Actors play the role of Charlemagne and his contemporaries. In an interesting twist to the dialogue, the actors sometimes converse with the narrator.   There are also maps showing the extent of Charlemagne's vast territorial holdings. The basic theme of the film is the way Charlemagne forced the Saxons to accept both Christianity and his political domination.   The film also considers Charlemagne's temporary success in reuniting much of the European part of the old Roman Empire as well as preserving some of the cultural legacy of the ancient world.

The greater portion of the film shows Charlemagne's campaign against the Saxons starting in 782. It begins with gory scenes following a massacre of some of Charlemagne's followers by rebellious Saxons. The narrator describes the process by which Charlemagne established a new unity in Europe out of the chaos following the fall of Rome. He discusses how Charlemagne, himself the descendant of Germans converted to Christianity, struggled to extend his sway to the pagan Saxons of eastern Germany.

To illustrate one aspect of Charlemagne's style of government, the film shows envoys from numerous areas coming to his German headquarters for orders. Meanwhile, the missi dominici, Charlemagne's officials, take the emperor's orders outward. The film also presents the views of Alcuin, the English cleric whom Charlemagne chose to build an educational system. Alcuin serves as spokesman for a moderate alternative to Charlemagne's policy of converting the Saxons by fire and sword. The first segment of the film concludes as Charlemagne calls together the nobles of Saxony, then has them murdered, and brutally subordinates the Saxon population. A brief second segment of the film shows the scene on Christmas, 800 A.D., when Charlemagne was crowned by the pope. This sealed his momentary success in uniting Europe.

Charlemagne is visually striking, with authentic forest locations, costumes, and artifacts. It conveys a wealth of basic information about Charlemagne and his empire. The narration raises an important issue by showing that scholars continue to disagree over questions such as the number of Saxon killed during Charlemagne's repression.

On the other hand, a description of the newly crowned Charlemagne in 800 as "the most powerful ruler in the world" is Eurocentric hyperbole. Moreover, the film is admittedly fragmentary, offering only two widely separated events from Charlemagne's career. Finally, there are episodes presenting the viewer with graphic violence.

The film should be highly useful as a follow-up to a consideration of the Carolingian era. It poses a valuable question for discussion: was Charlemagne's use of coerced adoption of Christianity either morally justifiable or politically effective as a tool for controlling the Saxons?

Christians, Jews, and Moslems in Medieval Spain
(Europe in the Middle Ages series)

33 minutes   color
1989   Films for the Humanities

Summary: A rambling, awkwardly constructed examination of cultural diversity and coexistence in Spain from the eighth to the fourteenth century

Grade: C

The film employs a narrator, dramatized scenes, and contemporary visits to sites of historical significance. The theme of the film is the way in which medieval Spain fostered the culturally fruitful coexistence of Western Europe's three major religious groups.

Christians, Jews, and Moslems rapidly presents scenes illustrating a number of issues: brief dramatic segments show the Christian population that lived under Visigothic rule around 700 A.D.; present-day views show monasteries and surviving examples of Moslem architectural achievements. At this point the film also describes the expulsion of the Jews from much of Western Europe.

There follows the major segment of the film, a discussion of the medieval center of Toledo. There populations drawn from each of the three faiths coexisted and interacted under Moslem rule. Scenes from the Sephardic Museum in Toledo introduce a discussion of the Jewish role in medieval Spain.

Beyond making the single memorable point about Spain's unique role as a meeting ground for Christians, Jews, and Moslems, the film is notably difficult to follow or to decipher. It never presents a clear chronology of events. It is generally inferior to the lucid treatment of the same topic found in The Crucible of Europe (q.v.), which tells the story from the Jewish viewpoint.

The Frozen World

See The Skin of Our Teeth

The Mother Tongue
(The Story of English series)

60 minutes   color
1986   BBC

Summary: An informative but diffuse discussion of the evolution of the English language from the invasions of England that followed the collapse of the Roman Empire to the start of the sixteenth century; strong in showing the atmosphere of this part of Europe during the worst of the Dark Ages

Grade: B -

The film employs a narrator, Robert MacNeil, maps and cartoons, visits to important historical locales, interviews with scholars, and scenes with ordinary

Britons who speak languages or dialects that reflect the various stages in the development of English. Finally, there is an extensive excerpt from a play dating back to the close of the fifteenth century.

The Mother Tongue begins with a striking scene of corpses recently exhumed from graves in Denmark. They were the sacrificial victims of a savage Germanic tribe, the Angles, who lived here more than fifteen hundred years ago. Narrator Robert McNeil makes the memorable comment that the language of the Angles has become the most widely spoken tongue on earth.

Following the titles, the film discusses the wide spread influence of Indo-European languages. A description of the migration of Germanic tribes from Central Europe to the North Sea coast comes with an example of how their descendants in northern Holland speak today.

The remainder of the first half of the film describes the coming of waves of Scandinavian invaders to Britain. Arriving in the fifth century, the Angles smashed the defenses left by the Romans and drove the Celtic inhabitants into corners of the island such as Wales. Pointing to the other influences on English during these centuries, the narration considers the arrival of Christianity and subsequent invaders such as the Danes and the French-speaking Normans.

The final portion of the film deals with the evolution of English through the Middle Ages, as Norman French added an elegant vocabulary to the existing store of English words. The Mother Tongue ends with several developments showing the English language on the eve of its triumphal use by Shakespeare. These are the writings of Geoffrey Chaucer, the work of the pioneer of English printing William Caxton, and several scenes from the late fifteenth-century play Mankind.

The film is engrossing. Its first half shows vividly the chaos--social and political as well as linguistic--that occurred following the collapse of Roman power in an important part of the old Roman empire. The photography, maps, and accompanying cartoon illustrations are notably effective.

Unfortunately, the film's description of how the English language evolved, colorful and entertaining as it is, will strike most students as a tangential topic.   The long discussions of grammatical development and the speech examples of modern Englishmen and Welshmen and others are well done. Nonetheless, they slow the pace of the narration and make the overall historical yield of the film unfortunately low.

The Skin of Our Teeth
(Civilisation: A Personal View by Kenneth Clark series)

54 minutes   color
1970   BBC

Summary: An examination of Western Civilization from the crisis following the collapse of the Roman Empire through the tenth century; sometimes slow paced and verbose, but enlivened by a number of striking visual images; frequently listed under the title The Frozen World

Grade: B -

The film employs a narration delivered by art historian Kenneth Clark, visits to important historical locales, as well as works of art and architecture of the time. The basic theme of the film is the way in which Western Civilization narrowly survived this period of internal collapse and outside invasion ending at a stage in which the Catholic church had become the key institution of the society.

As the first segment of Kenneth Clark's series on Civilization, this film begins with an extended introduction by Clark on the nature of civilization and the way in which we can recapture the essential spirit of an era through its art. Clark goes on to discuss the achievements of the ancient world, using a surviving Roman aqueduct and temple in southern France to illustrate the confidence, vitality, and durability of the classical world. He points to Roman friezes to illustrate the successful invasions by German barbarians and seventh-century paintings to show the even greater disruption that Islam brought to the Mediterranean world.

The remainder of the first half of the film stresses the survival of classical Christianity in such remote regions as the islands of Iona and Skellig Michael off the Irish coast. A view of the Viking ships now preserved in a Norwegian museum illustrates an additional threat to Western Europe. Clark makes the telling point that the prow of a Viking ship appearing an a European river like the Seine had the same ominous effect as the appearance of a nuclear submarine in the modern world.

The second half of the film focuses on the partial revival of Western culture in the era of Charlemagne. Clark shows the Church of San Vitale in Ravenna, where Charlemagne confronted the achievements of the Byzantine Empire, and the palace in Aachen that Charlemagne created in imitation of this eastern Mediterranean splendor. The Skin of Our Teeth ends with a view of the burgeoning art sponsored by the Catholic church of the tenth century. Clark notes that the Church was the new establishment destined to shape European civilization for centuries to come.

Clark effectively employs the resources of art museums and travel to present-day locations. The views of the remote islands off the Irish coast, with their surviving Celtic crosses and stone huts, illustrate the difficult passage Christianity passed through in the centuries after the fall of Rome. Likewise, The Book of Kells shows the fervor and the artistic skills of the Irish monks in preserving the Christian tradition. The film makes the contrast between the dying world of Imperial Rome and the ensuing disorder memorable.

Nonetheless, Clark's account is vague on the precise historical sequence of many of the events described. Given the numerous geographical sites to which the film refers, students will be put at a loss by the absence of any maps. Most important of all, at times the film's pace is deliberately slow to permit a detailed view of the art and buildings presented.

The film raises a number of issues for discussion: the personal experiences of an Irish monk, Roman aristocrat, or Viking sea raider in this era; why much of the ancient world could survive in the centuries before 1000 A.D.; why many elements of the ancient world could not remain viable after the fall of Rome.

LATER MIDDLE AGES

Art of the Middle Ages
(Art and Architecture series)

30 minutes   color
1963   Encyclopedia Britannica Educational Corporation

Summary: An ambitious but static and verbose effort to examine the thought patterns of the Middle Ages through the art of the time

Grade: C +

The film is a lecture by art critic John Canaday accompanied by views of medieval works of art, notably the sculptures found in six of the great cathedrals of France. Canaday's lecture also employs maps and cartoon models. The basic theme of the film is the intellectual distance separating our scientific age from the age of religious faith that the medieval era represented. Canaday attempts to analyze the components of that religious faith through medieval art.

Canaday begins the film by noting that we are intellectually far removed from the medieval era of mystical faith. In contrast we are closer to the practical concern and worldly ambition that characterized the societies of the ancient world and the Renaissance.

Using six French cathedrals, Canaday examines the nature of the Middle Ages. He considers the religious themes and the artistic styles seen in the statuary of the cathedrals. He attempts to define and explain the difference between the Romanesque architecture seen in cathedrals built before 1200 and the more elegant Gothic cathedrals that appeared in large numbers starting in the thirteenth century. Examining a surviving architect's sketchbook and the painting of the Annunciation by Robert Campin, Canaday explores medieval technology and religious belief.

The film encourages students to consider how individuals in different ages can see the world from drastically different perspectives. Nonetheless, the film's lecture format is static and uninteresting, and Canaday's analysis of the medieval era bogs down in a detailed consideration of questions of artistic style. Moreover, his depiction of medieval man as totally divorced from considerations of power and achievement is simplistic. The film Cathedral (q.v.) explores medieval life in a far more effective fashion.

Bruges: The Story of a Medieval City

59 minutes   color
1977   International Film Bureau

Summary: A visually brilliant and engrossing account of the city of Bruges stressing its cultural, political, and economic history in the latter stages of the Middle Ages

Grade: A -

The film revolves around a colorful narration given by Sam Stoneburner. It contains numerous views of the historic buildings and canals of Bruges, as well as a rich set of works of art from the medieval era. Much of the film presents present-day reenactments of the great parades and festive events marking the high points in the history of Bruges. The basic theme of the film is the rise of Bruges to wealth, culture, and prominence as a result of the wool industry and international commerce. Implicitly other such cities followed the same course. A second theme is the rich and diverse nature of medieval society.

Bruges begins with a series of striking views of the city today, emphasizing how much of the medieval city has survived down to the present. Sam Stoneburner introduces the history of Bruges by noting that men escaping from the misery the Dark Ages built this city, which then became the busiest port in Europe. At the old Customs House, now transformed into a library, Stoneburner shows examples of the great collection of pre-1500 manuscripts whose illustrations will be used throughout the film.

Following a spectacular reenactment of the festivities that accompanied the marriage of Duke Philip the Good, the ruler of Bruges in the fifteenth century, the film shifts to present a history of the city starting with its emergence in the midst of the population boom in Europe following 1000 A.D. The account features a discussion of the great flood of 1180, which opened a river route to the North Sea and set the stage for Bruges to become a great port. The film illustrates the wealth and culture of Bruges in the twelfth and thirteenth centuries with views of such spectacular constructions as the great Belfry of Bruges.

The first half of the film closes with a consideration of the deep religious roots of medieval society in Bruges as well as the era's brutality. The former is illustrated by traditional May parade, featuring a reenactment of Christ's Passion. The latter is shown in a series of grisly paintings displaying the judicial tortures and executions of the period.

The film then moves into the troubled fourteenth century, in which Bruges lost its status as an independent city and fell under the control of the Valois dukes of Burgundy. Following scenes of the lavish residences and entertainments of the time, the film takes up Bruges's role as a cosmopolitan center of international commerce and banking. A discussion of the last Valois dukes features a spectacular modern reenactment of the jousts between armored knights that took place on festive occasions in the Middle Ages. The film closes with a visit to the tomb of Charles the Bold, the last Valois duke. The narrator notes that by 1500 Bruges had lost its economic vitality and was sinking into poverty and weakness.

The film's visual qualities are first-rate, with splendid views of the community's buildings and civic festivals. The film moves at a brisk pace, and it presents the basic course of medieval history with admirable clarity. It makes the important point that the main features of the medieval world extended up to the fourteenth and fifteenth centuries in parts of Europe such as present day Belgium.

The film has only two weaknesses. It is longer than its subject matter requires, and it can fail to hold an audience's attention. Second, its generally lucid narration breaks down at the close, with a murky account of the death of Charles the Bold and the end of the medieval era. Students will need to be informed about the conflict between Charles the Bold and the French monarchy in order to make sense of this important development.

Castle

60 minutes   color
1983   PBS

Summary: A lucid and entertaining examination of the castle as the key "military machine" of the thirteenth century and as a tool enabling the English monarchy to hold down a rebellious Welsh population; not as clearly focused as its companion film Cathedral

Grade: B

Castle employs narrators David Macaulay and Sarah Bullen, animated cartoons, and numerous present-day views of historic English castles located in Wales. The basic theme of the film is the castle as a stronghold for English rule in the midst of a hostile countryside. A secondary theme is the way in which the castle and its surrounding community developed into a medieval town and then a city.

The film begins with a series of cartoons showing the Norman conquest of England, the warfare between England's rulers and their newly conquered Welsh subjects. There follows David Macauley's childhood recollections of visiting thirteenth-century English castles told against the background of present-day scenes of Castle Conway.

The film proceeds along two lines. A cartoon story recounts how the fictional English nobleman Kevin LeStrange built and defended a castle in Wales at the orders of King Edward I. Interspersed in the tale, the two narrators explore numerous surviving castles, analyzing them as military tools and as features of medieval life.

The cartoon saga shows Kevin and his experienced architect Master James building a military fortress in a carefully selected location. The film indicates the technical skills thirteenth century builders employed and considers the nature of society in that era. A key character is the ambitious blacksmith from Chester who volunteers to work in distant Wales in the hope of creating a better life for himself.

In their segments, the two narrators describe the structure of medieval society: its short life spans, rigid hierarchy, and reliance on religious institutions. They also consider the clever ways in which military builders made the castle into both a powerful stronghold and a home of relative luxury as well. Finally, they show the viewer the contrasting dwellings and lifestyles of the era's townspeople.

The second half of the cartoon story sees the castle completed and facing an unsuccessful attack by Welsh rebels. Here the story indicates how well the castle's military features work in a supreme practical test. Finally, the town that was first set up around the castle walls, and restricted to an English population, expands to become a thriving community with both Welsh and English inhabitants.

The cartoon story is witty and engrossing. The photography, especially aerial views of present-day castles, is admirable. Touring those together, the two narrators present an intriguing examination of how a building can be the most potent weapon of its era. Nevertheless, the film becomes muddled in its closing minutes, by mixing the story of the castle with the larger issue of the development of urban life in the Middle Ages. The survey of medieval society given by the narrators is rapid and superficial at best compared to Cathedral (q.v.). The Welsh attack on the castle contains a number of grisly scenes.

Cathedral

60 minutes   color
1985   PBS

Summary: A well-photographed and skillfully narrated examination of the great cathedrals constructed in northern France in the thirteenth century; it presents a superlative view of medieval society featuring the role of the Catholic church as well as medieval technology

Grade: A

  Cathedral blends two elements: the cartoon history of the construction of a cathedral from 1216 to 1267 in the fictional town of Beaulieu, and present-day scenes of Chartres and other great church edifices built during that time. It considers the architectural and engineering techniques needed to construct these great centers of the Church. The film pays even more attention to the nature of medieval society.
  The film begins with a cartoon prologue recounting the destruction by fire of the old cathedral of "Beaulieu" and the commitment of the townspeople to build an even grander structure to celebrate their faith. It then alternates between cartoon sequences and those in which narrators David Macaulay and Carolyn Berg examine the great cathedrals of northern France. The first to be considered, and the one that dominates the film, is the magnificent cathedral at Chartres.
  The cartoon story is told with a humorous touch by the fictional character Father Pierre of Beaulieu. It recounts how funds were gathered for this immense and expensive enterprise, and the role figures like the local bishop and the master builder played in the construction. There is also a description of the architecture of the typical cathedral.
  The remainder of the first half of the film brings the contemporary narrators back to discuss such issues as how the light and airy Gothic style of the thirteenth century emerged from the earlier, heavy Romanesque. As in other portions of the film, both in cartoons and present-day narration, there is an ongoing discussion of the nature of medieval society.
  The second half of the film starts with a cartoon sequence illustrating the tensions within the Catholic church. It focuses on the corrupt bishop Gervais, and the growing tension between him and the master builder and the cathedral chapter. The narrators return to discuss how the cathedrals reflected the increasing economic resources of European society in the thirteenth century, in particular in urban life.
  Cartoon sequences then show the technical aspects of building the cathedral's roof while the plot recounts how the bishop's corruption leads to the tragic death of the master builder and the bishop's removal. A subsequent

cartoon portion shows the final financial barrier to the cathedral's completion removed by the merchant Thibaut: in good medieval fashion, he is compelled by a vision of the Virgin Mary to donate his fortune to the cathedral and to join a religious order.

The narrators conclude with issues such as the cathedral as a teaching tool in an illiterate society and the role of the Virgin Mary as a comfort and inspiration for the typical member of medieval society.

The film is well-constructed, intelligently narrated, and brilliantly photographed. The views of the cathedrals' interiors are striking. Even more impressive are external shots including aerial photography. The film offers a wealth of material for anyone interested in the diversity of medieval society, the internal structure of the Church, and the technical and organizational skills needed for such a massive undertaking.

Some portions of the narration by Macaulay and Berg are overly compact and filled with facts. Students may have difficulty taking in all of the valuable points they make. The cartoon sequences, on the other hand, are generally lucid throughout. Nonetheless, some technical descriptions, e.g., on the making of stained glass and bells, are also too dense to be readily understood.

The film can serve to stimulate discussions on the degree to which thirteenth-century Europe was a society with an economic surplus and on the nature of the Catholic church and its internal tensions. Students may find it interesting to consider how medieval society was held together by the Church and how modern societies substitute other institutions for this purpose.

Chartres Cathedral

60 minutes   color
1962   Encyclopedia Britannica Educational Corporation

Summary: A well-conceived but poorly executed effort to show how the cathedral at Chartres served as a teaching tool of the Christian faith for a largely illiterate population; vivid views of the cathedral are accompanied by a verbose, murky narration

Grade: C +

Chartres Cathedral is a lecture by art critic John Canaday on the architecture of Chartres and its role as a symbol of Christian belief. The chief theme is how medieval man saw Chartres and how the cathedral, this "Bible for the poor," brought together the faith, the intellect, and the engineering skills of the Middle Ages. Virtually all scenes of the film show portions of the cathedral. The film is accompanied throughout by a concert of music from the Middle Ages.

The film begins with a description of the Beauce region west of Paris and the town of Chartres. Canaday notes that today, as in the Middle Ages, the cathedral is the center of the urban community. He then poses the question why this asymmetrical building with its parts of varying architectural styles is considered the greatest of the medieval cathedrals. The answer comes as a discussion of the building and rebuilding of the church at Chartres and in analysis of its structure.

The central element of the film is an extended discussion of how the medieval Church used the art and even the shape of the cathedral to represent Christian truth. Sculptures show scenes of Christ triumphing over evil or standing before humanity as a divine teacher. Canaday struggles to explain how the interior empty spaces of the cathedral symbolize the mystery of god.

The narration makes the interesting point that the portals, built in different centuries, show a changing image of saints and other religious figures: the heavy formality of eleventh-century statuary, in which individuals are shaped like columns, gives way to the greater humanity and realism of figures carved in the thirteenth century such as the warrior St. Theodore.

The final portion of the film takes the viewer into the cathedral for a discussion of its interior space, stained glass windows, and the intensified light that flowed through them. A brief discussion of the engineering skills shown in constructing the cathedral concludes the film. Here again Canaday attempts to show how such elements as the interior lighting and the very structure of the building appeared to medieval man as part of a divine mystery.

The goal of showing the cathedral as it appeared to a medieval individual is intriguing. Moreover, the film is effective in showing the cathedral in its urban setting; the observer unexpectedly catches glimpses of the great building from all over the city. Many of the views of the cathedral, from broad daylight to dusk, are memorable. The history of the cathedral's reconstruction over several centuries is lucid and helpful.

The weaknesses of the film center on Canaday's stodginess as narrator and the difficulty he has in explaining what lessons the cathedral taught to medieval society. A clumsy effort to compare the cathedral to a modern scientific laboratory (complete with shots of a space launch in the early 1960s) is crude and distracting. Finally, the treatment of the cathedral as an engineering accomplishment is tacked on to the film as a poorly written afterthought.

Students will receive a more lucid and informative picture of the medieval cathedral and the religious faith it represented in the superior film Cathedral (q.v.).

The Crucible of Europe
(Heritage: Civilization and the Jews series)

60 minutes   color
1984   WNET

Summary: A lucid, well-photographed survey showing Europe's most distinct religious minority in Spain and in the northern and eastern parts of the continent; ranging from the ninth to the late fifteenth century, it presents a view of European history from an unusual angle

Grade: B +

The film employs narrator Abba Eban, maps, actors reading important historical documents, paintings and buildings from this era, and contemporary views of historical locales. The basic theme of the film is the role of the Jews as constantly vulnerable outsiders in both Islamic and Christian regions. A second theme is the way in which religious hostility and economic resentment played a potent role in imperiling the security of Jews in Europe.

The film begins with an extended description of Jews in Spain. Speaking from the great synagogue in Toledo, Abba Eban considers the long era in which most Jews lived in Arab lands while the two groups maintained cordial relations. The career of the Jewish thinker Maimonides, "the second Moses" and physician to the Sultan Saladdin, serves to illustrate the high level of Jewish achievement and political influence.

The remainder of the first half of the film considers Jews in Christian Europe. Showing the emergence of urban life in this relatively poor and wild part of the continent, the film indicates Jewish economic success. Jewish merchants linked Christian Europe with the Moslem world. Some, like Aaron of Lincoln, even helped to finance the construction of cathedrals. Intellectual achievement flourished in Talmudic academies such as the one founded by the sage Rashi in northern France. At the same time Jewish vulnerability remained evident. Judaism was sometimes represented in cathedral art as a blind goddess unable to see the truth. The massacres of Jews that accompanied the Crusades show the Jews as victims of religious hatred that sometimes spilled over into state sponsored slaughter.

The second half of the film concentrates on the growing difficulty of Jews in Western Europe: the Catholic church put the Talmud "on trial," and political authorities used the Jews as their agents in collecting taxes, then abandoned them to popular anger. The catastrophe of the Black Death (1347-1351) put the Jews in the role of scapegoats and led to new massacres. The film shows Jews shifting from regions like Germany to the frontier territories of Lithuania and Poland where they hoped for a more secure existence.

The film ends with the tragic and powerful story of the forced conversion of thousands of Spanish Jews and the expulsion of the remainder from Spain in 1492. The narration stresses that this was noteworthy given the remarkable success Jews had long enjoyed in Spain.

The Crucible of Europe presents a vivid picture of events, especially when the focus is on Spain. The story of Christian Europe's powerful and culturally superior Islamic neighbor to the west is a vital element in our understanding of European history. On the other hand, the film treats sweeping and complex events such as the decline of the rural, feudal order in medieval Europe in only brief fashion.

Students can be asked to consider what trends in European history in the medieval period and thereafter isolated and threatened the Jews in a way that was not true in the era of Charlemagne.

Crusade: By Horse to Jerusalem
(Retracing History series)

54 minutes   color
1993   Films for the Humanities & Sciences

Summary: A charming, visually impressive, but rambling account of a modern trip by horseback retracing the route taken by the first crusaders

Grade: C +

Crusade employs several narrators, maps, medieval paintings, and numerous present-day scenes of important historical locales. The basic theme of the film is the extraordinary feat of the original crusaders in their unprecedented three-year journey from Western and Central Europe to Jerusalem.

The film begins with contemporary scenes of the Ardennes Forest including views of the breed of huge horses who helped to carry the crusaders to Jerusalem in 1096. In the first third of the film, Tim Severin and his traveling companion ride for four months in the summer and fall from Belgium through Germany, Austria, and the Balkans to reach Istanbul. From there they follow the crusaders' route, recounting the siege of the ancient walled city of Nicaea and the battle at Dorylaeum.

The remainder of the film begins the following spring. The travelers renew their journey through present-day Syria, stopping at Antioch where the crusaders engaged in a seven-month siege. They travel through Damascus, entering Jordan, and then Israel, completing the entire journey in eight months. The crusaders, delayed by the need to fight battles and to take fortified cities, needed three years for the same trip. The film concludes with a description of the siege and conquest of Jerusalem, a great Christian victory dishonored by the accompanying massacre of the city's population.

The film offers a unique opportunity for students to examine the landscape through which the crusaders traveled. Much of it beyond Istanbul turns out to be largely unchanged from medieval times. The photography is often striking, and the film's visual qualities are noteworthy. All in all, this is an opportunity to recapture part of the experience of the original crusaders.

Unfortunately, much of the film dwells on the selection and care of the horses involved in the trip. The accompanying historical account is pushed into the background. The colorful and historically enlightening segments of the film are thus buried in an account that is too slow moving to be fully useful.

The Crusades: Saints and Sinners
(Western Civiization: Majesty and Madness series)

26 minutes   color
1969   Learning Corporation of America

Summary: A slow paced, occasionally gory account of the origins and course of the First Crusade

Grade: C +

The Crusades employs a narrator, actors who sometimes address themselves directly to the audience, and maps. The basic theme of the film is the complex nature of the crusade, an event influenced by the diverse motives of its participants and bringing with it unintended consequences.

The film begins with graphic scenes of an army assaulting a city in the Holy Land. The narrator notes that this part of the world had been a battleground for centuries. He then considers political development here prior to the First Crusade: the shift the Middle East brought about by the rise of the Seljuk Turks and the consequent call by the Byzantine Empire for assistance from Western Europe.

Dramatic scenes show Pope Urban II preaching the crusade to various audience, and various great noblemen like Godfrey of Lorraine preparing to leave for the Holy Land. The film uses its various characters to illustrate the differing motives of the crusaders, ranging from religious zeal to hopes of acquiring wealth.

The final portion of the film shows the crusaders besieging Jerusalem. They take the city in scenes marked by uproar and gore. The narrator presents a gruesome extract from a chronicle describing the invading army's actions, then notes that Moslem forces would win the city back within a few years.

The film is a lucid introduction to the origins and course of the First Crusade. On the other hand it is disjointed and slow paced; the acting is merely adequate. The battle scenes, sometimes gory, have the quality of a mediocre made-for-TV movie. The film's basic theme of the crusader's diverse motives can be explored in a lecture more readily than it can be pictured on film.

Faith and Fear

See review under FOURTEENTH CENTURY

The Great Thaw
(Civilisation: A Personal View by Kenneth Clark series)

52 minutes   color
1970   BBC

Summary: An enlightening, sometimes slow paced, examination of Western Europe in the twelfth century stressing the role of the Church and Christian belief

Grade: B

The film is narrated by Kenneth Clark. It employs the art and buildings of the time, as well as visits to historical locales. The basic theme of The Great Thaw is the sudden leap (or awakening) of European civilization following the year 1100. Kenneth Clark, discussing this sudden warming, like "a Russian spring," stresses the power and influence of the Catholic church as the crucial factor in Europe's advance. An important sub-theme in the film is Europe's increasing contact with the outside world.

The film begins by showing edifices such as Durham and Canterbury cathedrals as evidence of a confident society equipped with significant technical skills and resources. Its chronological account goes back, however, to present the earlier Romanesque cathedral and the monastery as key developments of the era. It also notes the growing mobility of European society as seen in pilgrimages and the militarized pilgrimage of the crusades as well as the intellectual vitality represented by Peter Abelard, the "star" theology teacher of the era. The final portion of the film focuses on the Gothic style of cathedral building. Chartres illustrates this new, impressive product of the medieval world.

The film points clearly to several strengths of medieval Europe and the relative suddenness of their appearance. Some concepts, such as the ability of men of humble origins to rise to power in the Church, and the way in which senior Church figures were appointed to posts far from their native lands, add significantly to a student's understanding. Present-day scenes of monastic life and of the cathedrals themselves illustrate our link with this era. The theme of Europe's growing ties with the outside world can be seen vividly in Persian influences. Reaching Europe with returning crusaders, they are visible in the Romanesque art work of the twelfth century.

Regrettably, the stress on the development of architecture and art moves the film away from more central historical topics. Thus, the pace slows repeatedly to permit a leisurely examination of objects like cathedral sculptures. Meanwhile, the issue of the social underpinnings of the great leap forward is unfortunately ignored.

Students can be asked to consider, how resources were tapped to permit projects like the building of cathedrals. One could ask how great a percentage of the society's resources went to such activities and how the money was raised.

Magna Carta
Part 1: Rise of the English Monarchy
Part 2: Revolt of the Nobles and the Signing of the Charter

31 minutes   black\white
1959   Encyclopedia Britannica Educational Corporation

Summary: A solid, factual, but unimaginative dramatization of the conflict between the English crown and the country's nobility from 1066 to 1215; the acting is merely adequate and the film seems designed for an audience below the college level

Grade: C +

The film employs a narrator whose account of English history is illustrated by dramatized episodes as well as by scenes from the famous Bayeux tapestry. The basic theme of the film is the conflict between ambitious monarchs and the English barons. The former sought unhampered control over their kingdom; the latter hoped to limit the king by putting him under the rule of law. A subsidiary theme is the long-range effect of the confrontation: the extension of rights and the protection of the law to the common Englishman. The film also notes our reliance on the records made by historians of the time, individuals whose view of events may have been skewed by their political allegiances.

The film is split into two parts. The first, The Rise of the English Monarchy, begins with the unwilling King John forced to agree to the demands of his barons in 1215. It then moves backward to the Norman Conquest and its aftermath, shown by scenes from the Bayeux tapestry. Dramatic scenes and a chronological narration describe the reigns of English kings from William the Conqueror to the coronation of King John in 1199. William is shown imposing a tighter political control over his barons and financial control over the entire population than had been the case before 1066. A parade of kings augments royal control: Henry I establishes more efficient systems of taxation; Henry II spreads the power of royal courts of justice.

The second portion of the film, The Revolt of the Nobles and the Signing of the Charter, shows John oppressing his barons with measures like taking hostages from noble families. John's weakness vis-à-vis the power of the Catholic church emerges as Pope Innocent III forces him to accept Stephen Langston, the pope's choice as archbishop of Canterbury. Meanwhile, in a series of events the film does not present clearly, John is shown waging war in France. The nobles take the opportunity offered by John's lack of success there to force him to concede to their demands at Runnymede on June 15, 1215. The Church also benefits from the limits on royal power imposed on the monarch.

The film states clearly the fundamental issue of rivalry between the monarchy and the nobles. At the same time, it merely presents the political history of the English monarchs between 1066 and 1215 in the form of an illustrated, and not very imaginative lecture.

Medieval Guilds

21 minutes   color
1955   Encyclopedia Britannica Educational Corporation

Summary: A lucid and visually attractive examination of one of the key institutions in the life of the Middle Ages; its tone is not wholly appropriate for a college level class, and the treatment of economic change in this era is oversimplified

Grade: B -

Medieval Guilds employs a narration accompanied by silent actors who play the role of participants in medieval society. The action takes places in authentic locations in France. The major theme of the film is the growth of a medieval community from village to commercial town to early manufacturing city; the process is seen in the emergence and decline of the institution of the medieval guild.

The film begins by examining the simple community of serfs clustered around the castle of a local feudal lord in the Early Middle Ages. It goes on to show how the development of a food market and the growth of river trade could turn a village into a commercial town over the space of a century. Views of the great guild halls that have survived to the present introduce a discussion of the institution of the medieval guild. An extended dramatization illustrates the workings of the shoemakers' guild, examining the apprenticeship system and the process by which guild wardens regulated all aspects of the shoemakers' trade.

The final portion of the film describes how members of the leading guilds formed trading partnerships to engage in long distance commerce. The profits they gathered helped them in subordinating other guilds. These powerful guild leaders then brought the small craftsmen of weaker guilds into their employ as paid workers in an early factory system.

The film blends a clear narration with effective dramatic scenes to show the immense authority of the guilds in regulating economic life. The views of great guild halls that have survived to the present indicate the wealth that these organizations possessed. Nonetheless, the film is too slow in pace and too simple in tone for a college audience. It does not consider numerous factors such as demographic change, technological breakthroughs, and Europe's links with the outside world as causes for the rise and expansion of cities and commerce.

Students can be asked to contrast the degree and nature of economic regulation we consider appropriate at present with that accepted and used in the medieval era.

Medieval Manor

21 minutes   black\white
1955   Encyclopedia Britannica Educational Corporation

Summary: A stiff and oversimplified examination of a supposedly typical community of the Middle Ages; it shows the roles of the lord of the castle and his serfs, the operation of a local court, and noble marriage celebration

Grade: C

Medieval Manor consists of a narration accompanied by dramatic scenes with actors playing the roles of participants in medieval life. The film also employs animated maps and cartoons.

The film begins by showing the role of the lord of the castle and members of the community over which he presides. Using an animated cartoon, the film goes backward in time to show how this feudal community and a system of homage extending up to a medieval king emerged. It notes the system grew out of the chaotic conditions following the collapse of the Roman Empire.

Next, the film pictures the role of serf, the lord's seneschal, the village miller, and the local priest. It stresses the central role of the Church in tying medieval society together, as well as the ladder for advancement the Church offered individuals of non-noble birth. The film's last major segment shows the festivities as two noble families join in marriage. It concludes with a sweeping look to the future in which the emergence of nations and the voyages of exploration would end the closed world of the medieval community.

The film is clear and concise, but it is marred by awkward acting. A more serious flaw is its lack of precision about the Middle Ages: the isolated, self-contained community and social system it describes seems set in the early stages of the medieval period, perhaps around 1000 A.D., but the luxurious trappings of noble life and the technical level of the work of the blacksmith and armorer are more appropriate to the thirteenth century. Thus, it is uncertain what time period it is supposed to depict.

The Medieval World, revised edition

16 minutes   color
1980   Coronet

Summary: A brisk and lucid survey of the origins and nature of medieval society; its brevity and the simplicity of its narration make it more suitable for a pre-college than a college-level class

Grade: B

The film employs a narrator, maps, art and buildings from the medieval era, and a number of dramatic scenes. The basic theme of the film is the way in which a new and sophisticated society based upon feudalism and the Roman Catholic church emerged from the wreckage of the Roman Empire.

The film begins by showing the basic physical remnants of the medieval era: castles, town buildings, and cathedrals. It then turns back to the Roman Empire of the second century A.D., noting the relatively weak hold that Rome had over northern Europe. Describing the German invasions and Islamic invasions, The Medieval World notes that literary works survived due to the efforts of the Catholic church, while Europe owed its rudimentary political stability to a system of feudalism.

The second half of the film shows the more prosperous and confident Europe that existed by the close of the eleventh century. The Crusades, the revival of trade and urban life, and the construction of the great cathedrals like the one at Chartres show the new current of the High Middle Ages. A close look at Chartres indicates the beauty and confidence of medieval art based upon immersion in Christian belief.

The film contains splendid photography, with particularly impressive views of Chartres and the medieval buildings in the Belgian city of Ghent. The narration is notably clear and direct.

The Medieval World can serve best as a brief introduction to the subject. It fails to stand comparison with the more inclusive and sophisticated treatment given medieval life in <u>Cathedral</u> (<u>q.v.</u>). Students might benefit by being asked to see the two together and to note the issues and complexities that <u>Cathedral</u> takes up.

The Middle Ages: A Wanderer's Guide to Life and Letters
(Western Civilization: Majesty and Madness series)

27 minutes   color
1970   Learning Corporation of America

Summary: An amusing but thin and superficial introduction to numerous aspects of the Middle Ages

Grade: C +

<u>The Middle Ages</u> centers on the account of a young student-poet who directly addresses the audience on the subject of medieval life. It includes an excerpt from the play <u>Everyman</u> and a dramatization of the <u>Tale of the Wife of Bath</u> from Chaucer's <u>Canterbury Tales</u>. The main themes in the film are the central role that religion played in medieval life and the vast differences between our era and the world of 1350.

The film shows the narrator moving through the medieval world while commenting on its various aspects. The first half of the film includes an excerpt from the medieval play <u>Everyman</u>. This is followed by a brief dramatic scene in which knights and ladies discuss the rules of courtly love.   The second half of the film presents a dramatization of the <u>Tale of the Wife of Bath</u>, followed by a visit to an urban market day.

The film is well-acted and the patter of the narrator offers an accurate survey of medieval life presented with a light touch. The dramatic episodes enliven the course of the film. The film, however, touches on numerous topics in excessively rapid fashion. The episode from <u>Everyman</u> offers a useful view into the concerns of medieval man, but it suffers from a cursory introduction.

People of the Book
(The Christians series)

44 minutes   color
1976   Granada

Summary: A diffuse examination of the relationship among Christians, Moslems, and Jews from the birth of Islam to the expulsion of Jews and Moslems from the Kingdom of Spain at the turn of the sixteenth century

Grade: C +

The film employs a narrator, present-day visits to historically important locales, maps, paintings, and actors reading from important historical documents. The basic theme of the film is the spread of Islam across the Middle East, North Africa, and into Spain and the subsequent Christian and Jewish responses. The latter included a military and political counterattack in the form of the Crusades. But there was also peaceful contact and assimilation of Islamic culture in the Sicily of Frederick II and in the meeting ground of Islamic Spain.

People of the Book begins with a visit to the Monastery of St. Catherine's, a Christian institution at the foot of Mount Sinai in territory dominated for centuries of Moslems. A testimony to the meeting of the two faiths is a Moslem mosque within the monastery. The film goes on to discuss the basic tenets of Islam, noting how the relatively simple theology and lack of a clerical hierarchy facilitated its spread. There follows a description of how a dynamic Islam overwhelmed both Palestine and Syria, with Jerusalem and Damascus becoming the locations of new Moslem mosques established on the site of Jewish and Christian shrines. In both instances, Islam was welcomed by the local population as an alternative to the unpopular rule of the Byzantines. Present-day scenes of urban centers in Tunisia, Spain, and Egypt show the scope of Islamic expansion. Scenes from Cordova, the great Spanish center of Islam, illustrate the cultural heights Islam reached.

The second half of the film considers the subsequent Western response. It stresses the savagery of the Christian conquest of the Holy Land, the crusader castles, and the manipulation of the crusading impulse by the trading city of Venice in turning the crusaders into an army to conquer Constantinople. Non-violent contact between the Christian and Moslem worlds took diverse forms: the effort of St. Francis of Assisi to convert the Egyptians, and the blending of cultures seen in the cathedral at Palermo with its mixed Christian and Moslem motifs.

The film concludes with images of Christian intolerance toward Jews and Moslems, the other "people of the book." Spain, once a great meeting ground for Moslem, Christian, and Jewish culture becomes a center of the Inquisition. It appears in lurid prints of torture scenes. In the decade between 1492 and 1502, both Jews and Moslems confronted the harsh choice of conversion to Christianity or expulsion.

The film's goals are sound and intriguing. Unfortunately, much of the film is presented in a patchy and diffuse fashion.

Romance and Reality
(Civilisation: A Personal View by Kenneth Clark series)

52 minutes   color
1970   BBC

Summary: A well-conceived but poorly executed examination of the contrasting spirits of the thirteenth and fourteenth centuries; the film juxtaposes the chivalric ethos and spiritual concerns of the former with the bourgeois realism of the latter

Grade: C +

Romance and Reality employs narrator Kenneth Clark, the art and buildings of the time, and visits to important historical locales. The main theme of the film is the shift in Western culture at the close of the thirteenth century. Focusing on St. Francis and Dante representing the old and Giotto the new, the film stresses how the late Gothic themes of the thirteenth century were now jarred by the urban, commercial culture of the Italian city-states of the early fourteenth century.

The first half of the film explores the ornate art and architecture of the late thirteenth century, the chivalric tradition of courtly love, and the lavish lifestyle of aristocrats such as the Duke de Berry. The emphasis rests on European society's elite and the high culture it generated: tapestries, nature paintings, and ornate churches. The typical product of the era, examined at length in the film, is the Duke of Berry's famous illuminated manuscript, The Very Rich Hours.

Kenneth Clark then takes up the career of St. Francis of Assisi, the Italian dandy who embraced nature and poverty. He shows how St. Francis introduced a special kind of piety, based upon poverty and identification with the simple things of nature, into Western life. Thus, it is striking to see how Francis' followers rapidly honored him with vast and extravagant churches like the one erected to him at Assisi. It shows how rapidly religious innovation could be turned into bureaucratic interests and wealth.

The final third of the film shifts to include the vibrant merchant society developing in the northern city-states of Italy such as Siena. Clark stresses that this society gave birth to a new order of realistic art, epitomized in the dramatic Biblical scenes painted by Giotto. Nonetheless, Clark notes that Dante, Giotto's contemporary in early fourteenth-century Italy, was linked to the earlier era of celestial concerns.

The film is visually striking. It introduces the viewer to the contrasting but equally elite cultures of two significant eras: the last peak of medieval times and the first stirrings of the Renaissance. Unfortunately, a leisurely pace and uncertain organization mars the film. For example, Giotto is introduced early in the film, ignored, and then taken up later for extensive examination. Clark concerns himself solely with social elite and its artistic values, ignoring the full range of medieval society. Fundamental political developments that affected key figures such as Dante, e.g., the conflict of popes and emperors, do not appear at all.

A White Garment of Churches--Romanesque and Gothic
(Art of the Western World series)

60 minutes   color
1989   WNET

Summary: A wide-ranging and colorful examination of the role of the Church in medieval society during the eleventh and twelfth centuries

Grade: B -

White Garment of Churches uses a narrator, extensive views of the surviving cathedrals, maps, interviews with present-day experts, and the sculpture and paintings of the Middle Ages. The main theme is the influence of the medieval church as seen in the practice of pilgrimages, the great churches that grew up along the key routes for pilgrims, and monasticism. A second direction the film takes is to consider the changing architecture of the cathedral and the art it contained. It examines the expansiveness, optimism, and the greater artistic realism that developed as the older Romanesque style gave way to the Gothic.

The film begins by noting how medieval Christian civilization emerged following the fall of Rome. It shows the great era of church building in the eleventh and twelfth centuries as a signal of Europe's new stability. There follows and extensive consideration of the cathedral at Vézelay in Burgundy, which was the point of departure for pilgrims traveling to the shrine of Santiago de Compostela in Spain. The sculptures of the cathedral at Autun, centered on the theme of Christ and the Last Judgement, serve as the basis for a discussion of medieval religious belief. The remainder of the first half of the film explores monasticism. It notes that the great monastic empires like that of the Cluniac order, established in the Early Middle Ages, stretched across much of Europe. There is a also a consideration of the architectural features of the heavy Romanesque building style of the time.

The second half of the film takes up a number of issues: the growing prosperity and urbanization of Europe between 1100 and 1300, the role of the cathedral and religious ritual in the lives of the average inhabitant of medieval Europe, Abbot Suger and the shift from the Romanesque to the Gothic as exemplified in the Church of St. Denis. The film returns at several points to examine the cathedral at Chartres. It is both an example of both the Gothic style of building, and the Church's social role as the focus of civic life.

The film deals intelligently with the key features of the medieval world including the growing economy, the life of the average individual, and the splendor and power of the Catholic church. Visually much of the treatment is splendid: highpoints include aerial shots of various cathedrals and close-up examinations of the statuary and stained glass windows of individual churches. The film stresses the exuberance and vitality of the medieval intellectual world.

The film's weaknesses start with its tendency to engage in extensive technical discussions of topics like church architecture. Moreover, the chronology is sometimes muddled. For example, the narration jumps from a discussion of Chartres back to the story of Suger and St. Denis as the narration shifts from the Gothic to the Romanesque.

Students can be encouraged to consider the level of wealth and resources of the medieval era as manifested in the cathedrals of the time. Another interesting point to consider is the realism the film shows in some of the statuary of Chartres: does this show that some of the intellectual vitality normally associated with Renaissance Italy was already present in medieval France?

FOURTEENTH CENTURY

Chaucer's England (With a Special Presentation of the Pardoner's Tale)

30 minutes   color
1958   Encyclopedia Britannica EducationalCorporation

Summary: A colorful and well-acted set of dramatizations from Geoffrey Chaucer's Canterbury Tales; it touches on several topics of historical interest concerning in the fourteenth century, but its main focus is on Chaucer's literary achievement

Grade: C +

The film uses medieval manuscripts and present-day scenes of the cathedral at Canterbury, but its major technique is dramatization. Actors play the role of Chaucer's pilgrims, and the centerpiece of the film is a dramatization of the Pardoner's Tale from Chaucer's great literary work. An important theme of the film is human greed as represented by the characters in the Pardoner's Tale but also by the Pardoner himself. As a church official using high-pressure tactics to sell his holy relics, the Pardoner represents elements of the Catholic church that Chaucer wished to criticize.

The film begins with a lucid and informative description of England at this time, the career of Geoffrey Chaucer as a government official, and the significance of pilgrimages to Canterbury. The dramatic portion of the film starts by introducing the assemblage of Chaucer's characters en route to the great English cathedral.

The bulk of the film consists of the Pardoner's Tale in which three young Englishmen, having found a cask of gold, turn on one another in an orgy of greed and murder. The film ends with another scene of the assembled pilgrims, in which the Pardoner's own greedy and unscrupulous character appears in full force.

The film features good photography and fine acting, with the themes of Chaucer's poetry made clear in modern translation.   The introduction is informative, and the dramatizations captures the flavor of life at this time. Nonetheless, the overall historical content of the film is small.

Medieval England: The Peasants' Revolt
(Western Civilization: Majesty and Madness series)

31 minutes   color
1969   Learning Corporation of America

Summary: An oversimplified and gory account of the English Peasant Revolt of 1381; the acting varies sharply in quality, and the tone of the film is not appropriate for a college-level class

Grade: C -

Medieval England employs a narrator, a dramatized account of events, and film clips of later examples of social unrest such as the student riots in Paris in 1968. The basic theme of the film is the failure of the rebellion of England's oppressed peasants. Urged on by saintly leaders to create a just society, they could not sustain their revolt against treacherous and brutal representatives of the established order.

The film begins with the popular preacher John Ball speaking to a group of English peasants. He presents the vision of a just society based on man's goodness and equality. As a fleeing peasant is seized and brutalized by royal officials, the narrator describes the injustices of medieval England. It was, he notes, a realm in which land was wealth and one's rights depended upon the status one achieved at birth.

The narrator recounts how the social order was in flux at the close of the fourteenth century. This led to "the first clash of capital and labor" as English peasants revolted against unjust taxes. The film illustrates the point by showing peasants turning on one particularly brutal tax collector.

Other main characters of the film appear in the person of the rebel leader, Wat Tyler, and the young king, Richard II. The peasant revolt spreads, and the king and his ministers play for time. Meanwhile, Ball, the popular preacher maintains an idealistic vision of the future.

In the end, England's nobles murder Tyler, massacring his peasant followers, and torturing the survivors into confessions before they too are executed. But the narrator notes that the unjust feudal order faded as economic change took place.   Meanwhile, the spirit of righteous revolt seen in 1381 continues to surface in a montage of scenes from twentieth-century social upheavals.

Medieval England's principal attraction is the acting offered by Anthony Hopkins as Wat Tyler and Christopher Logue as John Ball. In marked contrast to these skilled performances, the other players offer only corny histrionics. The film is marked by gruesome (and gratuitous) scenes of violence including Tyler's murder and the torture of one of his lieutenants. Moreover, the narration goes overboard in declaring this event to be the first in the clash between labor and capital. The concluding scenes linking 1381 to later revolts are unconvincing.

Faith and Fear
(The Christians series)

40 minutes   color
1976   Granada

Summary: An unfocused but sometimes engrossing examination of the beliefs and experiences of Europeans during the High Middle Ages and the fourteenth century

Grade: B -

The film employs a narrator, visits to historic locales, the buildings and works of art of the time, maps, and present-day examples of religious practices directly linked to the Middle Ages. Actors read key passages from this time such as St. Francis of Assisi's Canticle of the Sun. The basic theme of the film is the way in which the Catholic faith helped alleviate the uncertainty and psychological insecurity of life in this era. A secondary theme is the tension between religious belief, as personified by St. Francis, and the organized church as a possessor of wealth and power.

Faith and Fear begins by visiting a Spanish village where the observance of Good Friday still revolves around a "dance of death" reminiscent of the practices of the Middle Ages. The remainder of the first half of the film presents the cathedrals constructed during the this era, and looks at such features of medieval life as the pilgrimage and the collection of relics. The sculptures carved into the walls of the cathedral of Bourges show the harsh image medieval Europeans had of God's judgement and the hell to which sinners would be consigned.

The second half of the film shows the students of present-day Paris taking their annual spring hike to the cathedral at Chartres. Following a further discussion of the medieval obsession with relics and the lavish buildings and reliquaries designed to house them, the film examines the life of St. Francis of

Assisi. The narration stresses the contrast between the Church as a vehicle for salvation and its role as a powerful worldly institution. The film shows the vast convent and basilica built where St. Francis had once lived in a simple hut. Faith and Fear closes by examining the grisly impact of the Black Death, the epidemic of the bubonic plague that devastated European society in the fourteenth century. It also stresses the growing pomp and worldly focus of the Church. The sale of indulgences and the vast sums spent on the construction of St. Peter's in Rome show a religious organization far removed from the simple piety of St. Francis.

The film illustrates vividly the living legacy of medieval piety, e.g., in scenes of today's Catholics climbing the Holy Staircase in Rome on their knees as pilgrims have done for centuries. The narration is eloquent and witty: comparing pilgrimages to modern tourism and describing relics like "the Holy Foreskin." The central theme of medieval Europeans clinging to religious faith as solace in a dark and frightening world is made memorable.

Faith and Fear is marred,, however, by its wandering among numerous topics. It lacks any clear sense of chronology: no student watching it will find indications about when key events took place. The basic theological achievements of the Middle Ages, such as the philosophy of Abelard or St. Thomas Aquinas, are omitted. As the narration jumps wildly from the Black Death to indulgences to the construction of St. Peter's, the film loses coherence.

THE RENAISSANCE

The Artist
(Renaissance series)

57 minutes   color
1993   Vision/Quest

Summary: A visually magnificent examination of the changing role of the artist in Europe from Brunelleschi to Velasquez; it is marred the limited way in treats the topic as well as by its attempt to discuss nearly a dozen individual artists

Grade: B +

    The Artist employs a narrator, commentators from academia such as Natalie Davis and Theodore Rabb, present-day figures from the art world, and actors playing the role and reciting the words of important artists. There is also a rich sampling of the art of the time (portraits, sculptures, buildings) as well as contemporary views of some of the great locales of the Renaissance. The basic theme of the film is the way in which the artist's social role changed from craftsman to a figure courted by monarchs and aristocrats. A secondary theme is the way in which artists not only glorify their own era but also serve the subversive role of critic and proponent of alternate realities.
    The film's impressive prologue quotes Leonardo da Vinci, against a background of great works from this era, on the artist's vast capacity to create either beauty or horror. The contemporary figures from the art world--artists, museum and gallery executives--also consider what an artist can offer his society.
    The film proper begins by tracing the career of the independently minded Filippo Brunelleschi in the early fifteenth century: an architect whose ideas provoked the ridicule of prominent citizens in his native Florence, he also

refused to knuckle under to the authority of the guilds in that city. Magnificent scenes of present-day Florence and Venice accompany a discussion of the stormy relationship between art patrons and geniuses like Michelangelo and Rafael.

During the second portion of the film, the scene shifts to include artists from northern Europe such as Albrecht Dürer. Peter Brueghel is shown as a powerful critic of Spain's religious persecution in the Low Countries. In Italy Titian, Veronese, Caravaggio, and Artemesia Gentileschi exemplify artists as, respectively, a wealthy entrepreneur, an embattled target of the Inquisition, a figure on the fringe of the criminal world, and a woman whose violent experiences with men shaped her artistic vision.

The film offers a multitude of extraordinary images ranging from the works of art of the time to memorable views of the locales that produced them. Scenes from present-day Florence are particularly striking. The narration is interesting, and the comments on the aims of today's artists and the obstacles they face are well-integrated into the flow of the film.

The film's major weakness is its stress on the artist's social position. The vital theme of the Renaissance as a transition to a new intellectual world from that of the Middle Ages is scarcely mentioned. The hasty treatment of numerous artists such as Veronese in the final portion of the film is rushed to the point of being breathless.

Dürer and the Renaissance

14 minutes	color
1962	McGraw-Hill

Summary: A brief, lucid, and informative study of how the artistic and intellectual trends of late Renaissance Italy spread northward as seen in the work of Albrecht Dürer

Grade: B

Dürer and the Renaissance employs a narrator, the prints and woodcuts of Dürer, as well as the paintings and drawings of the Italian artists who influenced him. The theme of the film is Dürer's role as a bridge between the artistic techniques of Renaissance Italy and the cultural and religious currents of Northern Europe. The film begins with Dürer's self portrait, prints showing Nuremberg during the early sixteenth century, and paintings showing the Venice of that era. It then describes how Dürer became a link between these two great European centers of civilization.

There follows an examination of Dürer's early works, such as his sketch of Erasmus. Next comes a description of Dürer's important visit to Venice.

The film concludes with an examination of Dürer's painting, showing how he blended techniques of Michelangelo with the religiosity and melancholy of his northern homeland.

The film elucidates a topic of fundamental importance, namely the spread of Renaissance culture beyond the bounds of Italy. Its chief weakness is its brevity. Moreover, the narration contains a crucial error. It contends incorrectly that independent towns, which reflected economic and intellectual changes, existed only in Italy at this time. This ignores the flourishing urban life in the Netherlands in this era.

Students can be asked to consider what other kinds of individuals traveling between Northern and Southern Europe were likely to transmit the ideas of the Renaissance to regions beyond Italy.

The Early Renaissance
(Art of the Western World series)

60 minutes   color
1989   WNET

Summary: An uneven but clear and valuable consideration of both Italy and Northern Europe from the mid-fourteenth century to the eve of the Reformation; the portion of the film dealing with Italy is more focused and adroit

Grade: B

Using contemporary scenes, the works of art of the time, and interviews with leading authorities, the film traces the development of a brilliant urban Italian culture. Florence is used as an important example of a community that blended a continuing connection to the Christian church with a rage for knowledge of the ancient world of Greece and Rome. The treatment of Northern Europe centers on the ducal court of Burgundy with its center at Dijon, the vivid and often morbid Christian practices of the North, and the works of Albrecht Dürer.

The first half of The Early Renaissance considers the nature of the city-states of northern Italy, beginning with scenes of present-day Siena and Florence. The narration notes the way in which the Black Death that arrived in 1347 decimated Italian society but opened opportunities to the survivors for economic advancement. The film traces the art of the period from Giotto to Botticelli and da Vinci. It indicates how the representation of religious subjects took on greater realism and then, borrowing from pagan antiquity, greater sensuality. All of this, as the film stresses, constituted a basic shift in Western thought: from the religious rigidities of the Middle Ages to the modern, individualistic culture of the Renaissance. The latter integrated classical culture and modern ambition.

The second half of the film has no comparably clear, overriding theme. It notes correctly that the Europe of this time had a second center of urban activity and artistic achievement in the Netherlands. This region had close commercial and artistic contact with northern Italy; but it lacked a classical interest comparable to Italy's. In the North religious tensions augmented by news about the Turkish onslaught against Europe, produced notable works: the horrible secular and religious imagery of Hieronymous Bosch, Matthias Grünewald's Isenheim Altar, as well as the moody introspection of Albrecht Dürer's woodcuts.

The first portion of the film can be shown by itself as a vivid and accessible introduction to Italy in the first stages of the Renaissance. It presents in fine fashion the development of a commercial society with an interest in human personality, individuality, and its own roots in pagan antiquity. Both halves of the film feature memorable and well-photographed works of art.

Nonetheless, the second section of the film lacks a clear theme. Moreover, the film suggest a number of dubious conclusions: that the Renaissance took place against the background of smoothly rising prosperity in fourteenth and fifteenth-century Italy; that the classical interests so evident in Italy were not present in such northern regions as Germany or England.

Students can be asked to weigh the relative significance of religious themes and classical (pagan) techniques in the art of the Renaissance to consider how strong Christianity remained in such circumstances. One could also consider possible explanations for the often morbid nature of northern art in contrast to the life-affirming images of the South.

Epitome of the Italian Renaissance: The Gonzagas of Mantua

60 minutes   color
19992   Films for the Humanities & Sciences

Summary: This visually appealing film treats a significant topic in the history of the Renaissance; nonetheless, it is marred by poor pacing and a lack of organization

Grade: C -

Epitome of the Italian Renaissance employs a narrator, extensive dramatic reenactments, visits to important historical locales including spectacular aerial views, maps, and rich samples of the art of the time. The basic theme of the film is how the Gonzaga rulers of the small city-state of Mantua came to power, then played a significant role in the course of the Renaissance.

The film begins with contemporary views of Mantua and its surrounding countryside. It shifts almost immediately to the first in a series of dramatizations of key events in the history of the city. Like many of these dramatizations, this one involving a local nobleman and a representative of the bishop of Mantua lacks any clear significance.

The story of Mantua continues through the civil wars that brought the Gonzagas to power, the construction of their great ducal palace, and the formation of their highly cultured court. There are extensive discussions of the achievements of the artist Andrea Mantegna at Padua, the role of Isabelle d'Este as wife of the Duke of Padua and patroness of arts, and finally of marital conflict within the Gonzaga family.

Despite the rich historical topic it takes up, the film cannot hold the viewer's attention. The numerous dramatic sequences, while they feature fine acting, have no obvious link with the mainstream of events. Overall, the slow pace is deadening. The vast contribution of the Gonzagas and their court to Renaissance art and culture is never made clear.

Florence: Cradle of the Renaissance
(Museum City Video series)

30 minutes   color
1992   PBS

Summary: A visually attractive but intellectually muddled introduction to the Renaissance through a tour of the city of Florence

Grade: C +

Florence: Cradle of the Renaissance presents the Renaissance through the examination of a number of the city's historic buildings. By considering structures such as the Baptistery, the Campanile, the Signoria, and the Uffizi Palace, the film attempts to explain how the Renaissance marked a break with Europe's medieval past.

The film's flaws are more striking than its virtues. The tone of the narration is gushy and breathless. It stresses an unsophisticated view of the medieval era as a prolonged period of ignorance and intellectual stagnation. It is equally simplistic in tying the start of the Renaissance to the prosperity of Florence's banking community. Thus, the Renaissance is seen as a sudden event, marking an abrupt turning point in European history.

The film fails to describe clearly the basic intellectual concepts of the Renaissance. It never follows up on brief references to "man, the measure of all things," or Florence's "love of liberty." Nor does it offer any comprehensible chronology. Events such as the Siege of Florence in 1509 are mentioned in passing. The narration casually refers to numerous individuals ranging from Petrarch to Benvenuto Cellini without placing them in any historical context.

The film's positive elements are contained exclusively in its visual images. Despite occasionally blurry photography, it offers an extensive view of the artistic and architectural heritage of the Renaissance in present-day Florence. Used with a detailed historical introduction, it would be understandable to most students.

A more ambitious possibility is to ask students to consider some of the contradictions within the film. If the Renaissance is so dramatic a break with the religious society of the Middle Ages, why does so much of the art center on religious themes?

The Hero as Artist
(Civilisation: A Personal View by Kenneth Clark series)

52 minutes   color
1970   BBC

Summary: A narrow and poorly paced examination of the artistic achievements of the Renaissance during the sixteenth century stressing the work of Michelangelo, Rafael, and Leonardo da Vinci; it is sharply divorced from any consideration of the political or social developments of the time

Grade: C -

The Hero as Artist features a narration by Kenneth Clark, the art and architecture of the time, and visits to important historical locales. The basic theme of the film is the splendid artistic achievement of the sixteenth century and its dependence upon the cooperation between such creators as Michelangelo and patrons such as Pope Julius II.

Showing present-day Rome, Kenneth Clark indicates how the scale of Renaissance creativity changed by the early sixteenth century. Artistic creation now took place in ways represented by the grandiose Vatican courtyard and the elaborate tomb intended for Julius II.

The film goes on to an extensive examination of Michelangelo's paintings on the Sistine Chapel, Rafael's School of Athens, and the scientific notebooks of Leonardo da Vinci. Unlike preceding portions of the Civilisation series, this episode is unrelated to significant political or social developments. No student watching it would get a hint of the invasions of Italy by France and Spain, the popes' roles as political and even military leaders, or the political and intellectual ferment that helped to produce a Machiavelli. Most important of all, the pacing is slow to the point of being soporific.

The High Renaissance
(Art of the Western World series)

60 minutes   color
1989   WNET

Summary: A visually attractive but verbose treatment of the artistic peak of the Renaissance in Rome and Venice; it displays little concern with the historical currents of the time

Grade: D

The High Renaissance uses classic works of art, brief lectures by noted art historians, and contemporary scenes of the locales where great art was produced. Stressing a technical consideration of the art of the time, the film initially focuses on Michelangelo and Rafael as the great artistic heroes of the sixteenth-century Roman Renaissance. The second portion of the film looks at the great painters and architects who worked in the Venice of this era; Titian, Palladio, Tintoretto, and Veronese.

The film begins with the works of Rafael and Leonardo da Vinci. There is a brief discussion of the impact of the sack of Rome by the army of Charles V in 1527. This introduces the somber artistic works and poetry produced by Michelangelo in the following decade.

The second portion of the film focuses on the city of Venice, described as a self-consciously modern and freethinking urban center of the sixteenth century. There Titian produced both visions of the Virgin Mary and erotic depictions of Venus, and Palladio built churches in the shape of classical temples. Meanwhile, the merchants of the economically declining city-state masked their concerns with expensive villas modeled on those of the ancient Romans.

The film is visually attractive and clearly organized. It briefly raises interesting issues: the impact of traumas like the sack of Rome in 1527 on Renaissance art and on the mood of society. It also considers the ability of Venice to shelter its artists from the force of the Inquisition. Regrettably, the dominant element in the film consists of technical discussions of the work of the artists of the High Renaissance.

Leonardo Da Vinci: Giant of the Renaissance

25 minutes   color
1957   Encyclopedia Britannica Educational Corporation

Summary: A sketchy but visually attractive study of the career of the great Renaissance artist; it stresses his vast intellectual curiosity and his success in creating works of lasting beauty

Grade: B -

The film uses Leonardo's own words and sketches, visits to locales where key events in his life occurred, and examination of his surviving works of art. The theme of the film is Leonardo's pursuit of his dual passions: a scientific impulse to understand the structure of the world around him, and the artist's desire to create masterworks of visual magnificence.

Leonard Da Vinci begins by showing scenes of the artist's home region followed by views of Florence, where he obtained his artistic education. There is an extensive consideration of the training he received in the workshop of the established artist Andrea del Verrocchio, including parts of Verocchio's painting probably done by this young apprentice. The film goes on to show Leonardo's growing interest in engineering and invention as he became involved in Italy's wars at the close of the fifteenth century. But this is combined with his study of a variety of faces, his interest in botany, and his skills at architecture.

The film follows Leonardo's great artistic achievement of The Last Supper from his preliminary sketches to the finished product. Stressing the range of his interests, the film shows Leonardo immersed in the study of anatomy at the same time he produced his brilliant paintings. In his final decades he appears building fortresses for Cesare Borgia and delving into the mechanics of flight.

The film vividly displays Leonardo's artistic achievement, and it emphasizes the range of his scientific interests. It employs Leonardo's own words and sketches from his notebook with great effect. On the other hand, there is no effort to connect Leonardo with the events of his time or larger artistic trends of the Renaissance. The wars into which he was drawn and the leaders he served such as Ludovico Sforza and Cesar Borgia are scarcely discussed.

The film can be used only following a substantial introduction to the basic features of the Renaissance. Students can be asked to consider whether Leonardo's scientific concerns were unique to him or tied to the concerns of other key figures of the Renaissance. Students should be informed that the narration is drawn largely from Leonardo's own writings.

Machiavelli on Political Power
(Man and the State series)

29 minutes   color
1972   Barr Films

Summary: A drama presenting Machiavelli's cynical and realistic ideas about the nature and conduct of an effective ruler; well-paced, effectively acted, and colorful but marred by a lack of clarity in parts of the narration

Grade: B

The film shows numerous dramatized episodes from Machiavelli's life; its centerpiece is an imaginary trial ordered by Duke Lorenzo de' Medici of Florence.   In this confrontation the actor playing Machiavelli quotes from his writings in response to challenges from a theologian, a humanist philosopher and a teacher of government.   The key theme of the film is how Machiavelli tried to analyze political life in terms of the brutal and power-hungry way in which he believed rulers actually conducted their affairs.   Another theme is the tumultuous and unstable political environment in which Machiavelli and other Italians lived at the start of the sixteenth century.

Machiavelli on Political Power begins with an extended prologue introducing the artistic and political world of Renaissance Italy.   It shows Machiavelli, imprisoned, tortured, and then exiled into the countryside outside his native Florence.   After writing The Prince, Machiavelli must return to Florence to face an offended Duke Lorenzo.   The Duke orders him to defend his ideas against proponents of the traditional view, stretching from Aristotle to Erasmus, that a prince must be a model of virtue and morality.

Machiavelli cites three episodes from the career of Cesare Borgia to show how an effective ruler should conduct his affairs.   Each of the three incidents pictures a cruel ruler who bases his actions on distrust of his subjects.   Machiavelli insists that such measures are necessary for a ruler, if not to come to power then to remain on top.

The film ends with Machiavelli seeking employment from the government of the Florentine republic after the fall of Duke Lorenzo. Florentine officials reject him as a traitor: they remind him that he once supported the republic, then groveled before the duke seeking work, and now turns once again to the republic he abandoned.

The film is colorful and well-acted. It effectively presents the dilemma of how to achieve political success. Its major flaw is one important dramatized episode showing Cesare Borgia crushing his rebellious subordinates.   Here the narration becomes totally confusing.   The film also neglects to present any background about Borgia and the events in which he used his power so brutally. The rapid change in government in Florence that victimized Machiavelli is also left unexplained.

The film can serve as a follow-up to a class treatment of the Renaissance and Machiavelli's role as a pioneer of modern political thought. Apart from the obvious discussion of the accuracy of Machiavelli's views of the political process, there is another topic to pursue.   Did Machiavelli see the prince acting only in his own interest? At several points in the film, Machiavelli seems to suggest that the population as a whole benefits from having this kind of realistic if brutal leader.

Man, the Measure of All Things
(Civilisation: A Personal View by Kenneth Clark series)

54 minutes   color
1970   BBC

Summary: A clear, colorful, but slow paced examination of the Renaissance in fifteenth-century Italy stressing the emergence of confidence and individualism

Grade: B

     Man, the Measure of All Things employs narrator Kenneth Clark, the art and architecture of the time, and visits to important historical locales. Its major theme is the way in which the urban world of fifteenth-century Florence and the smaller cities of northern Italy became the setting for a new interest in human capabilities. A subsidiary theme is the way in which similar developments in the arts took place in Flanders during the same era.
     The film starts by examining the light and airy Pazzi Chapel in Florence. This illustrates the shift in spirit from the Middle Ages to the new world of the Renaissance. As Clark puts it, the wealthy and pleasure-loving merchants of northern Italy now felt a new awareness of human possibilities. They wanted their own faces and their view of humanity incorporated in works of art that differed sharply from those of medieval Europe.
     The film considers the pioneers of the new culture such as Petrarch, the searcher after the texts of the ancient world, Cosimo de' Medici, who built a library to house these works, along with artists like Brunelleschi and Donatello. It points out how the new urban world generated an interest in town planning not seen since the era of Ancient Rome. The confidence of the era is captured by the sculptor Alberti's statement in his autobiography, "A man can do all things if he will." Clark's focus shifts briefly to northern Europe to show the painters of the Flanders school, but he returns to Italy for an extended examination of Botticelli. Botticelli's paintings like The Birth of Venus show the artistic highpoints of the period.
     The film concludes by broadening its perspective. First, it considers the smaller courts of northern Italy such as Mantua and Urbino. Secondly, it reminds the viewer that the Renaissance was the product of a wealthy minority living in a society still largely tied to an agrarian, religious style of life. Clark sees a sense of pessimism entering Renaissance art by the time of Giorgione.
     Man, the Measure of All Things is clear, and Clark skillfully employs the vast supply of art available to illustrate the period. Even with its focus on

the visual arts, the film manages to consider the work of political figures like Lorenzo de' Medici and writings like Baldassare Castiglione's prescription for gentlemanly conduct. Nonetheless, the film slows markedly for leisurely examinations of works by like Donatello and Botticelli. Its abrupt shift of focus to Flanders is confusing. The pessimistic note introduced at the close has no clear connection to the bulk of the film.

Michelangelo

30 minutes   color
1965   Encyclopedia Britannica Educational Corporation

Summary: A visually brilliant examination of the highpoints of Michelangelo's life and career; it omits any consideration of the historical times in which the great artist lived

Grade: B

Michelangelo employs a number of actors reading key documents of the time and numerous examples of Michelangelo's achievements as a painter and sculptor. The basic theme of the film is Michelangelo's extraordinary range and profundity as an artist.

The film begins with an actor reading from Giorgio Vasari's biography of Michelangelo, detailing his boyhood, his period as an apprentice, and his growing interest in sculpture. Other actors read passages from Michelangelo's letters as the artist's career proceeds through such sculptural achievements as the Pietà, David, and the statuary for the tomb of Pope Julius II. The second half of the film stresses Michelangelo's successes as a painter. It treats his work from the ceiling of the Sistine Chapel to the Last Judgement he did for Paul III in the latter stages of his career. The final topic considered is Michelangelo's role as the pioneer architect in the planning of St. Peter's basilica.

The film combines a lucid narration and memorable views of Michelangelo's work. Its major weakness is the absence of any consideration of the Renaissance and the Counter-Reformation as crucial events framing Michelangelo's artistic career. There is no effort, for example, to put Michelangelo's sculpture in the context of the Renaissance's fascination with the ancient world. Nor does the film tie Michelangelo's grim Last Judgement scenes to the thrust of the Counter-Reformation. Combined with a suitable historical introduction, however, the film can be used to illustrate such developments while it shows the artistic highpoint of this era.

Princes and Prelates
(The Christians series)

43 minutes   color
1976   Granada

Summary: A lucid and informative treatment of two significant, often neglected, topics: the opposition to papal power on the part of John Wycliffe and Jan Hus; the growing political and artistic sophistication and the parallel decline in spiritual prestige of the Renaissance

Grade: B +

Princes and Prelates employs a narrator, actors reciting passages from key figures of the time, portraits and other works of art from the period, maps, and visits to important historical locales. The basic theme of the film is the growing weakness of the papacy in this era. The institution found itself burdened by critics like Hus, the corruption of individual popes, and the tendency of popes to devote much of their energy to the arts and the Italian political scene.

Beginning with views of Vatican City today, the film uses the papal palace at Avignon to represent the extent of the papacy's physical power in the final stages of the Middle Ages. A discussion of the Great Schism of the late fourteenth and early fifteenth centuries, when the Church was tormented by having two and then three popes, leads to a consideration of the growing criticism of papal authority. First came the challenge posed by the Englishman John Wycliffe. Then, with greater impact, the Czech Jan Hus weighed in. The film shows the anti-papal paintings on the walls of Hus's chapel in Prague and the weapons used by his followers to fight off armies dispatched against them by the pope. Thus, the film presents a rare treatment of this first successful heresy in Catholic Europe.

The second half of the film focuses on the papacy in Renaissance Italy. Tracing the travels of Martin V, the pope whose election in 1417 ended the Great Schism, the film first examines Renaissance life in Florence. It points out the exuberant commercial and artistic world to be found in Florence. It uses the works of Botticelli and Michelangelo to show how knowledge of the ancient world stimulated Renaissance artists to glorify the human body and, more broadly, human potential. Following Martin to Rome, the film describes the success of popes in transforming the shabby city into a great center of majestic buildings designed to dazzle Catholic believers. It also shows the accompanying corruption: popes elevating their relatives to high church positions; popes like Alexander VI arousing gossip across Europe by the dissolute way they lived.

Finally, the film shows the papacy confronting the reforming priest Savonarola in the 1490s and, three decades later, the conquest of Rome by the army of Emperor Charles V. In the face of such catastrophes, the changing temper of art sponsored by the pope appears in the terrifying images of Michelangelo's <u>Last Judgement</u>.

<u>Princes and Prelates</u> shows clearly the forces challenging the papacy as well as the self-destructive actions of individual popes. The story of Hus and his movement is particularly lucid. Pagan imagery in Botticelli's painting shows how far the Renaissance world with its view of man's perfection diverged from that of the Middle Ages. The film, however, suffers from instances of ambiguity. There is no discussion of how the papacy came to be located at Avignon or how the resulting Schism took place. Until the film takes us to the career of Hus, it presents no dates to orient the viewer in time. The sack of Rome by the army of Charles V remains unexplained. A brief reference to Martin Luther is equally cryptic.

A useful topic for discussion is whether better leadership could have guided the papacy safely past the forces that weakened it in the fifteenth and early sixteenth century.

Renaissance--Its Beginnings in Italy

26 minutes   color
1957   Encyclopedia Britannica Educational Corporation

Summary: A clear and well-organized examination of the origins and development of the Renaissance; it stresses the magniture of the change that occurred when medieval culture gave way to the new ideas of Florence in the fourteenth and fifteenth centuries

Grade: B

The film employs a narrator, present-day views of Italian cities, the art and buildings of the Renaissance, dramatic reenactments, and actors reading from documents of that era. The basic theme of the film is the discernible shift in European culture, first from the medieval world of 1000 to the start of the fourteenth century, then from the early fourteenth century to the highpoint of the Renaissance at the start of the sixteenth century.

The film begins with views of Renaissance statuary. The narrator notes that the Renaissance bloomed throughout much of Europe, but it began in Florence. There follows a brief view of European culture at three crucial points: 1000, 1300, and 1521, setting up the framework for the remainder of the film.

Scenes of Chartres Cathedral and its religious statuary show how the medieval world view stressed the glory of an afterlife. Immediately thereafter views of happy children at play, the sculptured figures of Renaissance artist Luca della Robbia, show the leap art has taken in three centuries in glorying in the pleasures of the here and now. The narration then considers factors including the commercial wealth of Italy and its ties to the ancient world that facilitated a cultural rebirth based on classical civilization.

The narration then considers the role of Florence as the center of Renaissance culture, with an extensive consideration of the art of Leonardo da Vinci and Michelangelo. Leonardo's role in scientific investigation, a field which the film presents as a crucial part of the Renaissance, appears with sketches and quotations from his notebook on the human body and the possibility of flight.

The film is a useful summary of significant historical thinking about the Renaissance. Students can be asked to consider whether it overstates the distinction between the medieval world and the Renaissance. Similarly, they can be asked if Leonardo was part of an important wave of scientific discovery, or only an isolated indicator of the true Scientific Revolution that would follow him in the seventeenth century.

Van Eyck: Father of Flemish Painting

27 minutes   color
1974   International Film Bureau

Summary: A visually splendid but slow paced analysis of several major paintings by Van Eyck, the leading artist in Northern Europe in the fifteenth century; it depicts the splendor and religious devotion of the North during this era without considering specific historical events or trends

Grade: C -

The film is an illustrated lecture about the works of Jan van Eyck, employing a narration set against his various paintings and drawings. There is a particular emphasis on the symbolism and artistic techniques he uses in his Adoration of the Lamb painted in 1432. The main theme of the film is the success van Eyck had in moving away from the miniature illuminations on manuscripts that had constituted the main body of northern painting. Another theme is the way in which van Eyck filled his work with a combination of realistic detail, psychological insight, and religious devotion.

The film begins by describing how van Eyck joined the court of Philip the Good, the Duke of Burgundy, in 1425. It then considers a number of paintings showing how van Eyck produced portraits, wedding pictures, devotional works, with an increasing emphasis on realistic landscapes in the background. The second half of the film is devoted to an analysis of van Eyck's masterpiece, Adoration of the Lamb.

The film is visually attractive, and it can serve in an examination of urban society and court life in Northern Europe in this period. The marriage scene indicates both the presence of Italians in the North--the bridegroom is a Medici banker--and the fervor of religious belief as seen in the numerous examples of religious symbolism. Nonetheless, the film stresses van Eyck's artistic genius and accomplishments, and there is little concern with historical events.

The Warrior

See review under SEVENTEENTH CENTURY

REFORMATION AND COUNTER-REFORMATION

The Dissenter
(Renaissance series)

57 minutes   color
1993   Vision/Quest

Summary: A stimulating and lucid examination of the role of Jan Hus and Martin Luther in challenging the Catholic church's doctrines and organization in fifteenth and sixteenth-century Europe; the film contains a lively discussion of the role that dissent and dissenters should play in any society

Grade: A

      The film uses a narrator, commentaries by Professor Theodore Rabb and such notable contemporary dissenters as Betty Friedan and Solidarity activist Bronislaw Geremek, actors playing the parts and reciting the words of historical figures. There are also prints and paintings from the era under discussion, and visits to important historical locales. The basic theme of the film is the way in which first Hus, then Luther used Biblical authority and their own aroused consciences to attack what they considered the errors and abuses of church authorities. A subsidiary theme is the way in which many societies witness a creative tension between long-established institutions and courageous individuals who insist on following their own consciences.

      The first half of The Dissenter examines the career of Jan Hus, who appears in the first scene in the dungeon at Constance that will hold him until his execution in 1415. Narrator Ian Richardson addresses the audience to describe the dominant role of the Catholic church in Europe during this era, illustrated by scenes of the great cathedrals that stood at the center of Europe's cities. The film notes that the scholarly disputations characteristic of university teaching in the Late Middle Ages provided a basis for future challenges to the Church's doctrine.

The film then traces Hus's moves toward confrontation with the Church. The promising and ambitious young priest decides to challenge the Church's authority over issues such as the nature of communion, the sale of indulgences, and the authority of the pope. Interspersed with this account are statements by twentieth-century dissidents like Friedan and Gemerek on the elements that motivated them to challenge existing social and political norms. Actors give rich samples of Hus's stirring rhetoric.

The second half of the film focuses on the life and career of Martin Luther. An actor recites Luther's musings in old age about the surprising path his life had taken. The film describes him as a child tormented by fears of Hell, as a young man entering the monastery against his father's wishes, and as the novice priest who remained in the throes of spiritual torment. Theodore Rabb comments astutely on Luther's break with the past: he discerned in his Bible the view that Faith alone, not the mediation of the Church, would bring him salvation. As Rabb puts it, the psychological release Luther received at such a moment made his return to previous ideas impossible.

The film notes how the political support of Germany's princes saved Luther from the tragic fate that Hus suffered. It vividly displays samples in the "war of pamphlets" by which Luther's ideas spread and were challenged. Thus, the key role of the printing press in breaking the Church's monopoly on knowledge appears clearly. In dealing with the Peasant Rebellion of the 1520s, Luther turns dramatically to the political establishment that had protected him. Grisly contemporary prints demonstrate how the peasant uprising was repressed.

Interviews with twentieth-century dissidents add a modern dimension to Luther's career. One highpoint is Betty Friedan's comment that she, like Luther after 1517, would have been frightened to know in advance the dimensions of the change she was about to unleash. The film concludes with a brief treatment of the Counter-Reformation, the Wars of Religion, and Europe's first halting steps toward a system of religious toleration.

The film is well-paced, brilliantly photographed, and accompanied by an incisive narration. The historical speeches presented by the actors illustrate the ideas of reformers and traditionalists alike. The treatment of Jan Hus, less well-known than Luther but a crucial figure in European history, is clear and convincing. Luther's shift from a figure of rebellion to a pillar of a new (and intolerant) status quo following the Peasant Rebellion is an important point, well-presented.

Like other films in the series, this one employs the term "Renaissance" to cover a vast period more properly described as the era of Early Modern Europe. Moreover, the film overstates its case in one significant way: by identifying the collapse of the exclusive authority of the Catholic church as the sole cause of why we accept dissent in present-day society. Students should be reminded of the way dissenting ideas circulated at the time, with the Czech Hus drawing inspiration from the English scholar John Wycliffe. Similarly students should be directed to the way in which limited dissent, such as Hus's view of Communion and Luther's objection to indulgences, implied challenges to Church and papal authority as a whole.

Students can be asked to consider what personality traits or personal experiences help create a dissenter. What conditions permit the success of a challenge to a long-standing and well-established set of established institutions?

Grandeur and Obedience
(Civilisation: A Personal View by Kenneth Clark series)

52 minutes   color
1970   BBC

Summary: A disjointed but insightful examination of the resurgence of the Catholic church following the challenge of the Reformation; much of the final third of the film deals with the seventeenth century

Grade: B -

Grandeur and Obedience employs narrator Kenneth Clark, the art and architecture of the sixteenth and seventeenth centuries, and visits to important historical locales. Its major theme is the continuing power of the Catholic church and its confident spiritual reply to the Reformation.

The film begins by displaying the grandeur of the Church of Santa Maria Maggiore. Dating back to ancient times, it shows the confidence of the early Church prior to the barbarian invasions. Kenneth Clark sets the theme of the entire film by noting that such grandeur was now, following the blow applied by Protestantism, to be seen once again.

In its first two-thirds, Grandeur and Obedience uses great works of art such as Michelangelo's Last Judgement to show a somber but determined Church. Even though Rome had been sacked by foreign armies in 1527, the Catholic church reasserted its authority with daunting self-confidence. As architect of the new St. Peter's, Michelangelo stood at the center of the building program which was the revival's most tangible produces.

The film notes astutely the psychological sustenance the Church and its cult of the loving Virgin offered to huge numbers of Europeans. Similarly it stresses the confidence and skill with which Church leaders countered Protestantism by restating old doctrines, such as the power of saints and relics, which Protestants had found so repulsive.

The final third of the film deals with the Baroque art of the seventeenth century. The focus is on Bernini as sculptor and architect. Clark finds the

Italian's exuberance, flamboyance, and sense of drama to reflect the Church's restored confidence.

Much of the film is visually grand, notably the aerial shots of Rome's architectural monuments of this period. The film intelligently treats several basic features of Catholic Europe in the sixteenth century: papal leadership, the Council of Trent, and doctrinal authoritarianism. Clark indicates clearly that, in the midst of the Reformation century, many Europeans had good reason to remain psychologically attached to the security and comfort of the Catholic church. The film is severely marred, however, by its leisurely pace with long stretches devoted to religious architecture. The final third of the film immerses itself in a technical examination of artistic achievements of Bernini. Moreover, Grandeur and Obedience never touches upon the great military and political confrontations that helped shape Europe in this era: the Netherlands Revolt, the French civil wars, or the Thirty Years War.

Students can be asked to consider how the artistic achievements of this era reflected the Church's continuing financial resources. They can also ponder why so many Europeans responded positively to the Church's conservatism in dogma.

In Search of Tolerance
(The Christians series)

40 minutes   color
1976   Granada

Summary: An examination of radical Protestant movements in Europe during the sixteenth and seventeenth centuries and how such groups then found refuge in British North America; its first half is a valuable view of the Reformation era

Grade: B -

The film employs a narrator, prints from the time, visits to historical locales and to present-day practitioners of the religions under consideration. There are also actors reading from important documents of the time. The first theme of the film is the diversity of Protestant movements that sprang up in this era and the brutal persecution some of them encountered. The second theme is the way in which religious refugees to Massachusetts set up their own brand of religious intolerance, only to see it countered by the growth of religious diversity and toleration.

In Search of Tolerance begins with such images of dissent and religious toleration in contemporary America as Martin Luther King's Washington Speech of August 1963 and views of an Amish community in Pennsylvania. There follows a discussion of radical Protestant movements in Reformation Europe. It features a comparison of the Anabaptists, ordinary people without political ambitions who were martyred for their faith, with the Huguenots, some of whom were willing to lunge for power in late sixteenth-century France. A visit to a Huguenot stronghold in present-day France shows devices like disguised altars by which the dissidents hid their activities from the representatives of a Catholic state. Here worshippers still hold open air services to commemorate the practices of four hundred years ago.

The story of English Puritans starts in the Old World. It illustrates the tolerance of Holland where these English refugees first found shelter. Tracing the Puritans leads the film to colonial America. There a self-reliant immigrant community grew. It displayed its own intolerance against the Indians and against non-conformists in its own ranks. For example, the film describes the brutal treatment Massachusetts Puritans meted out to dissidents like the Quakers. It concludes by noting the triumph of toleration in the policies of William Penn, who was happy to tolerate even self-confessed witches! The Amish communities of today show the direct descendants of the Anabaptists of the sixteenth century.

The first half of the film is a lucid and informative depiction of the growing diversity of Protestantism and the mixture of persecution and toleration such groups found in sixteenth-century Europe. Unfortunately, the second half of the film is rooted in the history of colonial America and presents little of direct interest for a consideration of European history.

Students can be asked to consider the power of the emotional forces that incited their fellow Europeans to deal so harshly with the Anabaptists. They can also consider what factors tended to maintain Holland as a bastion of toleration.

<u>Protest and Communication</u>
(<u>Civilisation: A Personal View by Kenneth Clark</u> series)

53 minutes   color
1970   BBC

Summary: A loosely knit treatment of the sixteenth-century breakup of the medieval religious order and the response of contemporary thinkers to the ensuing turmoil; coherent in its first section, it wanders hopelessly thereafter

Grade: C

The film employs narrator Kenneth Clark, the art and artifacts of the period, visits to important historical locales, and excerpts from the era's literature. The first theme is the strong and growing religious impulse to be found in Northern Europe at the start of the sixteenth century in contrast to the more secular world of Renaissance. The second theme is the way in which

Europeans traumatized by the century's religious upheaval tried to keep their mental equilibrium.

Protest and Communication starts with the art of late fifteenth-century Germany. Clark claims that it shows a pious peasant society, intoxicated with religious feeling, and sharply different from the elegant culture of Renaissance Italy. The first portion of the film follows the career of Desiderius Erasmus, the northern Humanist whose satires of the Roman Church paved the way for the Reformation. It also traces the development of the printing press, which helped Erasmus to become Europe's first best selling author. Narrator Kenneth Clark uses an antique press to demonstrate how readily a single pamphlet could be reproduced to flood Europe with new ideas.

The film shifts to a leisurely examination of the works of Albrecht Dürer.   Clark finds this German's restless personality and artistic works mirroring the growing religious unrest of Northern Europe.   Next comes a consideration of the personality and religious rebellion of Martin Luther.

The final portion of Protest and Communication examines the violence unleashed by the Reformation.   It appears in present-day ruins of Catholic churches and pictures showing the bloodletting during the St.Bartholomew's Day massacre. The film indicates how Europeans like Michel Montaigne in France and William Shakespeare in England were unwilling to participate in the horrors of their time.   They deliberately stood aside from the dangerous fervor: Montaigne as a literary recluse and Shakespeare as a popular dramatist found refuge in intellectual endeavors.   Both called for individuals to bear up courageously in a world in which religious faith was no longer desirable.

The film has several useful portions, notably the early segment on Erasmus. The artifacts of the time, from the printing press to illustrated pages of Erasmus's writings, bring the sixteenth century to life.

On the whole, Protest and Communication is a ramshackle collection of murky elements. The segment on Dürer is a long digression on the artistic impulses that characterize his work. Clark's declaration that "the Germans are always looking for a leader" is tendentious. Luther's role in the early sixteenth century receives only modest attention. Most important of all, the final segment, with its long excerpts from Shakespeare's Hamlet and Macbeth, is virtually incomprehensible.   Its key point, that skepticism and deliberate lack of involvement were significant responses to religious change, remains unclear.

Protest and Reform
(The Christians series)

42 minutes   color
1976   Granada

Summary: A lucid and informative examination of the Protestant Reformation from Luther's challenge to the papacy in 1517 through Elizabeth I's establishment of a stable and relatively tolerant Anglican church

Grade: A

The film's writer and narrator, Bamber Gascoigne, discusses the main developments of the Reformation while showing the viewer the actual locales where key events took place. These range from the church door at Wittenberg to the monasteries seized by Henry VIII of England. The film uses numerous prints and paintings from the Reformation era, maps, and scenes showing present-day Protestant ministers at work. It ends with a glimpse of Northern Ireland in the 1970s, where the quarrels originating in the Reformation era remained a deadly force in society. The basic theme of the film is the dynamism of the Protestant Reformation, a dynamism that led to splits among the Protestants themselves.

The film begins by showing a Lutheran pastor and his family in West Germany. It moves quickly into a discussion of the sale of indulgences in early sixteenth-century Germany, the issue that led to Martin Luther's historic protest in 1517. Luther's career provides the centerpiece for the first half of Protest and Reform. It considers his confrontation with the Emperor Charles V at Worms in 1521, his translation of the Bible, his opposition to the Peasant Revolt of the mid-1520s, and his new personal role as a husband and father.

The second half of the film takes up the clash between Luther and his fellow reformer Uldrich Zwingli at Marburg in 1529. It shows how this presaged the divisions that would haunt Protestantism in the future. There follows a series of segments on John Calvin in Geneva and John Knox in Edinburgh, and a detailed treatment of religious changes in England in the first half of the sixteenth century.

The film concludes with a grim view of the ravaged province of Northern Ireland. It demonstrates the Reformation's continued ability to divide Europeans into warring camps. Balancing the hatred demonstrated here is an optimistic scene showing a husband and wife in Edinburgh, receiving ordination together into the Church of Scotland.

The film is written with wit and clarity, and Gascoigne skillfully ties events to their geographic location. In one memorable scene he shows the room in which Luther threw ink at the devil. Other highlights of the film include a description of Tetzel's techniques for selling indulgences as well as an account of how the lives of one group of nuns registered the complex religious changes dictated by England's various rulers.

The film is from a BBC series made for a British audience, and it employs terms such as "vicarage" and "nappies" that American students may find unfamiliar. Made in the mid-1970s, the film contains some dated references to a divided Germany and Moscow as an international center for revolution. These are insignificant failings.

SIXTEENTH CENTURY: WARS, POLITICS, THE AGE OF DISCOVERY

The Age of Gold
(The Buried Mirror series)

60 minutes   color
1991   Sogotel

Summary: A examination of Spanish history and culture in Europe and America from the sixteenth century to the eve of the colonial rebellions of the early nineteenth century; sometimes brilliant but more often diffuse and verbose

Grade: C +

The film centers on the narration by author Carlos Fuentes, along with maps, portraits and paintings, and visits to locales of historical significance. The basic theme of the film is the development of a powerful and culturally vibrant Spain in the sixteenth century and the parallel growth of a different but related set of societies in the New World.

The Age of Gold begins with an extended visit to present-day Bolivia. There Indian laborers continue to work the silver mines at Potosí whose origins date back to the Spanish Empire in the sixteenth century. The scene then shifts to Spain for a discussion of the rule of Charles V and Philip II, the challenge of English sea raiders like Sir Francis Drake to the Spanish Empire, and the cultural achievements of Spanish geniuses like the novelist Cervantes and the painter Velasquez.

The second half of the film ranges over an even wider set of topics. It begins by considering the style of Baroque art that developed in the Spanish churches of the New World, and moves on to consider the contributions of African slaves and their descendants to the culture of Latin American. In rapid fire order, the film takes up the transfer of agricultural products such as tomatoes, chocolate, and tobacco from the New World to the Old, the impact of the eighteenth-century Enlightenment on Spain, the work of the painter Goya, and, finally, the Napoleonic occupation of Spain.

Much of the film is well-photographed, and segments of the film illustrate important historical topics. Highpoints of the film include the contemporary views of Potosí as well as the fortifications set up in Puerto Rico to defend this valuable part of the Spanish Empire from raiders like Francis Drake. Unfortunately, the length of the film and the large number of topics it takes up makes it almost unviewable in its entirety. Significant portions of the film such as Fuentes' discussion of the work of Velasquez and the Baroque art in Spanish America are technical and abstract to the point of being incomprehensible.

The most manageable portion of the film for classroom use is the first half where the power and accompanying weaknesses of sixteenth-century Spain provide something close to a unifying theme.

Brueghel's People

19 minutes   color
1975   International Film Bureau

Summary: An examination of the works of Peter Brueghel, the great Netherlands painter of the sixteenth century who created numerous images of everyday life

Grade: C

The film consists of a narration accompanied by important works of Brueghel. The painter is presented as an artist who concentrated his efforts into showing the life of the common man in the Netherlands

Brueghel's People begins by noting how Brueghel's art and its depiction of human life differ from the optimistic views of Renaissance Italy. Brueghel's work makes no effort to overstate man's power and perfection. Instead, he stays close to the Middle Ages, showing humankind as limited, gross, and often misshapen. Even in the midst of events such as the Reformation Brueghel painted average figures going about their everyday business. Man's tools and efforts give him some successes in these works of art. But such successes are limited in the face of nature's storms and harsh winters.

The second half of the film presents Brueghel's artistic reaction to the horror of the invasion of Spanish troops under the Duke of Alva. Brueghel shows the carnage resulting from this effort to crush the Protestant challenge to the supremacy of Catholic power. But this brief concern with a specific historical event soon gives way to a renewed consideration of Brueghel's fascination with laboring peasants in everyday life.

The depiction of the life of peasant villagers of Northern Europe in the sixteenth century is vivid and interesting. It can serve as a useful counterpoint to considerations of urban society both in Renaissance Italy and the prosperous communities of Flanders. The film also serves to remind student's of the normal life that moved quietly along in the midst of changes like the Reformation that loom large in textbook accounts. Nonetheless, the film is marred by a pompous narration. With the exception of the portion on the Duke of Alva's invasion, the film does not connect clearly with any specific historical event.

The Conquest of Souls
(The Christians series)

41 minutes   color
1976   Granada

Summary: A witty, lucid, and informative examination of the expansion of Europe led by Portugal and Spain in the sixteenth century; it shows the blending of culture that ensued between Catholic Europeans and the Indians of Mexico and Central America

Grade: B

The film employs a narrator, maps, paintings and other works of art from this period, actors reading from key documents of this era, and visits to important historical locales. The main theme of the film is the way in which the Spanish imposition of Roman Catholicism on indigenous peoples led to a religious synthesis far different from the beliefs and practices of European Catholicism. Others themes include the sudden expansion of Europe's contact with the outside world that took place around 1500, and the renewal of the Catholic church in the era of the Counter-Reformation.

The Conquest of Souls begins with a visit to Lisbon harbor, showing the port from which the first great European explorers set out into the Atlantic. The first third of the film describes European expansion under Portugal and Spain, including an examination of the Aztec society Spain encountered in Mexico and the reasons for the success of Hernando Cortés in conquering it.

The second third of the film takes up several issues. It considers the way in which Catholic priests supported by the Spanish government rapidly converted the Indians of Mexico to Christianity, then tried to protect the Indians against overly harsh exploitation. Next, it examines features of the Catholic revival in the face of the Reformation: Loyola and the Jesuit Order, the Council of Trent, and the attitudes of triumph and puritanism seen in the art and architecture of sixteenth-century Rome.

The final third of the film returns to the confrontation between Catholic missionary activity and the non-European world. The narration indicates how Catholicism obtained only a shaky foothold in Asia, where missionary activities could not be backed by Western military power. In contrast, Catholicism enjoyed apparent success in regions such as Mexico where church and state power could support one another. Scenes show how present-day Indians blend their Catholicism with aspects of their pre-Columbian culture. Thus the film leads to crucial questions. Did the Spanish merely enjoy a superficial success? Or, did Christianity triumph by proving capable of combining effectively with non-European elements?

The Conquest of Souls is well-paced, and it features a witty narration and splendid photography. Visual highpoints are the scenes of Lisbon harbor, the vast temple city of the Aztecs, and the grim illustrations from the book by Bartholemé de Las Casas showing the horrors inflicted on the Indians. The film's main weakness comes with the extended attention it devotes to present-day Christian practice by the Indians. Interesting in itself, the issue is peripheral to major historical topics.

The first two-thirds of the film can stand alone to illustrate European expansion as well as the atmosphere of triumphant Catholicism in Europe. The final third of the film can be used for a discussion of how deeply European culture penetrated indigenous societies.

The Defeat of the Spanish Armada: Twelve Summer Days, 1588

55 minutes   color
1990   Films for the Humanities & Sciences

Summary: A clever and entertaining depiction of the English defeat of the Spanish invasion fleet presented as a breaking television news story; overly long, but incisive in showing the confusion and uncertainty involved in trying to make sense of a rapidly developing historical event

Grade: A -

The film employs several professional newscasters filling the roles of television anchorwoman, defense analyst, and reporter on the scene as they present the daily "Armada Report." It also uses maps, modern paintings of the key participants, and computer-generated simulations of naval action. One theme of the film is how the invasion threat would have looked to an English public in 1588 with access to the tools of modern news coverage. A second theme is the way in which historical events that seem clear and conclusive in retrospect were confused and complex at the time.

The Defeat of the Spanish Armada is presented as a series of newsbroadcasts over a twelve-day period in the summer of 1588. Anchorwoman Fiona Armstrong, whose clothing ensemble changes daily, summarizes breaking news of the Armada's progress. Chris Rogers, the defense correspondent, discusses the military significance of events. John Kiddey is the reporter following events from various locations on the English coast close to the action. After the broadcast for the last day, the participants give a brief summary of the fate of the defeated Armada as it was driven by winds into the North Sea. Fiona Armstrong reads Elizabeth I's stirring address to her people at the close of the event.

The presentation is lucid, crisp, and colorful with all parties playing their roles to perfection. Each of the techniques of modern television news coverage is put to good use, including the computer model simulations of combat maneuvers. Most important of all, the film makes the viewer aware of how long it took before even an informed contemporary participant could be sure what was happening. Thus, the film brings home the confusion, atmosphere, and immediacy of a historical event.

The film's sole weakness is its excessive length. Despite the deftness with which the story is presented, the approach wears thin over a twelve-day time span. Unfortunately, some viewers will probably find their attention exhausted before the film reaches its conclusion.

Students can be asked to consider how a similar approach would look for other significant historical events in which participants were emotionally upset, confused by breaking developments, and uncertain about the outcome.

Elizabeth: The Queen Who Shaped an Age
(Western Civilization: Majesty and Madness series)

27 minutes   color
1970   Learning Corporation of America

Summary: A verbose and poorly constructed examination of the background and character of this key ruler of the sixteenth century

Grade: C -

The film employs a narrator and a series of dramatized scenes from the life and times of Elizabeth. The key theme is Elizabeth's success in creating an era of peace and expanding influence for England.

In the film's prologue, the narrator describes a weak, divided England in 1558 at the time of the death of Queen Mary. He goes on to indicate

Elizabeth's background, the problems she faced, and the successes she brought to her country. Following the titles, the film's dramatic episodes show Elizabeth's stratagem of dangling herself as a marriage partner in front of a number of European rulers. Also during the film's first half, she appears to crowds of adoring subjects who present her with doggerel poetry written in her honor.

The second half of Elizabeth focuses on the coming war with Spain. The queen confronts the dilemma of her cousin Mary, Queen of Scots, imprisoned in England and a center of plots against England's monarch. The film ends abruptly by describing, although not showing, how Englishmen, both Protestant and Catholic, rallied to defend their country successfully against Spanish Armada.

Elizabeth is poorly paced, marred by mediocre acting, and is disfigured by a gratuitous torture scene showing a plotter against Elizabeth being interrogated. Key events such as the achievement's of English mariners in exploring the non-European world are scarcely mentioned. In all, this treatment of the subject is inferior in every way to The England of Elizabeth (q.v.).

The England of Elizabeth

26 minutes   color
1960   International Film Bureau

Summary: A brief, vivid, and eloquent interpretation of Elizabethan England stressing the role of the queen, the work of playwright William Shakespeare, and England's successes in exploration and maritime power

Grade: B +

The film uses a narrator, paintings, artifacts, and visits to historical locales. The main theme of the film is the way in which religious compromise, inspired royal leadership, cultural genius, and the talents of the country's seamen combined to create an age of wealth, peace, and artistic creativity.

The England of Elizabeth begins by showing still visible remnants of the English past such as a sign marking the site of London's traditional outdoor gallows at Tyburn. It shows that farming practices and the lifestyles of the Elizabethan past can still be found in the English countryside. In rapid fashion, the film considers the great seafarers of the late sixteenth century and the wide ranging intellectual achievement of William Shakespeare. It takes up in detail the early life of Queen Elizabeth, Francis Drake's fighting circumnavigation of the earth between 1577 and 1580, and the childhood and early adult years of Shakespeare.

The second half of the film describes the defeat of the Spanish Armada, England's growing contact with the farthest reaches of the outside world, and the new wealth now visible in everything from ceramics to great country homes. The film closes by quoting Shakespeare's great characters in <u>Romeo and Juliet</u>. and <u>Macbeth</u>, noting that they remain the most lasting legacy of this great age.

The film successfully presents a positive, but not overly glamorized, view of Elizabethan England. The church music accompanying many scenes combines with an exuberant narration to capture an atmosphere of excitement and optimism. The film's sole weakness is its brevity. Thus, basic historic events like the English Reformation and the conflict with Spain can only be mentioned but not properly described. Nonetheless, this is a splendid accompanying piece for a study of Elizabethan England. The film's positive presentation of Europeans penetrating the outside world can be put in contrast to the view shown in other films such as <u>Francisco Pizzaro</u> (q.v.).

<u>Francisco Pizzaro</u>
(<u>Ten Who Dared</u> series)

31 minutes   color
1976   BBC

Summary: A colorful, entertaining, and emotionally engaging dramatization of Pizzaro's conquest of the Inca Empire of Peru in 1532; a negative view of European expansion that nonetheless shows the drive and abilities present on the European side

Grade: A

The film features a narration by Anthony Quinn and readings by another actor from the diaries of Pizzaro. The bulk of the film consists of a dramatization of Pizzaro's career and conquest of the Incas. The basic theme of <u>Francisco Pizzaro</u> is how well-organized, politically astute, and militarily superior Spanish forces conquered the vast but complacent and divided Inca Empire.

The film starts with actor Anthony Quinn describing the early career of Pizzaro. There is also a dramatized scene of Pizzaro and his partners planning the advance into Peru and the division of any wealth to be found there. Thereafter, the film stretches from Pizzaro's first penetration into the high Andes in 1532 to his death at the hands of his rival conquistadors nine years later. In all the dramatized scenes, the historical characters speak in their own language rather than in English.

The story follows Pizzaro's small, well-armed force of Spaniards advancing over rivers, desolate plains, and mountain trails into the Inca realm.

After making contact with the Incas, the Spanish won a one-sided, gory battle and captured the Inca king, Atahualpa.

The second half of the film narrates how the Spanish received a rich ransom in gold and silver for the captured king whom they then executed. Despite military reverses in a second bloody battle, the Spaniards advance on the Inca capital of Cuzco. With the aid of Inca collaborators they win control of the entire empire. Quarrels over the division of the vast wealth to be found there lead to Pizzaro's death. At the close of the film, Anthony Quinn speculates about various historians' explanations for the relatively easy Spanish victory over this impressive indigenous society.

The film is lucid, well-acted, and brilliantly photographed. It shows vividly the costumes and weapons of the time and the physical locale in which these dramatic events took place. The use of Spanish and the Inca language in the segments when the actors speak adds to the realism of the film. The view of Inca customs surrounding the person of the king and the nature of Inca worship is notable.

The film raises important questions about the relative importance of the role of Spanish religious zeal, greed for Inca wealth, and the weaponry of the time in deciding the outcome of the encounter between the Spaniards and the Incas. Students can be encouraged to consider whether the motives and methods of the Spaniards can be understood (or condemned) without taking into account the nature of Spanish society and the recent experiences of Spain in fighting the Moors and in expanding into regions like the Azores.

Hieronymus Bosch

38 minutes   color
1992   Films for the Humanities & Sciences

Summary: A visually brilliant account of the painter whose work reflected the violence and emotional turmoil of the decades preceding the Reformation; focused on an analysis of Bosch's artistic achievement, the film offers little direct consideration of the era in which he lived

Grade: C +

The film employs a narrator and a detailed examination of several of Bosch's most significant paintings. The basic theme of the film is the way Bosch, a member of a radical religious sect known as the Adamites, presented a harsh and troubling view of human nature and the human experience

Hieronymus Bosch shows the painter's vision growing darker and more bizarre as his life proceeded. It begins with a sampling of scenes from Bosch's work as the narrator notes that Bosch must be viewed within a specific and troubled historical context: burgeoning heresy, mass violence, and the threat of Turkish invasion. The narration continues to discuss Bosch's membership in the Adamite religious sect and the way in which that group's views toward nudity and sex helped shape his artistic vision. The film examines at length several of Bosch's major works from Seven Deadly Sins to Garden of Earthly Delights.

The film's images are memorable and feature vivid details of Bosch's work. The narration explains clearly the symbolism Bosch employed in choosing his grisly images. But, despite a brief description of the era in which Bosch lived, historical issues disappear once the consideration of the artist's specific works begins. The film even fails to indicate the dates when the artist was born and died. Students viewing Hieronymus Bosch will be struck by the psychological turmoil and pain the artist's images displayed, but they will get no information from the film about events that may have helped to bring Bosch to produce such works.

The film could be employed following a presentation of the tensions in the European world during the artist's lifetime (1450-1516). It offers numerous opportunities for a consideration of the personal pain an average European might have felt during such an era.

Pepper: The Master Spice
(The Spice of Life series)

26 minutes   color
1985   Beacon Films

Summary: An amusing study of pepper that puts more emphasis on its use in contemporary cooking than on its key role in history

Grade: C

Pepper employs a narrator, an interview with a pepper merchant, contemporary scenes to show the cultivation of pepper and its use in food preparation, as well as maps and paintings to illustrate the role of the spice in European history. One basic theme of the film is pepper's role in promoting European exploration and dominion over the non-Western World. Another theme is the spice's huge role in present-day cooking.

The film begins by showing a spaceship launch, noting that the European desire for pepper set off another such age of discovery centuries ago. The scene then shifts to hunters in present-day Quebec hunting down and cooking a wild boar with pepper. This represents scenes that have been repeated in European life over the centuries. Crucial for both preserving and flavoring meat, the spice, as the film informs us, was once so valuable only princes could enjoy it regularly.

The second third of the film is largely historical, tracing the use of pepper from Ancient Rome through voyages of Marco Polo and the establishment of a spice trace dominated by the city-state of Venice. It goes on to show how the need to circumvent the Venetian monopoly spurred the Portuguese to find a sea route to India and to create a vast empire based upon buying and shipping the spice to Europe. The final portion of the film mingles the later history of pepper, including the British role in the spice trade with the Far East, with scenes of pepper's use in today's kitchens and dining rooms.

The film indicates vividly how a particular commercial need helped to stimulate Europe's connection with Africa and Asia from the fifteenth century onward. Nonetheless, the overall historical content is not extensive enough to hold the interest of a class in European history. The simplistic suggestion that the quest for pepper in itself was a sufficient explanation for European exploration and conquest is misleading.

The Prince
(Renaissance series)

57 minutes   color
1993   Vision/Quest

Summary: An examination of the emergence of powerful centralized forms of government in Europe from the era of Cosmo de' Medici to Oliver Cromwell; visually impressive with useful individual segments, but marred by questionable generalizations and irrelevant segments

Grade: B

The film employs a narrator, commentaries from Professor Theodore Rabb, actors, works of art from the time, and visits to important historical locales. There are also present-day figures from the worlds of politics and historic political dynasties. The basic theme of the film is the application Machiavelli's prescriptions for vigorous, effective, and unscrupulous political leadership took in Italy, Spain, and England.

The Prince begins by introducing the harsh and cynical ideas of Machiavelli. A minor Florentine official, he produced a book, also entitled The Prince, that shaped his era's views of how political power should be won and exercised. The first half of the film focuses on the brutal political world of Renaissance Florence. Visits to the palaces of the great Florentine families alternate with a description and dramatization of the rise of the Medici family. The film introduces living descendants of the great families of Renaissance Italy to recount memories of their ancestors. Rabb's commentaries stress the danger of holding political power in that time and place, a factor that helps explain Machiavelli's cynical maxims for would-be princes.

The remainder of the film analyzes the contrasting political styles of Philip II of Spain and Elizabeth I of England. Philip appears as a "Renaissance Prince" who wielded power as both a tireless chief bureaucrat and a harsh enforcer of religious unity. The paintings of Peter Brueghel show the response of an artist repelled by the repression Philip directed in Northern Europe. Elizabeth on the other hand appears as a master of public relations, a queen whose public appearances and utterances were calculated to promote her love affair with England's population. The film concludes with a brief examination of England's monarchy after Elizabeth. Parliamentary opposition challenges her unpopular Stuart successors, leading to the execution of one of them, King Charles I. Oliver Cromwell, leader of the Parliamentary side, in turn finds the pressures of governing effectively push him to become an uncrowned despot. Interspersed in the film are comments from such political figures as former British foreign minister Geoffrey Howe, former American attorney general Ramsey Clark, and New York Times correspondent Flora Lewis.

The film's main theme appears clearly. Students will come away from the film with a sharp idea of what Machiavelli had to say and how rulers in fact acted in the sixteenth century. The individual segments on both Philip II and Elizabeth are strong enough to be shown separately.

Nonetheless, the basic view of the film that figures like Philip II, with his devout religious belief, can be defined as "a Renaissance prince" stretches the term beyond all meaning. As in other episodes from this series, the term "Renaissance" is made to cover a vast sweep of centuries in a way that will confuse students. Many of the commentaries such as those by Flora Lewis or Ramsey Clark are merely fillers, banal snippets of irrelevant information. At its close, the film makes a half-hearted effort to introduce a discussion on how centralized political power can be limited.

Shakespeare: A Mirror to Man
(Western Civilization: Majesty and Madness series)

27 minutes   color
1970   Learning Corporation of America

Summary: A witty, well-written, and brilliantly acted introduction to Shakespeare as a literary figure; unfortunately, it is devoid of historical content

Grade: D

Shakespeare consists of an actor and actress directly addressing the audience to explain the author's literary importance, then playing key scenes from a number of his plays. The themes of the film are Shakespeare's insight into the human personality, his technique of building his plays around great conflicts within the lives of his characters, and the sweeping range of emotion he was able to present to his audience.

The film begins with the two players acting a scene from The Taming of the Shrew. Each then speaks to the audience about the continuing appeal of Shakespeare's work for today. In a brief historical reference, the actress notes that the character Kate represents "the new woman" of the Elizabethan age, inspired by the example of England's great female monarch. Lengthy scenes from Macbeth and Othello take up the remainder of the film.

The two players, Brian Cox and Eileen Atkins, speak lucidly about Shakespeare. Their performances of his works are impeccable. Unfortunately, the discussion of Shakespeare's literary skills dominates the film to the exclusion of explaining Shakespeare's era or his own place in it.

With an extensive introduction to the time period, the film could serve as an illustration of the Elizabethan literary culture and England's artistic achievements in the Renaissance. Most students, however, will find the connection difficult to make.

Suleyman the Magnificent

58 minutes   color
1987   Metropolitan Museum of Art

Summary: A visually superb and informative consideration of Europe's powerful Islamic neighbor in the sixteenth century

Grade: A

Suleyman the Magnificent employs a narrator, buildings and works of art from the time, and visits to important historical locales. Its main theme is the power and influence of the Ottoman Empire and the achievements of the Ottomans' most powerful leader, Sultan Suleyman the Great.

The film describes the emergence of the Turkish Empire from its origins in the tribes of Central Asia to the climactic event that signalled its power: the successful assault on Constantinople in 1453 and the conversion of the great Church of Santa Sophia into a mosque. Extraordinary aerial shots of the walls surrounding the city, which had held out invaders for a thousand years, are one highpoint of this sequence. Scenes of the great mosque, in which the conquering Turks first celebrated their victory, are another.

Next comes a description of the Europe in the early sixteenth century, and the film focuses on the career of Suleyman, the first of the Ottoman sultans to involve himself deeply in European affairs. Pages from the contemporary

<u>Book of Suleyman</u> are mixed with scenes of present-day ceremonial soldiers to indicate the military potency represented by Suleyman's elite force of Janissaries. The accompanying music is mesmerizing.

The film balances a discussion of Suleyman's great military and naval campaigns--up the Danube into Central Europe, into the eastern Mediterranean, eastward into today's Iraq--with a consideration of the architectural, legal, and artistic achievements of the Turkish Empire during Suleyman's four decades on the throne. Much of the splendor of the Ottoman Empire of the early sixteenth century is still brilliantly preserved. The film presents extensive samples: its calligraphy, the great buildings of Istanbul (such as the Topkapi Palace), and the bridges and buildings constructed by Sinan, Suleyman's great engineer. The contrasts between Ottoman Turkey and the Europe of that era, seen in terms of European weakness, the small size and decentralized character of European kingdoms, and the absence of religious toleration in Europe, are striking.

Filmed with clarity and imagination, <u>Suleyman</u> shows the military strength, artistic achievements, and governmental skills of the greatest state of the sixteenth century. It shows how this outside force intersected with European events. It influenced European affairs during an era stretching from the Fall of Constantinople in 1453 to the Reformation and the Dynastic Wars in the first half of the sixteenth century. The splendor and power embodied in the Ottoman Empire places helps place the struggles and successes of its European neighbor into a larger world perspective. The film's special strengths are to be found in the pace and clarity of its narration, the remarkable photography, and the skilled used of contemporary scenes to draw the viewer back to the sixteenth century. Suleyman's droll letter to the imprisoned King Francis I of France, in which he refers to France as a mere "province," is one example of the new perspective on sixteenth-century Europe the film provides.

A barely discernible weakness is the occasional intrusion of travelogue elements (the film was made with the support of the Republic of Turkey). Moreover, while the film is clear in referring to many key events in European history, the influence the Turks had on others such as European exploration and the Reformation is not discussed.

The film offers rich possibilities for discussion. Points to pursue are the contrast between the Ottoman Empire and Christian Europe at this time. It would be stimulating to place Suleyman's state side by side with the Roman Empire under Augustus to draw some conclusions about what makes for successful imperial systems. Finally, students will be pushed to some interesting insights in European history by considering how the Europe of Martin Luther, Charles V, and Loyola appeared to its powerful Islamic neighbor.

<u>The Voyage of Martin Frobisher: A Quest for Gold</u>
(<u>Archaeology</u> series)

23 minutes   color
1992   Films for the Humanities & Sciences

Summary: An interesting account of the first English explorer in North
America and the first European to penetrate the Arctic; it shows the range of
European exploration in the sixteenth century as well as the interaction between
European and non-European societies

Grade: B

        The film employs narrator John Rhys-Davies, contemporary views of the
Arctic locales Frobisher visited, along with prints and portraits from his time.
There are also interviews with present-day experts including archaeologists, an
anthropologist, and a geologist knowledgeable about the Arctic. Included as well
are excerpts from a diary kept by one of Frobisher's shipmates, and extensive
film footage showing the today's lifestyle of the indigenous Inuit population
Frobisher encountered. One theme of the film is the way in which England's
motives for exploration changed. A search for a Northwest passage to Asia
became a frantic scramble to find gold. Another theme is the reciprocal
influence that developed between the Europeans and the Inuits.
        <u>The Voyage of Martin Frobisher</u> begins with views of present-day ships
moving into the Arctic to exploit its mineral resources. The narrator notes that
the first such expeditions took place under the direction of Martin Frobisher four
centuries ago. Spectacular aerial shots of Canada's Baffin Island show the area
that Frobisher encountered. The film then traces his three voyages from 1576
through 1578. It recounts how he returned from his first voyage, in which he
had sought the Northwest passage, with an Inuit prisoner as well as black rocks
that seemed to indicate the presence of gold. The account of the voyage is
illustrated by present-day views of the harsh sea coasts and Arctic environment
Frobisher must have encountered.
        The film discusses the mining operationsand the housing Frobisher's
efforts left behind. It notes the way in which the Inuit made use of the debris
abandoned by these first European explorers. At its conclusion, archeologist
William Fitzhugh summarizes the significance of Frobisher's efforts for
England's future naval supremacy: an English foothold in the New World, the
development of experienced navigators, and advances in naval technology.
        The film features vivid scenes of the Arctic that emphasize the hardships
these European explorers faced and overcame. The aerial photography is
particularly impressive. It reminds the viewer how early European exploration
extended into the most inhospitable northern areas. However, much of the
second half of the film moves away from a historical focus to deal with the
archeological techniques now employed to investigate the remnants of Frobisher's

voyages. Similarly, the historical account is interrupted by interesting, but only marginally relevant, material on modern Inuit life. As a result even this relatively brief film devoted to Frobisher produces a relatively low, albeit intriguing, yield of historical information.

Students can be asked to consider the contrast between the extent of Spanish and Portuguese imperial possessions at this time and the results of these first English efforts.

SEVENTEENTH CENTURY

The Burning Times
(Women and Spirituality series)

58 minutes	color
1990	National Film Board of Canada

Summary: A diffuse but emotionally gripping and provocative examination of the "witchcraft craze" that began in the sixteenth century; a good example of European history presented from a feminist perspective

Grade: B +

The Burning Times employs a narrator, interviews with self-proclaimed witches and authorities on feminist history, visits to important historical locales, as well as works of art and historical artifacts. There are also contemporary views of the legacy of the witchcraft craze, e.g., halloween images of witches, and present-day feminist celebrations. The theme of the film is way in which women's social prestige, autonomy, and healing powers were subjected to a devastating assault by masculine authority represented by the witchcraft craze. Thus, the craze was a "women's holocaust."

The film's first third explores the idea of witches and witchcraft without extensive reference to a historical framework. It shows modern women celebrating their innate powers in areas such as healing. It suggests that women historically have been repressed from exercising such powers.

The remainder of the film focuses on the witchcraft craze that began in the mid-sixteenth century. It suggests that Christian churches and political authorities have traditionally acted in concert to destroy male-female equality and fertile folk traditions. The Burning Times draws its evidence from the fourteenth-century Black Death, the career of Joan of Arc, and the eras of the

Renaissance and the Reformation. The film's message becomes particularly gripping with views of torture implements, excerpts from legal and personal documents, and descriptions of the torments of those who were targeted for persecution.

The film offers a compelling and novel, if debatable, view of European history. Its visual and verbal images make the story come alive. Unfortunately, The Burning Times is overly long and resolutely unchronological. The narration is often unclear about the precise era of European history to which it is referring.

Nonetheless, this documentary offers a rich set of possibilities for discussion. Classes can consider whether European history will invariably look different when seen from the standpoint of relatively powerless groups. Students can be asked to evaluate the theory of a golden age of folk traditions and sexual equality at some point in the European past.

The Civil War in England: 1645-1649
(Turning Points in History series)

36 minutes   color
1990   Films for the Humanities and Sciences

Summary: A mistitled film, it is partly a poorly paced and confusing survey of English history in the first half of the seventeenth century, partly a depiction of the Battle of Naseby in the English Civil War

Grade: C +

The film uses a narrator, dramatized scenes, maps, portraits, prints, and weapons from the time. It features an extensive reenactment of the encounter between Royalist and Parliamentary forces at Naseby. The basic theme of the film is how Naseby turned the tide in the English Civil War.

The Civil War in England begins with scenes of the armies gathering for the combat at Naseby in June, 1645. The narration then presents a panoramic survey of the causes leading to war. This survey is accompanied by portraits of figures such as Cromwell, dramatic scenes showing parliamentarians arrested by the king's orders, and present-day views of a church like the one used by the Puritans in Parliament. The film describes the events at the start of the conflict and displays the weapons and uniforms used at the time. It then moves on to the centerpiece: a re-enactment of the climactic battle accompanied by an analysis of the course of the fighting complete with model soldiers.

The final five minutes of the film presents a rapid fire survey of events after the parliamentary victory in the Civil War. In murky fashion it describes the conspiracies of King Charles I that led Cromwell to order his execution. It then jumps to describe the Restoration under Charles II and concludes by recounting the migration of refugee English noblemen to North America. Its final flourish is a brief reference to the American Civil War as a continuation of the seventeenth-century clash between English aristocrats and backers of Parliament.

The film is a rare effort to show the English Civil War on film. The reenactment of Naseby, while overly extensive, shows another topic infrequently encountered on film: seventeenth-century warfare. Nonetheless, this account is flawed by an odd rhythm: important issues like the background to the war and its consequences are skipped over in hasty and confused fashion. Meanwhile, events on the battlefield of Naseby appear in lengthy detail. The statements at the film's close on the alleged connection between the English and American civil wars are dubious at best.

The Dutch Miracle

50 minutes   color
1990   Films for the Humanities & Sciences

Summary: A rambling and verbose film on a topic of immense significance, the role of the Dutch Republic in seventeenth- century European history

Grade: C +

The film uses a narrator, paintings and prints from the seventeenth century, dramatizations of important events, and reconstructed sailing ships. There are also antique nautical instruments and visits to significant historical locales. The basic theme of the film is the development of Holland, newly freed from Spanish domination, into Europe's greatest trading center and the possessor of a world wide empire.

The film begins with a brief episode entitled "The Flying Dutchman." This introductory segment describes life aboard a seventeenth-century sailing vessel. The major portion of the film then starts by discussing Holland as a community of traders and herring fishermen. They were distinguished by their tradition of freedom of thought and their daring as world explorers.

A dramatized episode recounts the exploits of two early Dutchmen, one a seafarer, the other a merchant, in opening the Far East to Dutch trade. The film moves forward without any clear structure, taking up Dutch settlement in Java, Brazil, and the Western Hemisphere, the founding of the East India Company, and the operation of the spice trade. It discusses the fortified trading stations that can still be found around the world as relics of the Dutch Empire, the city of Amsterdam, and Holland's formal acquisition of independence from Spain in 1684.

The film features moments of fine photography, notably in aerial views of historic Dutch sailing vessels. The topic with which The Dutch Miracle deals is immensely significant, and this is a rare effort to treat it on film. Nonetheless, the film frequently bogs down in trivia such as the invention of the herring knife and the techniques for using seventeenth-century navigational tools. Meanwhile, crucial issues such as the ongoing conflict with Spain remain untouched. Overall, the slow pace of the film and its lack of coherent organization deprive The Dutch Miracle of any substantial value.

Galileo: The Challenge of Reason
(Western Civilization: Majesty and Madness series)

26 minutes   color
1969   Learning Corporation of America

Summary: A crisply written, lucid dramatization of the conflict between the seventeenth-century scientist and the Roman Catholic church; the film features witty dialogue and a gripping sense of the danger into which Galileo's views plunged him

Grade: A

The film shows actors playing Galileo, the audiences to whom he presents his views, and the Church's authorities articulating the traditional scientific views associated with Catholic teaching. The basic theme of the film is the crisis created by Galileo's curiosity about the physical world, his reliance upon experimentation, and his challenge to the religious teachings of the time. A secondary theme is the shift in Galileo himself, from the jocular and confident young scientist to the imperiled, elderly sage who is forced to recant his opinions.
Galileo begins with a representative of the Catholic church vigorously disputing Galileo's contention that the sun stands still while the earth revolves around it. The elderly Galileo, on trial in 1633, appears to defend himself against accusations of undermining the teachings of the Church.
The film then shifts to show a younger Galileo, happily conducting his experiments. Denying he is toying with heresy, he tells his students he is a mathematician, not a theologian. One scene dominates the entire film: Galileo, his aristocratic friends, and a number of Catholic cardinals meet for dinner. They debate the relative value of sources of knowledge ranging from the Church's tradition to experimentation. The film catches the emotional force of the Church's traditionalists. One cardinal asks Galileo if Jesus would have appeared on a minor star revolving around the sun as Galileo purportedly describes our plant.

Subsequent scenes show religious leaders shifting their response to Galileo's ideas. They move from discomfort to fierce, frightened opposition. In the end an elderly Galileo appears before the Inquisition, then receives a discreet suggestion that he recant. His alternative is to face the Church's terrifying weapons of torture and death by burning at the stake. At the film's conclusion Galileo dramatically recants his scientific views. The narrator notes that he continued his scientific investigations and published his findings.

The film is well-paced and features fine writing and acting. Moreover, it brilliantly evokes the strong feelings of both sides in the confrontation between Galileo and Church officials. Its only flaw is its fleeting reference to Aristotle. It thereby fails to make clear the role of the ancient Greek philosopher. Since the Middle Ages, the Church had, in fact, followed his views about the structure of the universe.

Galileo will add flavor and color to any class examination of the Scientific Revolution. Students can be asked to consider whether there are circumstances in which society's representatives do have the right to silence an opinion dangerous to the existing order.

Grandeur and Obedience

See review under REFORMATION

In Search of Tolerance

See review under REFORMATION

The Light of Experience
(Civilisation: A Personal View by Kenneth Clark series)

53 minutes   color
1971   BBC

Summary: An unevenly paced but useful examination of seventeenth-century Holland and England; it shows the growing influence of scientific thinking and capitalist values in the leading Protestant states of Northern Europe

Grade: B -

The film employs narrator Kenneth Clark, the architecture, scientific implements, and works of art of the period, as well as visits to important historical locales. A main theme of the film is the modernizing trends visible in seventeenth-century Holland and England. A secondary theme is the continuing influence of religious values, as seen in the paintings of Rembrandt.

The film begins with beautiful images of the Dutch landscape, illuminated by a clear light that seems to heighten its physical reality. Clark then demonstrates the astonishing realism of Dutch art: he shows a painting of the square at Haarlem followed by identical film footage of the same scene. Holland, he notes, was the first society where divine authority had been replaced by the scientific values of experience and observation. It was also a model of toleration where controversial books from the rest of Europe could be freely published.

Clark uses the realistic painting of Hals and Vermeer, as well as the bourgeois architecture of Haarlem and Amsterdam, to illustrate the modernizing trends of the time. One can see a practical society open to talent represented by paintings of prosperous bourgeois merchants banding together to perform civic tasks. The narration also presents some of the complexities of the time: the tulip craze, the tendency of artistic realism to degenerate into pictures of animals shown in textbook detail, and, most significant of all, the continuing religious passion evident in Rembrandt.

The final third of the film shifts the focus to England after the restoration of Charles II in 1660. Here Clark describes a newly energized society opening vistas of intellectual success. He notes the achievement of Newton's Principia Mathematica, which provided a mathematical model of the structure of the universe. Christopher Wren's observatory at Greenwich and the operation of a seventeenth-century microscope and telescope likewise show the scientific impulse at work. Clark ends the film on a somber note. He asks if the successes of the Scientific Revolution and the economic wealth it made accessible in turn produced industrial squalor and narrow materialism.

The film presents its basic theme with force and clarity. The photography is superlative. Nonetheless, apart from a fleeting reference to Galileo, the film offers no background or explanation of the Scientific Revolution itself. Moreover, the film has a tendency to ramble. A long interlude devoted to Rembrandt about a third of the way through the film slows the pace considerably. Allusions to the modern realism of painters like Mondrian may puzzle most students. Clark's final point concerning the long-range consequences of bourgeois prosperity--slums, squalor, and narrowly focused materialism--comes at the cost of a sudden and confusing jump in the narration.

Students will benefit from comparing the society and values illustrated by this film with those of the Counter-Reformation shown in Grandeur and Obedience (q.v.), a previous episode in the series.

The Making of Russia, 1480-1860
(The World: A Television History series)

26 minutes   color
1985   Landmark Films

Summary: A lucid, colorful, but sketchy survey of Russian history from the medieval Kievan state to the abolition of serfdom in the mid-nineteenth century

Grade: B -

The film employs a narrator, maps, historical prints and paintings, archival film, recent scenes of Soviet life, and visits to locales of historical significance. The basic themes of the film are the development of a powerful Russian state presiding over a population of backward and impoverished peasants as well as Russia's tenuous relationship with the rest of Europe.

The Making of Russia begins with recent scenes of urban and rural life in the Soviet Union. It then launches itself on a frenzied narration describing Russian history from the era of medieval Kiev and Russia's conversion to Eastern Orthodox Christianity in 988. The bulk of the film deals with the era from the rise of the principality of Moscow to 1860. It focuses on the development of Muscovite power and the expansion into Siberia, Russia's ties to Europe in the seventeenth century, and the intensified westernization under Peter the Great. The film closes with a rapid description of Russia's territorial expansion under Catherine the Great, Russia's dominant role on the European continent following the Napoleonic wars, the emancipation of the serfs, and the start of industrialization

The film is lucid, informative, and incisive in its interpretations. Moreover, it draws a vivid picture of Russian history with its effective use of old film footage and historical paintings. Nonetheless, The Making of Russia takes on a nearly impossible task in trying to introduce so complex a story into the time allotted. Only students who are already well versed in the basic course of Russian history will be able to follow the account presented here. For students with such a background, however, the film can serve admirably to illustrate and reinforce information they already possess.

It should be noted that the film covers a considerably larger time span than the one indicated in its title.

Newton: The Mind That Found the Future
(Western Civilization: Majesty and Madness series)

21 minutes   color
1970   Learning Corporation of America

Summary: An unengaging, highly technical examination of the work of the great scientist of the seventeenth and early eighteenth centuries

Grade: C

The film's narrator is an actor playing the role of Newton's friend Edmund Halley. The film employs old prints, modern scientific diagrams, and dramatic scenes. It also shows film clips of recent scientific successes like the space launches. The basic theme of the film is the epochal nature of Newton's scientific achievements, notably his formulation of the law of gravity, and its influence down to the present.

The opening scene shows Newton walking in the country. Halley, the narrator, lauds the great scientist's unique mind. Following the titles, Halley sketches the background of Newton's achievement in formulating the law of gravity. He notes that traditional thinking about science described the movement of heavenly bodies as different from movement of bodies on earth. In the seventeenth century the lessening hold of tradition and the growing prestige of scientific investigation opened the way for Newton's thought.

Newton examines an apple that has just fallen at his side, and Halley goes on to explain the theory of gravitation that Newton subsequently set down. Halley also describes Newton's rivalry with Robert Hook, a conflict that revolved around the differing importance each gave to the value of experimentation. Halley ends his account by noting the fame and prestige that marked the last decades of Newton's life. He uses shots of our era's space launches to show the ongoing influence of Newton's contributions to science.

Newton offers a clear overview of this scientific genius's greatest achievement. On the other hand, Newton's position vis-a-vis other scientific giants of the era like Galileo gets no consideration. Most important of all, the film is too technical, its writing too flat, and its tone too low key to engage an audience's attention. The calm intellectual and political environment in which Newton did his work does not makes for a dramatic story. This is in sharp contrast to the stormy circumstances of Galileo's later career. Thus, this film could be shown in conjunction with Galileo: The Challenge of Reason (q.v.), although its intrinsic interest remains limited.

The Prince

See review under SIXTEENTH CENTURY

Realms of Light: The Baroque
(Art of the Western World series)

60 minutes   color
1989   WNET

Summary: A vivid, complex, and uneven examination of Europe in the seventeenth and early eighteenth centuries; it examines the resurgent Catholic church, Catholic absolutist monarchies in Austria and Spain, and the contrasting model of bourgeois Protestant wealth and influence in Holland

Grade: C +

Realms of Light uses the works of art of the time, architectural monuments as the Belvedere Palace, and lectures by recognized art authorities like Simon Schama. The film's first theme is the renewed confidence and authority of the Catholic church as reflected in the art and architecture of the seventeenth century. Secondly, the film considers the ascending power of Catholic Austria following its defeat of the Turks at Vienna in 1683 as well as the faltering Spanish monarchy. Finally, Realms of Light focuses on the urban, tolerant society of the Protestant Netherlands with its governing class of prosperous burghers.

The film begins by considering the Catholic church after 1600. The era lay under the shadow of Reformation, assaults on the city of Rome, and the newly expanded world view created by global exploration and the Scientific Revolution. Nonetheless, the Church's wealth and confidence expressed themselves in the exuberant architecture of Bernini. The film cites the works of Caravaggio to show how artistic realism could reflect both a scientific view of the world and continuing religious devotion.

The middle portion of the film begins with a consideration of the Baroque style in Austria. There the Belvedere Palace stands as an allegory of religious journey to spiritual salvation. Next comes a discussion of the splendor of the absolute monarchies of the time and the way in which court painters like Rubens were used to depict them. This section features an extended examination of a single painting, Velasquez's Maids of Honor, by Simon Schama of Harvard University.

The final portion of the film uses present-day scenes and the work of Vermeer and Rembrandt to describe the Protestant Netherlands of the seventeenth century. The area was novel for its widespread prosperity as well as its role as the first mass market for art. Nonetheless, even in this non-Catholic stronghold the century's religious strictures held true: paintings contained clear messages about the transitory nature of wealth and the continuing presence of a divine standard for measuring conduct.

Brilliantly photographed, the film is rich to the point of overflowing with vivid images and important ideas. The narration holds consistently to an important basic theme: power, both religious and secular, in the seventeenth century. The first portion of the film could be shown by itself. It offers a valuable discussion of the Catholic church during this era. Regrettably, the film's pacing is frequently slow, with long discussions on the technical features of the works of art presented. Schama's extensive discussion on the hidden meanings in the work of Velasquez is a stellar example.

Students can be directed to consider the ways in which art and architecture were used to demonstrate the power of both religious and secular authority. Students should also consider why and how seventeenth-century Holland produced a society so different from most of the other states of Europe.

The Scientist
(Renaissance series)

57 minutes   color
1993   Vision/Quest

Summary: A rich, lucid, and provocative examination of science and its relationship to other ways of understanding the world from Paracelsus to Newton

Grade: A

The film employs a narrator, commentators in the person of Professor Rabb and a number of present-day scientists, as well as actors playing the role of historical figures. There are also maps, models, portraits, and sketches by the scientists under consideration. One theme of the film is the sharp challenge that scientists often unintentionally posed to existing methods of understanding the world, e.g., organized religion. A second theme of the film is the combination of elements, ranging from scholarly inquiry to an interest in magic and alchemy, that combined to produce modern science.

The Scientist begins by noting that the sixteenth and seventeenth centuries saw a dramatic change in ideas. Europeans struggling to survive in the face of incomprehensible natural forces came to employ the tools of science. They thereby gained the power to understand the world in a new way, perhaps even to control it.

The first half of the film considers the careers of Paracelsus, Copernicus, and Kepler. It also notes how science developed from a variety of sources: magicians and alchemists, artisans involved in practical problems, and natural philosophers debating the wisdom of ancient texts. The alchemist Paracelsus appears as a pioneering figure. He challenged ancient Greek authorities like Galen. He put his studies to such practical purposes as the treatment as the treatment of syphilis. Meanwhile, at the University of Padua, artisans and natural scientists had begun to merge their talents. There the Polish priest Copernicus advanced the revolutionary idea that the sun, not the earth, was the center of the universe. By the close of the sixteenth century, Johannes Kepler described the world as a gigantic machine and analyzed the laws of planetary motion. The narration draws an important distinction between different scientists. Kepler and Paracelsus attacked a vast range of ancient beliefs with gusto. More cautious scientists like Copernicus sought new ways to solve old problems.

The second half of the film stresses the career of Galileo. His clash with the Roman Catholic church constitutes the clearest example of scientific innovation colliding with existing orthodoxies. Galileo was more cautious by nature than Kepler. The latter had to urge him to express his theories more boldly. Nonetheless, Galileo employed the telescope, the first of the great new scientific implements, to provide direct evidence of the accuracy of Copernicus's view of the universe. Writing for both a popular and a scholarly audience, the great Italian investigator faced growing disapproval by Church authorities. In 1633, he was compelled to recant his beliefs. One of the dramatic highpoints of the film is the recitation, by a skilled actor, of the statement Galileo was compelled to make in his moment of desperate confrontation.

The film concludes with a rapid view of scientific giants who followed Galileo. René Descartes emerges as a cautious thinker influenced by Galileo's fate. Blaise Pascal combines scientific accomplishments with a conviction that religion provides different and even more profound truths for mankind. Isaac Newton appears to describe his great discoveries as akin to those of a small boy picking up pretty sea shells alongside a vast and unknown sea. The final segment of the film makes the important point that, in the political turmoil of the seventeenth century, the certainties of science had a growing influence. It was visible in a fascination with statistics, publicly attended anatomy lessons, and the construction of scientifically planned systems of fortification. Interspersed with the narration are comments from scientists like astronomer Margaret Geller and biologist Eric Lander on the nature of scientific curiosity, the eccentric personality of many scientists, and the role of intuition in scientific investigation.

The film lucidly presents the meandering course of scientific development. It shows how difficult it was for scientific pioneers to escape fully from the intellectual world around them. Copernicus, for example, did not wholly reject the planetary pattern set down by the ancient Greeks. The comments by the professional scientists show how the problems of challenging existing beliefs continue to exist in today's scientific culture. Like other films in the series, this one uses the term "Renaissance" in a confused fashion. The era it is describing here is far better described as Early Modern Europe.

Students can be asked to reconsider the dilemmas faced by the scientists and their opponents in this era: was Pascal right in declaring that science cannot connect us to higher truths? Can an argument be made in favor of Church authorities concerned about the intellectual and spiritual turmoil Galileo's ideas would cause?

The Search for Deliverance

See review under EIGHTEENTH CENTURY

The Warrior
(Renaissance series)

57 minutes   color
1993   Vision/Quest

Summary: A colorful but muddled examination of the changing role of the fighting man in Europe from the Late Middle Ages through the seventeenth century

Grade: B -

The film employs a narrator, commentators on military affairs such as Admiral William Crowe and Colonel David Hackworth, and historians Theodore Rabb and Natalie Davis.   There are also authorities on the art and medical practice of the time, as well as paintings and prints from the era under examination.   The theme of the film is the development of warfare from a relatively undestructive pastime dominated by landowner-knights to a socially calamitous enterprise.   The key agents of change were technology, in the form of gunpowder weaponry, and religious differences that produced an atmosphere of unprecedented hostility.

The Warrior begins with a survey of opinion about warfare from military leaders like Crowe to critics of armed conflict like Seymour Hersh. The bulk of the film consists of a survey of European military affairs starting with the Late Middle Ages.

The story begin with the knight in armor, a landowner whose social position was solidified by his role as warrior. Engaged in campaigns limited by social mores--a knight on a battlefield would not stoop to fight someone of lower social rank--such warriors did little to disrupt the workings of society. The film grows confusing as it moves on to the Renaissance. It claims that Renaissance conflict was ritualized and bloodless, but it identifies this as the moment when gunpowder's destructive potential revolutionized the battlefield.   A brief discussion of Baldassare Castiglione, the author of the Renaissance handbook on gentlemanly conduct, introduces the idea of warriors who were also expected to take up the role of patron of the arts.

The final third of the film describes the horrors of warfare in the age of gunpowder and religious division. It notes the growing revulsion toward warfare expressed by writers like Montaigne and painters such as Peter Brueghel.

It also includes a knowledgeable discussion of the war wounds and surgical treatment for them in this time.

The film is clear in showing how one technological change, namely gunpowder, raised the destructive force of warfare to an unprecedented level with immense consequences. Nonetheless, the chronology of the film is confused and uncertain. Discussions jump back and forth from medieval to Renaissance warfare, while the uniforms, weapons, and tactics used by the actors in the film are drawn primarily from the seventeenth century. The numerous insertions of expert commentary are often interesting. Nonetheless, they appear in random and confusing fashion. Given the film's length, its yield of useful historical information is surprisingly thin.

The film seems designed to encourage students to consider the balance between the usefulness of the warrior and armed conflict versus the costs such individuals and activities impose on society. It is unlikely students will need to go back to this murky presentation of military change dating from the fifteenth century to approach such a topic.

EIGHTEENTH CENTURY, FRENCH REVOLUTION, AND NAPOLEON

Adam Smith and the Wealth of Nations

28 minutes   color
1976   Liberty Fund

Summary: A verbose and technical introduction to the ideas of the great economist of the eighteenth century

Grade: C

The film employs a narrator, prints from the time, quotes from Smith's writings, visits to historical locales, and scenes of present-day economic activity. The theme of the film is Smith's role as an intellectual innovator whose views stressed the need to limit government's role in directing the economy.

Adam Smith and the Wealth of Nations starts with a view of a construction site. It is accompanied by a quotation from Smith describing the complex nature of economic activity and the advantages of a division of labor. The narrator then describes Smith's position criticizing the prevailing doctrine of mercantilism, which provided for government control over trade.

The bulk of the film consists of a sketch of Smith's life. It shows his birthplace in Scotland and the universities where he studied and taught, and it describes his grand tour of Europe that led him to write his great book of economy theory, The Wealth of Nations. The film goes on to analyze Smith's views on the division of labor, his opposition to restrictions on the economic activity of Britain's North American colonies, and his general alarm at expanding governmental power.

The film contains fine photography. Scenes showing the buildings and works of art from this era evoke the atmosphere and culture of the eighteenth century. Nonetheless, heavy and verbose doses of economic theory dominate the film, which seems designed more for the economist than the historian. Students will be hard pressed to see how Smith's theories can be linked to basic trends in eighteenth-century thought such as the Enlightenment. The first half of John Kenneth Galbraith's film Prophets and Promise of Classical Capitalism (q.v.) is marginally superior in dealing with the same issues.

An Age of Reason, An Age of Passion
(Art of the Western World series)

60 minutes   color
1989   WNET

Summary: A rambling examination of European culture from 1715 to 1830; the breadth of the film and its focus on the technicalities of artistic development detract substantially from its value

Grade: C +

The film uses a narrator, the works of art of the time, interviews with leading art historians, and present-day shots of important historical locales. Its basic theme is the shift from an eighteenth-century culture dominated by aristocratic norms to the more middle-class society of the first third of the nineteenth century.

An Age of Reason film begins by describing the death of Louis XIV. At the same time it shows the massive buildings and gardens of his palace at Versailles. From there the first half of the film describes the pleasure-loving lifestyle of the English and French upper classes as seen in the erotic paintings of Watteau. It notes the contrasting society to be found in the salons of the Enlightenment. Philosophes like Diderot, the film notes, criticized the art of the aristocrats as nothing more than "bottoms and breasts." Such intellectuals favored instead the classicsim of Jacques-Louis David with his paintings of heroic Roman warriors.

The second half of the film discusses the rise of Napoleon. Paintings show him in such contrasting locales as the plague house at Jaffa and at his coronation. The film juxtaposes two images from Napoleon's last years in power: the eroticism representing by Ingres's nude Odalesque and contemporary paintings showing the corpses and mutilated warriors on the battlefield at Eylau. The dramatic highpoint of the film is Goya's work displaying the horrors of the French occupation of Spain from 1808 to 1814. The film concludes by introducing the intellectual change represented by Romanticism. It notes that a new era which exalted feeling over reason could also produce criticism of the status quo. It uses Géricault's <u>Wreck of the Medusa</u> and glorifications of revolution like Delacroix's <u>Liberty Leading the People</u> to illustrate the point.

The film introduces clearly the basic historical themes from 1715 to the post-Napoleonic period. Its visual quality is very high. The segment on Goya, accompanied by a lucid narration and featuring graphic atrocity scenes, is memorable. Nevertheless, the film slows excessively for extended technical discussions of art and architectural monuments. Moreover, its scope precludes doing more than mentioning most key events. Students are unlikely to follow whimsical digressions such as analysis of the floor decorations of an eighteenth-century English mansion.

The Battle of Cholet: 1794
(Turning Points in History series)

38 minutes   color
1991   Films for the Humanities

Summary: Although overly long and unevenly paced, this is a useful film examining a crucial topic: the rebellion of the rural population of the Vendée in northwestern France against the radicalism of the French Revolution

Grade: B

The Battle of Cholet employs a narrator, present-day views of important historical locales, maps, paintings, dramatic reenactments, and the music of the time. The basic theme of the film is the growth and eventual suppression of a powerful conservative movement in the Vendée in the years 1793-1794.

The film begins with contemporary scenes from the region of the Loire Valley. Following a rendition of the peasants' conservative parody of the Marseillaise, the narrator recounts the grim statistics of the loss of life in the civil war here. There follows a description of the tradition of turbulence in this part of France and the opposition to the Revolution that developed by 1793.

The bulk of the film deals with the ensuing rebellion and the military conflict between the peasant forces of the Vendée and the French army. The narration describes how a variety of leaders, including members of the local nobility, emerged to direct the movement. The centerpiece of the film is the bloody military encounter at Cholet where Frenchmen slaughtered Frenchmen. The narration and dramatization follow the fate of the defeated Vendée rebels as they retreat temporarily to Brittany, then turn to guerrilla warfare back in the Vendée. The Battle of Cholet stresses the atrocities committed by both sides and the lasting bitterness the conflict provoked.

During the first two-thirds, the film is engrossing. It slows down and its impact diminishes only in the final portion as its dwells on the details of the suppression following the rebel defeat at Cholet. Somewhat mistitled, the story reaches far beyond the Battle of Cholet (fought in October 1793) to consider the larger issue of the Vendée revolt. Students should be informed that the revolt went beyond the 1790s and was finally suppressed in the early years of Napoleon Bonaparte's dictatorship.

Students can be asked to consider why the standard accounts of the French Revolution and the Reign of Terror pay so little attention to this fascinating episode.

<u>The Battle of Quebec: 1759</u>
(<u>Turning Points in History</u> series)

32 minutes   color
1990   Films for the Humanities & Sciences

Summary: An informative account of the struggle between Britain and France for the control of North America in the mid-eighteenth century; marred by mediocre photography and poor maps

Grade: B -

The film employs a narrator, visits to important historical locales, paintings, and maps. There are also reenactments of major events in the settlement of North America and the subsequent Anglo-French colonial warfare. The basic theme of the film is the spectacular success that Britain achieved in capturing the city of Quebec. Thus, they expelled the French from vast holdings in Canada and the Mississippi Valley. A secondary theme is the nature of eighteenth-century warfare.

The film begins with present-day views of the Quebec countryside where the descendants of the original French colonists still live. The first half of the film traces the development of French settlement in Canada: woodsmen explore the vast interior, a string of forts is set up to block English expansion, conventional French military forces train while a ferocious guerrilla war goes on within the American woods. Scenes show the important link between the French and their Indian allies.

The second half of the film focuses on the campaign of 1759. British forces under General James Wolfe besiege and bombard the city of Quebec and ravage the countryside. As winter closes in, Wolfe achieves the spectacular feats of placing his forces on the heights near the city, then defeating the French army under General Louis de Montcalm after a mere quarter of an hour of combat. <u>The Battle of Quebec</u> ends with another view of the French Canadians of today. Now six million strong, they remain unreconciled to living in an English society.

The film has numerous strong elements. It presents vivid scenes showing the training of the individual soldier and his military unit. There are memorable scenes of eighteenth-century European military force marching through the vast Canadian outdoors. Nonetheless, there are a number of important failings. The photography is poor. Since the maps are so inadequate, British and French strategy in North America and the precise significance of Quebec as a strongpoint will not be clear.

Students can be asked to consider how well Europeans in general, and European military leaders in particular, adjusted to the geographic and climatic conditions of North America

Burke and Paine on Revolution
(Man and the State series)

28 minutes   color
1978   Barr Films

Summary: A witty, well-written, and provocative examination of the French Revolution; it presents the course of events and debates the value of the decisions taken at the time

Grade: A

Burke and Paine on Revolution employs a narrator and shows prints from the time, but it depends chiefly on skilled actors. They play the roles of leading participants in the Revolution and the roles of the commentators on events, Thomas Paine and Edmund Burke. One theme of the film is the deepening, uncontrollable development of a more radical revolution after the old order was overthrown. A second theme is the deep difference in the perception of events between observers sympathetic to the Revolution like Paine and those like Burke who were hostile to it.

The film begins with the narrator introducing the main characters of the film. They are all supposedly present at a dinner party given by the English political leader Charles James Fox in 1790. Burke is shown as a political figure who supported the American Revolution but detests the events transpiring in France. Paine is presented as a fervent supporter of both the American and the French revolutions.

Early in the play, Fox's servants seize control of the dinner party. They go on to play the role of participants in the Revolution. Fox is compelled to play the role of King Louis XVI. Paine and Burke find themselves forced to debate the key issues the Revolution raises.

Burke and Paine cite excerpts from their own writings to debate the value of tradition versus the popular will in guiding the state. Meanwhile, one servant, the valet Horace Jones, takes on the power-hungry paranoia of a Robespierre and increasingly dominates the Revolution. The film concludes with the servants taking up their former roles. The drama of the evening is explained away: it was merely a witty play written by one of the guests, Richard Brinsley Sheridan.

The film presents the basic questions of revolutionary politics with force and clarity. In particular, it offers the views of Burke and Paine on such salient questions as the nature of society and the possibility of radical reform. At the same time, the film vividly traces the basic events of the Revolution. Depictions of the king's flight to Varennes and the domination of the revolutionary crowd by skilled demagogues indicate the emotions and confusion of the participants.

The film offers an ideal opportunity to stimulate discussion on the very issues that Burke and Paine debate.

The Eighteenth Century Woman

55 minutes	color
1987	Metropolitan Museum of Art

Summary: An entertaining but superficial examination of French, British, and American women in the century of the Enlightenment; based on an exhibit at the New York Metropolitan Museum of Art, it emphasizes changing styles in clothing and home decoration

Grade: B -

The film employs a number of narrators, including actress Marisa Berenson, fashion expert Diana Vreeland, and museum director Philippe de Montebello. Apart from the costumes and figurines taken from the exhibit, there are numerous examples of the great paintings of the eighteenth century, extensive contemporary views of important historical locales such as Versailles, as well as quotations from writers and diarists of the era. The basic theme of the film is the growing power that women enjoyed in the eighteenth century: as mistresses of intellectual salons, as monarchs like Catherine II of Russia, but especially because of their mastery in decorating themselves according to the latest fashion. This final skill gave them increasing control of the men who were the real decision makers of the time. A secondary theme is the opulence and extravagance during this era, especially in France.

Following a brief prologue, the film begins with views of the clothes in the museum's exhibit. Various narrators comment on the nature of the eighteenth century: they stress the intellectual changes brought by the Enlightenment, as well as the alleged sweetness of life, as Talleyrand described it, of the ancien régime.

The film proceeds chronologically, starting with a discussion of French life under Louis XIV and his mistress, Madame de Maintenon, who would later become his wife. It proceeds with the regency era following Louis's death in 1715 and the era of Louis XV and the Marquise de Pompadour. The film stresses the influence she had even in the realm of foreign policy. There follows a brief discussion of the two great female rulers of the time, Catherine II of Russia and Maria Theresa of Austria.

The second half of the film moves to the less rigid societies of Britain and America, discussing upwardly mobile Englishwomen like the actress Sarah Siddons. Abigail Adams is heard in her plea to her husband as America moved toward independence, admonishing him "not to forget the ladies." The film's historical treatment concludes with an examination of the royal lifestyle of Queen Marie Antoinette, along with her tragic fate after the Revolution of 1789. The film itself ends with a view of our own era's beautiful people, such as Raquel Welch, at the gala ball celebrating the exhibit's opening.

The Eighteenth Century Woman is visually impressive. There are splendid paintings by artists like Boucher and views of the great buildings of the time. It combines a lighthearted tone with a lucid description of the course of events, notably in France, during this century.

The film is excessively long, but its greatest weakness is its superficiality. It has little to say about social life in general, focusing instead of the lifestyles of the rich and powerful. There is no effort to note key events like the Seven Years War or the looming financial crisis of the French government in the 1780s. The greatness of rulers like Catherine II of Russia and the influence of figures like Marquise de Pompadour are mentioned without being explained. Moreover, the credentials of several of the narrators as authorities on the eighteenth century are dubious.

The film can be used to illustrate the physical circumstances and social atmosphere of the eighteenth-century elite. Students can be encouraged to consider how many vital elements in the history of the century the film omits. The main premise of the film--that women were influential primarily as a result of their skills in decorating themselves--should evoke some lively discussion.

The Fallacies of Hope
(Civilisation: A Personal View by Kenneth Clark series)

53 minutes   color
1971   BBC

Grade: B -

Summary: The first portions of the film present a useful, if sketchy, picture of the era of the French Revolution and Napoleon; the final third takes up a wide-ranging discussion of Romanticism through the nineteenth century and lapses into incoherence

The Fallacies of Hope employs narrator Kenneth Clark, the works of art and architecture of the time, and visits to important historical locales. In its final section, it displays film footage from the revolutions of the twentieth century. The basic theme of the film is the revolutionary challenge to the old order in Europe begun during the French Revolution and extending into our own time.
    The film begins with a view of an orderly eighteenth-century drawing room. The narrator, Kenneth Clark, moves immediately into the wild outdoors to illustrate how the European mood shifted to an "escape from reason" with the rise of Romanticism.
    The film then traces the French Revolution from its outbreak and moderate stage in 1789 to the escalating radicalism of the early 1790s. Contemporary paintings show the desecration of churches, the effort to found a new religion to replace Christianity, and the grisly revolutionary massacres.
The second portion examines the career of Napoleon. Contemporary scenes show his council chambers and study at the Malmaison Palace. The development of the young general into the crowned emperor appears in a striking series of paintings. Clark emphasizes how Napoleon disappointed the hopes of idealistic proponents of revolution like Beethoven by adopting the trappings of monarchy and combining them with a new brand of repression. The results appear in a visit to the dungeons Napoleon's security police employed at the Fortress of Vincennes. Goya's paintings show Spanish patriots being executed by their French oppressors.
    A central theme of this portion of the film is how the legacy of the revolutionary era, 1789-1815, set an example of revolutionary action for other revolutions stretching from France in 1830 to 1968 in Czechoslovakia. Background music from Beethoven's Fidelio, taken from the opera's climatic release of prisoners from their dungeon, shows the emotional urge to revolutionary action. The remainder of the film, however, wanders in a confused manner through a series of topics dealing with the nineteenth century: Romantic pessimism of Byron and Géricault; the alienation of artists from bourgeois society; Rodin's sculpture of Balzac as an illustration of a final surge of Romanticism.
    The film succeeds in capturing the sense of the possibility of revolutionary change that entered European life starting in 1789. It is similarly useful in illustrating the changing response of Europeans like Wordsworth and Goya to the Revolution. It shifted from enthusiasm to hostility as the Revolution moved to bloody execution and dictatorship and foreign conquest.
    Nonetheless, the chronology of events and the identity of the main historical participants are often unclear.   Moreover, the film omits any explanation for the revolutionary explosion in 1789 beyond the rise of a mood of Romanticism. Most important as a flaw is the loss of focus during the final

third as Clark explores, in murky fashion, the European mood in the nineteenth century.

The French Revolution: The Bastille
(Western Civilization: Majesty and Madness series)

21 minutes   color
1970   Learning Corporation of America

Summary: A crisp, lucid, and well-acted dramatization of the events leading to the outbreak of the French Revolution in 1789

Grade: B +

The film employs a narrator, dramatized scenes, prints, and contemporary scenes of Bastille Day celebrations. The basic theme is the rising tension in France as various social groups express their discontent while the monarchy dithers.

The Bastille begins with pictures of a modern Bastille Day celebration followed by a dramatized scene of the crowd in 1789 marching to the fortress. This desperate act was a landmark event in both the history of France and Western Civilization, and the narrator asks why it took place.

After showing present-day views of the royal palace at Versailles, the film presents a series of dramatized scenes. These depict various elements in French society in 1789. The king meets his economic advisers, and Jacques Necker describes the financial strains on the French government. Nobles maneuver for position at the royal court and discuss how to squeeze more income from the peasants under their control. Meanwhile, street corner orators declare that oppression has destroyed any bond between the people and their rulers. Scenes at the royal court, in which nobles plot and the queen urges the king to dig in his heels against reform, alternate with views of rising anger and resentment in the urban middle class.

At the close of the film, leaders of the middle class, placed between the king and the mass of the population, swing over to support the masses. A final scene shows the Fall of the Bastille. The crowd mauls the prison's commander, a harbinger of both the spread of the Revolution and its deepening violence.

The film features a clear narration and witty dialogue. Beautifully photographed, it covers most of the growing tensions in France without lapsing into superficiality. The Bastille gives due attention to the influence on events of an ambitious nobility, which combined stubbornness and ambition to disastrous effect. Events move so rapidly, however, that their exact sequence is sometimes muddled. Thus the film needs to be preceded by a discussion of the growing crisis in France at the close of the decade of the 1780s.

The French Revolution: The Terror
(Western Civilization: Majesty and Madness series)

21 minutes   color
1970   Learning Corporation of America

Summary: A fast paced, but sketchy depiction of the era of violence in the French Revolution from 1792 until the fall of Robespierre in 1794; marred as well by mediocre acting and graphic violence

Grade: C

The Terror uses a narrator along with numerous dramatized scenes from this period. The basic theme is the growing violence of the Revolution as Robespierre freely employs force in his effort to create an ideal republic.

The film begins with revolutionary scenes featuring the erection of street barricades. The narrator notes that the Revolution that began with high ideals has descended by the year 1792 into increasing repression. Robespierre brutally dismisses a woman who has asked for his help in freeing her imprisoned husband. He informs her that her duty as a wife is secondary to her obligations to the Revolution.

Brief scenes recapitulate the storming the Bastille in 1789, the astronomical rise in the price of food, and the outbreak of war between France and the conservative powers of Europe. The film moves forward to show the execution of the king, the conservative revolt against the Revolution in Brittany, and the growing power of Robespierre. It reaches its climax by showing how Robespierre sacrifices his fellow revolutionary leaders. Then, Robespierre in turn falls victim to the revolutionary crowd.

The film touches briefly on many of the most significant events that transformed the moderate revolution of 1789 into the bloody terror filled era of 1793-94. Nonetheless, the rapid succession of very brief dramatic scenes confuses the course of events. At several points the film's chronology is inaccurate. For example, the execution of the king (January 1793) precedes the outbreak of international war (spring 1792). The acting is undistinguished, and some grisly scenes of public executions are included without serving any obvious purpose.

The Making of Russia, 1480-1860

See review under SEVENTEENTH CENTURY

Politeness and Enthusiasm
(The Christians series)

41 minutes   color
1976   Granada

Summary: A clear, witty, and brilliantly photographed examination of religious trends in the era of the Enlightenment ranging from Voltaire's criticism of the French church to the evangelism of George Whitefield and John Wesley

Grade: B +

Politeness and Enthusiasm uses a narrator, maps, visits to important historical locales, works of art from the eighteenth century, and actors reading important documents from that era. One theme of the film is the way in which the polite, emotionally sterile nature of the Church of England in the eighteenth century gave rise to an emotional, evangelical countertrend in the form of Methodism. A second theme is Voltaire's success in discomforting the religious authorities of his country. He promoted precisely the kind of rational belief against which Wesley was revolting.

The film begins with a contemporary Methodist revival meeting in England conducted by a visiting American evangelist. Next, the narrator contrasts the emotional appeal of such a form of worship with the splendor and worldliness of eighteenth-century Catholicism as seen in the monastery and abbey of Ottobeuren in Germany. There follows an account of Voltaire's admiration for the natural, rational form of worship promoted in the country house and parsonage environment of eighteenth-century England. Quotes from the diary of parson James Woodforde provide an insight into the kind of gentleman and local church leader whom Jane Austen depicted in her novels.

Next, the film introduces the harsh life of the average Englishman with prints from Hogarth. It then considers the emotional, hell-fearing form of Christianity developed by the "Holy Club" at Oxford, personified by its leaders Wesley and Whitefield. The film shows the open-air pulpit where Whitefield first preached about the flames of hell to audiences of weeping coal miners. A map of western England shows the astonishing scope of John Wesley's travels as he established his Methodist "meeting houses" over vast areas.

The final third of the film returns to Voltaire. It discusses how he promoted the idea of a rational God, the Catholic church's effort to take posthumous vengeance by burying him in degrading circumstances, and his final triumph in 1791 when his body was returned to Paris. The film also revisits the topic of Methodism. It discusses how Wesley's brand of Christianity grew increasingly conservative after his death. Returning to the contemporary American evangelist speaking emotionally to an English crowd, Politeness and Enthusiasm shows how Wesley's original impulse nonetheless remains alive.

The film features lush photography of the English countryside and its great manor houses, and a witty narration. It describes clearly the eighteenth-century impulse to replace traditional forms of belief with a view of god acceptable to minds influenced by modern science. Moreover, it is equally lucid in capturing the emotional counterappeal of Methodism. The quotations, notably those from the diary of Parson Woodforde, demonstrate the ideas and lifestyle of the English gentleman who chooses a church post merely as a convenient profession.

The film has two central weaknesses. Despite references to Voltaire's conflict with the Church, there is no indication of the bitterness and ferocity with which he attacked traditional Christian theology. Moreover, the pace of the final portion of the film slows significantly as it takes a last look at contemporary Methodism.

The Prophets and Promise of Classical Capitalism
(Age of Uncertainty series)

57 minutes   color
1977   BBC

Summary: A witty, colorful, but diffuse discussion of economic ideas and European society in the eighteenth and nineteenth centuries

Grade: C +

The film employs narrator John Kenneth Galbraith, visits to important historical locales, skits and computer graphics, portraits and other works of art of the time. The basic theme of the film is the evolution of economic ideas in a Europe changing from its agricultural origins to a society influenced by colonial trade and the Industrial Revolution.

Prophets and Promise starts with a prologue by Galbraith that introduces the entire series.   Speaking from the rooms the noted twentieth-century economist John Maynard Keynes occupied at Cambridge, Galbraith stresses the importance that economic ideas have had whether they turned out to be right or to be wrong. He also discusses the techniques, such as dramatized scenes, the series will employ.

The film itself begins with contemporary examples of unmechanized agriculture. Galbraith notes that such scenes dominated the world as a whole until only two hundred years ago. Most of the first half of the film analyzes the life and ideas of Adam Smith, with excursions into the career of Voltaire and the ideas of the Physiocrats. Galbraith emphasizes the way in which advanced thinkers like Smith and the Physiocrats tried to limit the role of the state in controlling the nation's economic life.

The second half of the film focuses on the changes brought by the Industrial Revolution. Skits illustrate the division of labor upon which factory production depends. Scenes of the Scottish Highlands show the human cost of economic change connected with textile manufacturing. There, rural laborers were brutally expelled to maximize the production of wood in what Galbraith calls a "final solution." There follows a consideration of factory reform under the aegis of Robert Owen, and then a technical discussion of the labor theory of value and the iron law of wages.

The closing portion of the film stresses the disaster to the Irish population of the potato blight. Beginning in 1845, it became a tragedy intensified by the unwillingness of the British government to take action in the face of prevailing economic doctrines. Galbraith shows the island in the St. Lawrence River near Quebec where thousands of Irish immigrants, who had managed to cross the Atlantic, died of cholera. The film concludes with an image of economic success, pictures of the Chicago Exposition of 1893.

Prophets and Promise is a useful overview of economic change, and it contains vivid and memorable individual scenes. The first half is a colorful introduction to European life in the eighteenth century. Nonetheless, the number of issues with which it deals is excessive, and the discussion of economic doctrines is often opaque. There is a jarring contrast between the wit of the narration and the juvenile skits the film employs to illustrate economic ideas.

The Pursuit of Happiness
(Civilisation: A Personal View by Kenneth Clark series)

54 minutes   color
1971   BBC

Summary: Visually sumptuous with an elaborate musical score, the film is almost totally detached from the historical issues of the eighteenth century; it is also marred by a tortuously slow pace and a murky narration

Grade: D

The film employs narrator Kenneth Clark, the works of art, music, and architecture of the time, and visits to important historical locales. The major theme of The Pursuit of Happiness is the development of the fragmented German world--divided into hundreds of separate states--into a more vibrant cultural world than the monumental and monolithic French kingdom. The film also stresses the frank love of sensual pleasure that segments of eighteenth-century society espoused and demonstrated in the Rococo style.

At first, the film presents a series of scenes contrasting the ponderous state architecture of the French monarchy with the light, flamboyant interiors of buildings produced in the diverse German community. Kenneth Clark points out that, following the devastation of earlier centuries, Germany was now stable enough to make its mark on the art of Europe. The narration plunges deeply into the technicalities of eighteenth-century architecture, focusing on the buildings of Balthazar Neumann and the paintings of Tiepolo. Clark claims that, in contrast to the secular nature of eighteenth-century thought, the art of the era was still largely religious.

After contrasting the personal and professional lives of Bach and Handel, the film shifts abruptly at its halfway point to examine the sensual Rococo painting of the Flemish artist Watteau. The remainder of the film continues to explore Rococo, which Clark finds expressed from English drawing rooms to the churches and palaces of Bavaria. The Pursuit of Pleasure concludes with a lengthy examination of Mozart and the opera. Clark contends that Mozart's melancholy and his passionate interest in human relations transcended the Rococo musical tradition.

The film's visual qualities and the musical score are exceptional. Moreover, the film touches on a rare topic for documentaries: the Germany of the eighteenth century. Ironically, it would best serve students in advanced classes in German culture and German history. Nonetheless, the pace of the film is disastrously slow. The narration is pitched at a level of artistic analysis beyond the undergraduate level. No other film in the Civilisation series is so divorced from historical currents and immersed in art for art's sake.

The Search for Deliverance
(Heritage: Civilization and the Jews series)

60 minutes   color
1984   WNET

Summary: A brisk but diffuse survey of basic changes in European life from the close of the fifteenth century to the eve of the French Revolution; it views events from the perspective of Europe's most prominent and vulnerable minority

Grade: B -

The film employs narrator Abba Eban, actors reading from important historical documents, contemporary views of historical locales, art from this era, and a segment from the eighteenth-century play Nathan the Wise. The film deals with the European and Islamic worlds from the Renaissance to the Enlightenment. Its basic theme is the Jews' continuing vulnerability alleviated by occasional opportunities for toleration and prosperity A subsidiary theme is the set of diverse strains that developed within Judaism such as the Biblical criticism of Baruch Spinoza and the Hasidic movement in Eastern Europe.

The Search for Deliverance begins by recapitulating the shock of the Jewish expulsion from Spain. It notes that the largest community of Jews in the world and one that achieved notable success in the larger society had now been forced from its homeland after five centuries. It goes on to consider how Jews now found themselves in the changing world of the Italian Renaissance and the German Reformation. The former segregated them into ghettoes, the first of which was in the port city of Venice; the latter, with its religious zealotry, endangered their existence.

The precise course of Jewish history disappears as the film notes such events as the opening of Atlantic trade routes, the revolt of the Netherlands against Spain, and the defeat of the Spanish Armada. The Jews reenter the picture as the film considers life in the newly formed Dutch Republic, where Jews found a refuge and where the philosopher Spinoza challenged aspects of Jewish Orthodox thought.

The second half of the film focuses on the precarious position of Jews in Eastern Europe. A visit to a thirteenth-century synagogue in Prague shows the depth of Jewish roots in Eastern Europe. But the basic trend saw religious differences combine with economic tensions to lead to events like the hideous massacres of Jews in seventeenth-century Poland. Despair gave rise to movements of renewal like Hasidism.

The film concludes by examining Western Europe in the eighteenth century. There the Jews' commercial skills, and even their geographic dispersal, made them valued members of many communities. Meanwhile, the Enlightenment, as represented in Gotthold Lessing's Nathan the Wise, pointed the way toward toleration of religious differences.

The film touches on the major changes in Jewish life in various parts of Europe. It suggests how the vast shifts in European life such as the Reformation and Counter-Reformation could have a particular harsh impact on this vulnerable minority. Its discussion of the roots of Jewish life in Eastern Europe is a rare treatment of an important issue in Jewish history. Nonetheless, the film barely has the time to mention some of the most momentous and complex events in European history. The overall impression most viewers will get is of a merry-go-round of events passing with extraordinary speed.

The Smile of Reason
(Civilisation: A Personal View by Kenneth Clark series)

53 minutes   color
1971   BBC

Summary: A vivid, panoramic view of Western Europe in the eighteenth century, stressing the role of Enlightenment ideas in France and England and their transfer to British North America

Grade: B +

The Smile of Reason employs narrator Kenneth Clark, the works of art and architecture of the time, and visits to important historical locales. Its main theme is the sweeping shift of ideas which took place in the European world of the eighteenth century.   It also stresses the vast geographic stage where intellectual change took place, ranging from remote European areas like Scotland to the wilds of North America.

The film's narrator Kenneth Clark sets the tone for what follows by displaying the busts in the foyer of France's National Theater. The smiling faces of leading French literary figures of the eighteenth century, he notes, illustrate the optimism and tolerance of that era.   Moving to England, the film uses architecture and painting to present the society that the exiled Voltaire found so free and appealing.   The harsh images of William Hogarth balance the rosy picture that the French writer describes.

As the scene shifts to France, the palace of Versailles serves to illustrate the massive wealth and ponderous nature of the French state.   The paintings of Boucher show the affluent upper class society that produced Parisian salons where Enlightenment ideas circulated.

The centerpiece of the film is an extended consideration of Voltaire's role in the Enlightenment.   A spokesman for free thought and the critical examination of institution, he struck his harshest blows at the Church. Nonetheless, the growing acceptance of his ideas let him leave his hideaway near the Swiss border for a triumphant return to Paris shortly before his death in 1778.

The final portion of The Smile of Reason looks at hints of rising revolutionary fervor in the paintings of David during the 1780s. Next it focuses on the roles of Thomas Jefferson--shown as one who absorbed the full cultural variety of Enlightenment--and George Washington in winning American independence.

The film captures some of the most important historical trends of the eighteenth century on both sides of the Atlantic world. Its visual images, ranging from a visit Voltaire's small hideaway at Ferney to a look at the original tomes of the Encyclopedia, will transport students back to this era. A highlight of the narration is a detour to Scotland. This illustrates how a remote part of Northern Europe not only absorbed the ideas of the Enlightenment but contributed dramatically to them in the persons of David Hume and Adam Smith.

The film contains some flaws.   Allusions to such fixtures of the eighteenth century as Blenheim Palace may puzzle many viewers. Clark's brief description of Hume's philosophical views is opaque, and the stress he puts on architecture pulls the viewer away from many of the most important themes the film investigates.

Students can be asked to consider why the ideas of the Enlightenment rooted in the urban civilization of Western Europe found such a welcome in the wilder environment of Britain's North American colonies.

The Worship of Nature
(Civilisation: A Personal View by Kenneth Clark series)

55 minutes   color
1971   BBC

Summary: An examination of European art in the eighteenth and the first half of the nineteenth century; poorly paced and laden with a murky narration, it is serenely detached from all of the major events of the era

Grade: D

The Worship of Nature uses narrator Kenneth Clark, the works of art and architecture of the time, and visits to important historical locales. It also contains extensive excerpts from the poetry of this period. Its main theme is the replacement of religious values in European life by an emotional concern for the beauty of the physical world.

At the film's start Clark notes that organized religion had become a comic anachronism in England by the early eighteenth century. An infatuation with nature was displacing religion. The first half of the film considers the growing interest throughout Europe in the beauties of the physical world. Luminaries of the time like Rousseau, Goethe, and Wordsworth asserted the moral purity of nature. This portion of the film features spectacular footage of the Swiss Alps. This was an area European thinkers saw as a source of beauty and inspiration for the first time.   A brief interlude shows Europeans impinging on the unspoiled tropical paradise of Tahiti.

The second half of film focuses on the nature painting of Turner and Constable. There is an extensive consideration of their fascination with the sky and their use of color rather than traditional line as a main organizing element. The film ends with a brief discussion of the early French impressionists.

The Worship of Nature would be useful for a course on the History of Art. The nature scenes and the outdoor paintings of Turner and Constable are striking. Nonetheless, it is largely ahistorical, devoid of any connection to key events in any area of European life over this period. The pacing is leaden, the narration features poetic excerpts that make no clear point, and Kenneth Clark himself feels impelled to defend portions of the film for dealing with artistic trivia. Moreover, The Worship of Nature contains dubious assumptions. For example, it claims that nature worship replaced organized religion throughout this era. This ignores both the residual force of religion during this time and such revivals as eighteenth-century Methodism in England and the reinvigorated Continental Catholicism of the early nineteenth century.

NINETEENTH CENTURY

An Age of Reason, An Age of Passion

See review under THE EIGHTEENTH CENTURY

The Changing World of Charles Dickens
(Western Civilization: Majesty and Madness series)

26 minutes   color
1969   Learning Corporation of America

Summary: A witty, well-acted, but slow dramatization of the life and work of the nineteenth-century author; it shows Dickens's fascination with the changes the Industrial Revolution brought to England but focuses on his literary achievements

Grade: C +

     The film employs a narrator, dramatized scenes from several of Dickens's novels, and nineteenth-century prints. The basic theme of the film is his role as a shocked observer of the pain inflicted on Victorian England by the Industrial Revolution. A related theme is the suffering of children in a society in which the demands of compassion have yielded to a frenzied race for money.

     The Changing World of Charles Dickens begins with the narrator describing Dickens's role as the most popular English writer of his day. Contemporary prints show England moving rapidly from a predominantly agrarian to an urban, industrial society. Dickens, the narrator notes, served as a spokesman for middle-class horror in the face of the pain such change brought. He died disenchanted and discouraged.

Dramatized excerpts from works like <u>Oliver Twist</u>, <u>Great Expectations</u>, and <u>Hard Times</u> show Dickens portraying the greed and the absence of compassion he observed. The final portion of the film focuses on the character of Josiah Bounderby, the self-made industrial tycoon of <u>Hard Times</u>. The narrator notes that Dickens personally traveled to northern England to get background material for the book and met real-life versions of Bounderby. Here Bounderby appears as a comical and charming man totally blind to the suffering of his workers.

The film contains generally fine acting, with the performer who plays Bounderby performing brilliantly. Both the prints and the dramatized scenes capture the atmosphere of newly industrialized England. This is clearly a society in pain, observed by a writer who was sensitive but who had no real solutions to offer. Nonetheless, the film yields relatively little historical information. Like Dickens's works, this presentation focuses on the remarkable personalities of his characters. Moreover, several of the dramatic excerpts that dominate the film turn out to be lengthy and uninformative.

<u>The Fallacies of Hope</u>

See review under EIGHTEENTH CENTURY

<u>The Colonial Idea</u>
(<u>Age of Uncertainty</u> series)

56 minutes   color
1977   BBC

Summary: A brilliantly constructed and witty examination of European imperialism from the Crusades through the collapse of the British Empire in India

Grade: A

The film employs narrator John Kenneth Galbraith, dramatic reenactments, visits to important historical locales, as well as photographs and newsfilm footage. The basic theme is the multiplicity of motives for colonial adventures, with economic gain generally looming largest. A second theme is the way in which colonial possessions are doomed by a eventual lack of interest on the part of the home population.

<u>The Colonial Idea</u> begins with a series of images ranging from a mounted knight to American forces in Vietnam. Narrator Galbraith then describes the patterns he sees in the history of Western colonialism. He notes

the phenomenon of short-term successes in establishing empires followed by a diminishing will at home. The population of the home country will no longer sacrifice in order to maintain an empire. Similarly, he finds that colonial enterprises tend to end in messy, bloody fashion as the imperial power withdraws.

The film goes on to consider the Crusades of the Middle Ages. The narration notes the numerous motives behind the Crusades, but it stresses the role of economic opportunity. The messy end to colonial ventures is illustrated by a dramatization of the collapse of the last Crusader stronghold at Acre in 1291. There follows an examination of the Spanish Empire, seen from the repository of its vast written records at Seville. Galbraith characterizes the Spanish possessions in the Western Hemisphere as an empire characterized by a multitude of exact regulations issued in Europe that turned out to be impossible to enforce in the New World.

The centerpiece of Galbraith's discussion is the British Empire in India. He considers this a vastly different, more loosely organized empire than the Spanish example. The narration follows the career of one British official, John Beames, from his training period at the East India Company's school at Haileybury, through his career in India. Dramatized episodes show the work and lifestyle of such a provincial official in the Indian Civil Service, the tiny group of British bureaucrats who governed the subcontinent.

The second half of the film shows the height of the British Empire in India, the visit by King George V to Delhi in 1911. It quickly moves on to trace the decline of British enthusiasm for empire after World War II and the precipitous and bloody withdrawal of British forces in 1947. Newsreel and dramatized sequences illustrate how the railroads, the symbols of British modernization in India, became the center of horrifying massacres as Hindus and Moslems turned on each other.

The final portion of The Colonial Idea surveys other messy withdrawals by Western nations in the late twentieth century ranging from the Congo to Vietnam. Galbraith concludes the film by visiting the Vermont home of Rudyard Kipling, the great British spokesman for imperialism. There he reminisces about his own experiences in post-imperial India.

The film features a lucid narration, fine photography, and well-performed dramatic episodes. Beames's career serves as a splendid focal point for an examination of the whole phenomenon of a European hold on the non-Western world.

Students can be asked to consider the relative significance of economic versus other motives in the Crusades, the Spanish Empire, and British India.

A Fresh View: Impressionism and Post-Impressionism
(Art of the Western World series)

60 minutes   color
1989   WNET

Summary: An analysis of Western European painting in the second half of the nineteenth century emphasizing the achievements of artists such as Courbet and Gauguin; it is visually appealing but slow-paced and only tangentially involved in significant historical developments

Grade: D

The film uses a narrator and the art of the time, including photographs and bits of contemporary music. There are also interviews with leading art critics of our day. An important theme is the shifting nature of artists' concerns. Some artists like Gustav Courbet challenged their bourgeois contemporaries directly. Others like Degas and Renoir sought an internal truth in Impressionism. Two muted themes, worthy of greater emphasis than they receive, are the impact of urbanization on nineteenth-century society and Europe's growing contact with the non-Western world of Japan and the South Seas.

A Fresh View begins with an extensive examination of the work of Courbet.   He was a radical critic of the existing bourgeois order and the conventional idealized art it sponsored. The film continues, stressing the work of one artist after another, with the achievements of Manet, Degas, Renoir, and Van Gogh. The narration notes the growth of Paris during the second half of the nineteenth century. Nonetheless, its emphasis rests upon an analysis of the techniques of these giants of European art. The second half of the film features an extended treatment of Gauguin's career. It raises but fails to explore interesting points such as his attitude toward the non-Western world and his domineering view of women.

The film's visual qualities are high, and it mentions issues of considerably significance. Nonetheless, its slow pace and lack of interest in basic developments in Europe in this era make it only marginally interesting.

Heroic Materialism
(Civilisation: A Personal View by Kenneth Clark series)

55 minutes   color
1971   BBC

Summary: A diffuse and uneven examination of the Atlantic world of the nineteenth and twentieth centuries; it contains a valuable treatment of the early development of industrial society and the variety of responses it evoked

Grade: B -

Heroic Materialism employs narrator Kenneth Clark, the works of art and architecture of the time, visits to important historical locales, photographs and newsfilm footage. The major theme of the film is the immense set of changes that came to the society and artistic values of the Western world with the advent of the Industrial Revolution. Another theme is how the growing sense of control over society was linked to the era's great industrial and engineering achievements. This appeared, for example, in the anti-slavery movement of Victorian England. Still another thread in the narration is the despair about industrial society displayed by figures like Tolstoy.

Kenneth Clark begins the film with paintings of the first factories and iron foundries of the Industrial Revolution. Next, he notes that this landmark economic development coincided with a wave of reform activity like William Wilberforce's anti-slavery crusade. For all of its smugness concerning the social byproducts of industrial and urban growth, nineteenth-century England developed a sense of kindness that it put to use in hospitals and prison reform.

Clark visits the great iron bridges of early nineteenth-century England and describes the rapid construction of the railroads from the 1830s onward. He compares such undertakings to a great military campaign. The spectacular career of I.K. Brunel, the builder of a tunnel under the Thames, a major railroad, and the first large passenger steamship to cross the Atlantic, shows the personality of the era's entrepreneurs.

The second half of the film takes up the effect that industrial society had upon painters of genius such as Courbet. Clark notes, however, that even greater artists such as Seurat and Renoir showed no awareness of such changing currents affecting the majority of their fellows. Clark devotes much of the rest of the film to examples of the uneasiness industrial life produced in sensitive spirits like Tolstoy, who returned to the land to live like a peasant. Clark's own uneasiness appears in a panorama of images from the Super Sonic Transport and the computer to the dive-bomber and, finally, the atomic weapons of World War II. The final portion of the course is taken up by the narrator's statement of the human and artistic values he treasures most.

Much of Heroic Materialism is vivid and memorable. It touches a valuable set of topics from the nineteenth century: industrialization, social reform, population growth, and the rise of new social prototypes such as Brunel. Visual highpoints of the film include branding irons and slave ship models from Wilberforce's collection and Gustav Doré's prints showing the London slums. Clark makes cogent points. He notes, for example, that an anti-slavery movement was possible precisely because it addressed a clearly defined evil. Unlike poverty, this was a practice that one could hope to end through a reasonable, organized effort.

Nonetheless, the narration is often verbose, and much of the film is static with the narrator directly addressing the camera. The film jumps abruptly into the twentieth century, and Clark details his personal concerns and ideals at great length. Heroic Materialism loses all cohesion toward the end.

The film offers several possibilities for discussion. Clark makes an interesting comparison at the start: the Gothic cathedrals of the Middle Ages and our century's skyscrapers took the same amount of time and relatively the same effort to building. Students can be encouraged to compare the social ideals reflected in such different uses of a community's resources. The optimism of Brunel and the deep pessimism of Tolstoy open the way for a consideration of the benefits versus the evils of the changes the film presents.

Karl Marx: The Massive Dissent
(Age of Uncertainty series)

57 minutes   color
1977   BBC

Summary: A lucid and entertaining introduction to life and ideas of Karl Marx

Grade: B +

The film uses narrator John Kenneth Galbraith, dramatized scenes from Marx's life, visits to important historical locales, photographs, and actors in skits illustrating economic ideas and principles. The basic theme of the film is the way in which Marx and his ideas were shaped by the political, intellectual, and economic environment of the nineteenth century.

Karl Marx begins with Galbraith discussing Marx's family, his early life, and his education. He illustrates these themes by visits to historic sites like Marx's grave in London and the Marx family home in Trier. The film then considers Marx's life and ideas up to the Revolution of 1848. That revolutionary surge in European society is the occasion for the narrator to discuss the nature of revolution and the conditions for its success.

The second half of the film focuses on Marx's life in London after 1848. It considers the founding of the First International, the Paris Commune, and the publication of Das Kapital. Interspersed in the narration are skits and discussions dealing with Marx's concepts such as the theory of capitalist accumulation. The film ends with narrator's declaration that Marx's ideas long outlived him. Chief among those surviving ideas was the view that economic institutions are the key to the history of all societies.

This is a clear and witty introduction to Marx's life. It focuses on many of the major political and economic developments of the nineteenth century, and it features sparkling photography of the key locales important in that era. But, despite its overall clarity, the film bogs down at a number of points when it wrestles with abstractions. In the first half, it stumbles in explaining the difficult philosophical concept of the dialect; in the second half it has difficulty with capitalist accumulation and the impoverishment of the masses.

Forewarned against the occasional dead spots in the narration classes can easily benefit from viewing the film as a general introduction to the key sites and historical trends of the nineteenth century.

The Making of Russia, 1480-1860

See review under SEVENTEENTH CENTURY

Man and the Industrial Revolution
(History of Man series)

20 minutes   color
1970   McGraw-Hill

Summary: A dated, unimaginative, and simplistic account of Britain's development of an industrial economy and the consequent social effects; more suitable for an audience below college age

Grade: C

The film employs a narrator, contemporary views of industrial cities and contrasting rural areas, visits to important historical sites, pictures and prints from the era in question, as well as film illustrating industrial techniques. The main theme of the film is the Industrial Revolution's role as the greatest single event to transform human history.

Man and the Industrial Revolution begins with contemporary views of Manchester, the original example of a modern industrial city. From there the film presents a historical account of how an agrarian society was transformed by developments like the cotton mill, water power, coal mining, and the steam engine.

During its second half the film shows the social trauma that the Industrial Revolution created: children and women working longer hours, industrial accidents, poor housing, and labor unrest. The film concludes with a complex picture of the industrial city of the 1970s. It shows pollution, the renovation of old neighborhoods, and community centers for retired workers. In describing the care modern society takes for elderly former workers, the film shows how a new attitude of caring for the weak may have developed along with of the creation of an industrial society.

The film has a clear goal. Occasional scenes, like a view of old factory buildings and a canal dating back to mid-eighteenth century, are intriguing. On the whole, however, the film is marred by a simplistic narration of events, mediocre photography, and a juvenile tone. Its examples of modern technology in fields like electronics reflect the era of the 1970s and look absurdly out-of-date to a viewer in the 1990s.

Marx and Rockefeller on Capitalism
(Man and the State series)

27 minutes   color
1977   Barr Films

Summary: A brilliantly conceived but poorly executed film in which the leading capitalist and the leading socialist revolutionary of the nineteenth century debate fundamental issues of modern society

Grade: C +

Marx and Rockefeller on Capitalism employs actors in a series of dramatic scenes. Two play Karl Marx and John D. Rockefeller, while the rest pretend to be members of a future society curious about the views of these spokesmen for differing ideas. The basic theme of the film is the sharply different way in which Marx and Rockefeller saw such issues as the nature of society, the role of the individual, and the course of historical change. A secondary theme is the question of how humans will organize themselves centuries into the future.

The film begins as a member of a future society describes how his community can recall figures of the past. At that point, Marx and Rockefeller are brought into this future world. The narrator from the future describes the background of both of these involuntary visitors.

Most of the remainder of the film consists of a series of verbal confrontations between the two nineteenth-century spokesmen. They debate issues like the nature of human beings, the characteristics of an ideal society, and the validity of private ownership of property. Their heated ideological interchanges are interrupted by scenes in which their hosts show them what the future will look like. These scenes include a dinner party featuring edible algae and a school in which children absorb information through the antennae of their "learning caps."

The debates become increasingly animated over the future of capitalism, the oppression that accompanies the Marxist state, and the waste and pollution typical of bourgeois societies. Marx and Rockefeller end by accusing one another of sponsoring societies characterized by repression, bureaucracy, alienation, and imperialism.

The film's greatest virtue is the basic idea of placing the ideas of Marx and Rockefeller side by side in sharp contrast. Unfortunately, the film is flawed in two crucial respects. First, Marx and Rockefeller debate using brief and rapid bursts of conversation that are difficult to follow and impossible to analyze. The result is a verbal muddle. Second, the acting of the members of the future society is stilted and corny; the amount of attention the film devotes to describing life in the future is wasted, detracting attention from the inherently interesting debate between the film's two protagonists.

Missions Abroad
(The Christians series)

40 minutes   color
1976   Granada

Summary: A lucid, informative introduction to British missionary activity in Africa from the nineteenth century to the present; the first part of the film is historical while the remainder shifts completely to the contemporary scene

Grade: B -

The film employs a narrator, paintings and prints from the nineteenth century, and visits to important historical locales ranging from England to East Africa. There are readings from key documents of the period. The basic theme of the film is how the European urge to bring Christianity to Africa in the second half of the nineteenth century has had unanticipated results. It has led, for example, to an African Christianity with its own forms and energy.

Missions Abroad begins with contemporary scenes of the coast of East Africa. The narrator notes signs of Africa's twin legacy of slavery and the anti-slavery crusade: slave compounds and the graves of nineteenth-century missionaries. Using paintings, the film shows the power of mid-nineteenth century Britain as witnessed by the Crystal Palace Exhibition of 1851. A visit to the steel town of Sheffield sets the stage for a description of how traditional religious devotion in England seemed threatened by anonymous urban life. The narration describes how a boom in church construction was one answer to this need.

Nonetheless, the greatest example of the missionary impulse was directed outward. An actor reads the influential speech David Livingston gave at Cambridge University in 1857 as the film shows the meeting room in which Livingston spoke. These stirring words capture the idealism and the determination of missionaries who felt called upon to wage war on the slave trade. The remainder of the first half of the film traces missionary activity ranging from the island of Zanzibar to the first great inland mission set up by the Anglican church.

The second half of the film shows the daily routine of missionaries in this area today: teaching school, visiting their congregants, dealing with

Moslems, pagans, and missionaries of other Christian denominations. It also shows how an African church, in which white priests and ministers are still prominent, is developing vibrant rituals of its own based upon African culture.

The film's first half is brilliantly written. It deals effectively with both the decline of religious zeal in England in the era of the Industrial Revolution and the parallel growth of missionary activity in Africa. Pictures of the Crystal Palace Exhibit and present-day views of the grim landscape of industrial Sheffield show two sides of the Industrial Revolution with consummate skill. The central weakness of Missions Abroad is the total concentration on the contemporary scene during its second half. Even though it attempts to show how nineteenth-century influences are still evident in missionary activity, its central concern is the workings of present-day religious activity.

The Paris Commune: 1871
(Turning Points in History series)

32 minutes   color
1990   Films for the Humanities & Sciences

Summary: A vivid, sometimes gory account of the great urban uprising of 1871 and its brutal suppression; it is presented from a point of view sympathetic to the rebels

Grade: B

The Paris Commune uses a narrator, dramatized scenes, maps, as well as contemporary photographs and portraits. The theme of the film is the way in which the poor of Paris, victimized by the Industrial Revolution and isolated from the majority of their countrymen, rose in a futile rebellion following France's defeat in its war against Prussia.

The film begins with a dramatized scene of armed workers manning a barricade in May, 1871. This is the eve of the final defense of the Paris Commune. The first third of the film turns backward to examine the previous twenty-year period. It describes the reconstruction of Paris by Baron Georges Haussmann, which split the population geographically along the lines of wealth. It shows the glitter and glamour as well as the industrial growth of the Second Empire of Napoleon III. Finally, it gives a brief description of the Franco-Prussian War of 1870-71 in which the French suffered catastrophic defeat leading to the occupation of Paris by the invading Germans.

The second third of the film describes the effort of the conservative French government under Adolfe Thiers to disarm the Parisian population. It shows the subsequent revolt led by an assortment of radicals within the city of

Paris, and the gathering of an army drawn from the rural population of France aimed at suppressing the Commune.

The final portion of the film traces the bloody suppression of the Commune. The rebels are pushed back into the eastern portion of the city to make a final standard in the suburb of Belleville. While both sides perpetrate atrocities, the film shows how most of the victims, including tens of thousands executed after their capture, came from the rebel side.

The Paris Commune examines a crucial example of the urban unrest that influenced European history in the nineteenth century. The maps employed show the battle for Paris clearly, and the brutality of the confrontation between rebels and conservatives appears vividly in prints and photographs. Views of the destruction wrought on the beautiful city are striking. Unfortunately, this depiction is hampered by a flat and uninspired narrator. Some of the dramatic scenes, e.g., showing a poor worker's family in the period leading up to the Commune, slow the pace of the film substantially.

The Paris Commune will be particularly useful in considering how the cities of Europe have served as centers for radical eruptions. Students can be encouraged to consider how these events, presented from a point of view sympathetic to the rebels, would have appeared to a more conservative Frenchman outside the environment of Paris.

The Prophets and Promise of Classical Capitalism

See review under EIGHTEENTH CENTURY

The Railway Age
(The Industrial Revolution series)

20 minutes   color
1992   Films for the Humanities & Sciences

Summary: An unimaginative but informative examination of the impact railroads had on English life in the first half of the nineteenth century

Grade: B -

The Railway Age uses a narrator, an interview with an authority on railroad history, prints, posters, and paintings from the era in question, and present-day scenes of important bridges and railroad locales. The film relies heavily on surviving models from this early era in railroading, some shown in museums and others still capable of being operated. The basic theme of the film is how an invention first used to transport coal came to have a complex set of effects on life in England within the space of a few decades.

The film begins with the story of the changing role of the first steam engines. Designed to transport coal from mine heads in Wales at the start of the nineteenth century, they were transformed into a means of travel from one city to another. Prints of antique trains appear along with surviving examples of these classic machines. The film describes the speed with which nearly ten thousand miles of track were built by the middle of the century using an army of 250,000 construction laborers (navvies). Old posters indicate the way that the railroad was publicized as a cheap means of transportation within the reach of almost everyone.

The second half of the film investigates the specific changes in lifestyle brought about by the railroad. They include standardized food products distributed on a national basis, a standardized system of time for the entire country, and a changed landscape filled with tracks, bridges, and new towns centered around making equipment for the railroad.

The film is particularly clear in stressing the many ways in which all members of the English population were affected by this new invention. It is lucid and informative for most of its length. In the closing moments, however, it diverges into views of deserted railroad yards and decaying equipment without making any clear point. On the whole, the numerous scenes illustrating antique trains and their operation will appeal more to railroad buffs than to the average viewer.

The film's narrator poses a valuable discussion question: did the railroad or television have the greater effect in breaking down local barriers and creating a homogenous national population?

Romanticism: Revolt of the Spirit
(Western Civilization: Majesty and Madness series)

25 minutes   color
1971   Learning Corporation of America

Summary: A   poorly written and ill-acted treatment of a major European intellectual movement of the late eighteenth and early nineteenth centuries; the film grapples unsuccessfully with the problem of presenting a set of colorful but murky ideas

Grade: D

Romanticism employs a narrator who plays the role of the typical young Romantic of the time; he converses directly with the audience. The narrator is also shown in conversation with such key romantic figures as the poet Lord

Byron. There are also a number of dramatized scenes from literary works such as Les Misérables and Jane Eyre as well as examples from Wordsworth's poetry, the paintings of Turner and Constable, and Chopin's music. The key theme of the film is the way in which this essentially non-political movement stressed a rejection of reason, the embrace of human feelings, and exaltation of the common man.

Romanticism begins in 1822 with scenes of the sea coast where the drowned poet Shelley is about to be burned on a funeral pyre. The narrator, Richard, describes some of the basic concepts of Romanticism, e.g., its revolt against convention and reason. Following the film's titles, there appears a scene from Les Misérables to illustrate how Romantic writers like Victor Hugo were intrigued by the character of the era's common people. Next, the scene shifts to a workers' household during the Industrial Revolution where the narrator regales a worker's family with inflammatory lines from Shelley's Men of England.

In its second half the film turns to Wordsworth's poetry and the paintings of Turner and Constable. These indicate Romanticism's craving to escape urban life, and to return to the rural landscape and untouched nature. Following a dramatized scene from Bronte's Wuthering Heights, the film returns to Shelley's funeral pyre.

On the whole, Romanticism is poorly organized and marred by mediocre acting and unimaginative writing. Individual scenes, notably the one from Wuthering Heights, will only puzzle students with their lack of apparent purpose. In a crucial historical lapse, the narration fails to indicate how this movement was a reaction against the rationalism of the eighteenth-century Enlightenment.

Roads from the Ghetto
(Heritage: Civilization and the Jews series)

60 minutes   color
1984   WNET

Summary: A rich and fast-paced examination of basic changes in European life from the French Revolution through World War I as experienced by the Jewish minority in various parts of the Continent; necessarily brief in dealing with numerous major developments

Grade: B

The film employs a narrator, Abba Eban, portraits, photographs and newsfilm, maps, and various contemporary scenes including views of present-day Jewish communities. The basic theme of the film is the way in which the ideas of the French Revolution and the economic impact of the Industrial Revolution brought much of European Jewry out of its traditional isolation. Jewish life was

challenged and changed. Jews, as modern Europeans, made a major contribution
to the life of the continent. A second theme is the way in which old resentment
of the Jews received a new impetus as they were identified by the discontented
as the agents and main beneficiaries of unsettling changes.

Roads from the Ghetto begins with views of the Venice ghetto. It
represents the isolation for the Jews of Europe which was now passing away.
Eban discusses the political liberation of the Jews in France and elsewhere as the
message of equality embodied in the revolution of 1789 spread. He also notes
the economic opportunities offered by industrialization. The success of the
Rothschild family and the emergence of modernist trends in Judaism leading to
the Reform denomination show Jews taking on new roles and struggling to
reconcile their traditional values to a changing world.

An extensive segment in the middle of the film examines the very
different experience of Russian Jewry. These Jews were isolated in market towns
amidst a non-Jewish peasantry. Jews in this part of the Continent are shown at
the mercy of repressive government policies under Nicholas I (1825-1855) and
again under Alexander III (1881-1894), while the liberalizing views of Alexander
II (1855-1881) provided an interlude in which doors opened to them in Russia
as well as in other parts of Europe.

There follows a consideration of the rising tide of anti-Semitism. Roads
from the Ghetto attributes this to the dislocation many Europeans felt in this era
and their tendency to make the Jews a symbol for the frighteningly new world
of cities and industries. The film shows the Dreyfus case as a highpoint of
official anti-Semitism. Next it considers Theodore Herzl's decision, stimulated
by Dreyfus's ordeal, to found the Zionist movement.

The film ends with a rush of topics: the revival of Yiddish culture in
Eastern Europe, the prominence of luminaries of Jewish background like Einstein
and Kafka, the devastation of the Pale of Settlement in World War I, and the
British pledge in the midst of the war of a home for the Jews in Palestine.

There are memorable images to be found here ranging from Roman
Vishniak's photographs of life in the Eastern European shtetl to French anti-
Semitic election pamphlets from the last decades of the nineteenth century.
Views of contemporary Jewish communities, ranging from a Reform synagogue
to Hasidic Jews debating religious law in Yiddish, are likewise colorful.
Regrettably, the film takes up a multitude of topics that it can consider only
briefly and superficially. Thus, it seeks to consider both overall changes in
Europe and the parallel Jewish experience. The final third of the film, in
particular, is too rushed for most viewers to absorb.

Students can be asked to consider why modernization led to increased
anti-Semitism and whether other groups or nationalities were similarly made
targets for such resentments.

The Roots of Disbelief
(The Christians series)

40 minutes   color
1976   Granada

Summary: A diffuse and uneven examination of the way in which science has undermined religious belief since the sixteenth century; only the first half of the film has a useful historical focus

Grade: C

The Roots of Disbelief employs a narrator, visits to important historical locales, and views of present-day religious practices. The basic theme of the film is the impact a stream of scientific discoveries, from Copernicus to Darwin, has had on religion. Initially it shook organized religion; then, it evoked a deliberate antimodernism from Catholic church leaders like Pope Pius IX. A second theme is the continuing vitality of religious belief, sometimes in modernist form, sometimes in communities akin to those of the earliest Christians.

The film begins with images of current belief and disbelief: street preachers, Salvation Army workers, unconcerned loungers in the park. There follows a discussion of the rise of science, starting with Galileo's use of the telescope. The narration considers how his examination of the solar system exploded the Biblical view of the earth at the center of an unchanging universe. The film goes in a novel direction to show present-day Jesuit astronomers at work at the papal observatory outside Rome. It notes that the Catholic church accepted Galileo's views on the solar system in 1822.

Next the film discusses nineteenth-century scientific advances in geology and biology. These indicated the earth was far older than the Bible could explain. They also presented the unsettling view that man and animals like chimpanzees had a common ancestor. The first half of the film ends with Pius IX taking deliberately traditionalist positions such as the claim of papal infallibility. Meanwhile, popular Catholicism in Europe was influenced by comforting images like the appearance of the Virgin at Lourdes and Fatima.

The second half of the film examines signs of religious vitality in the modern world. The first of these is the continuing faith in miracles by Catholics stricken with illness who go on pilgrimage to Lourdes. The film takes up the reform of Vatican II, the computer analysis of biblical texts by ministers of the Church of Scotland, and the remarkable meeting of Pope Paul VI and the Archbishop of Canterbury in the late 1970s. It also considers the emergence of experimental Christian groups, akin to those of the early Church, in present-day France.

The first half of <u>The Roots of Disbelief</u> is a lucid introduction to the role of science in challenging traditional religious faith. It moves briskly from the sixteenth through the nineteenth century vividly recounting how Darwin's champion Thomas Huxley routed the opposition in the famous Oxford debate of 1860. The film's second half, however, is fragmentary and unfocused. For example, scenes of pilgrims walking the last part of the distance to Fatima on their knees are unsettling but fail to make any notable point.

<u>Tools of Exploitation</u>
(<u>The Africans</u> series)

60 minutes   color
1986   BBC

Summary: A bitter examination of Western imperialism in Africa from an African point of view; it emphasizes the nineteenth and twentieth centuries

Grade: B +

<u>Tools of Exploitation</u> uses visits to historical locales, cartoons, maps, photographs, and newsfilm footage. Its centerpiece, however, is the running commentary presented by African writer and historian Ali Mazrui. The basic theme of the film is the exploitation of Africa's peoples and resources by European and American outsiders who possessed greater military and economic strength. A subsidiary theme notes that other outsiders, such as the Arabs who influenced events in East Africa, were less racially exclusive and less brutal than intruders from the West.

The film begins with an extended, angry commentary on the Western exploitation of Africa. It is set against present-day scenes of Western companies mining African resources. Mazrui insists that there has been no equal exchange between Africa and the West: in return for its treasure-trove of raw materials Africa has received only Western tastes, not Western skills.

The remainder of the film analyzes the African past beginning with the arrival of Portuguese explorers in West Africa in the sixteenth century. The first key development Mazrui describes is the European slave trade, which he considers more brutal and disruptive than the slavery practiced among Africans. In his view, slavery drained Africa of its manpower, benefiting areas like the American South while aborting economic development in Africa itself. This portion of the film features a visit to the fortress dungeons in present-day Ghana where slaves were confined before being sent to America.

The second issue he explores is the European division of Africa in the closing decades of the nineteenth century. Mazrui uses cartoons to show how Europeans rationalized this action as an effort to stamp out the evils of a persistent slave trade conducted by Arabs. His own family history serves as an example of the relatively humane form of slavery practiced by Arabs in areas like Zanzibar. The most graphic portion of the film shows the policies of King Leopold of Belgium. That monarch used terror and mutilation to force the population of the Congo to work for him. Mazrui also condemns Western missionaries and their school system for turning Africans away from modern skills.

The film is clear and grimly memorable in illustrating important aspects of the African relationship with the West. It offers rare newsfilm footage such as the sections on missionary schools. On the other hand, the amount of attention put on the present condition of Africa weakens its historical value. Mazrui's tone of outrage dominates the film throughout.

Students can be asked to consider whether the West's relationship with Africa was as one-sided as Mazrui suggests. What parts of the history of imperialism, e.g., the varied motives of European powers, does Mazrui omit from his account? The film could be shown in conjunction with John Galbraith's The Colonial Idea (q.v.), a version of imperialism seen from a Western perspective.

The Worship of Nature
(Civilisation: A Personal View by Kenneth Clark series)

See review under EIGHTEENTH CENTURY

EARLY TWENTIETH CENTURY

The Day of Empires Has Arrived: The Ruling Houses, 1900
(Europe: The Mighty Continent series)

52 minutes   color
1974   BBC

Summary: A detailed, incisive but unfocused picture of Europe in 1900; it stresses the role of monarchial states such as Russia, Austria-Hungary, Germany, and Ottoman Turkey

Grade: B

The film employs two narrators, John Terraine and Peter Ustinov, who speak directly to the audience.   There are also photographs, maps, newsfilm footage, and visits to important historical locales.   One basic theme of the film is the domination of European affairs by states still directed by crowned heads. Their collisions with one another were key events.   A second theme is the division within European societies between privileged and ostentatiously playful elites and masses of impoverished Europeans.

At the start, the narrators introduce the theme of a Europe with four great empires whose rulers were often linked by marriage. The film moves into an extended examination of the largest of them, the Russian Empire under Nicholas II.   Peter Ustinov visits Leningrad and recounts episodes from his family's history, illustrating the pomp, power, and social rigidity of the Russian Empire.   Examining the personalities of Tsar Nicholas and his wife Alexandra, he uses views of the Palace of Tsarskoe Selo to show the splendid isolation in which they lived.

Next, The Day of Empires considers Russia's chief antagonist, Austria-Hungary under Emperor Franz Joseph. It examines the severe weaknesses of this system, notably its ethnic diversity.   A more novel element is the film's discussion of the strength of the Austro-Hungarian state: the ceremonial and active role of the emperor, the state's religious link to the pope, and the economic vitality of the Danube Valley.

The most novel element in the film is its discussion of the Turkish Empire. Ustinov visits a Turkish cemetery outside Budapest to show how deeply the Turks penetrated Central Europe. The survey of European empires ends with a briefer consideration of Austria-Hungary's lone ally, the German Empire under William II. The narration makes the incisive point that the alliance was a recent and shaky one: Germany's unification under Prussian control had come at Austria's expense.   There is also an analysis of German power.   Based on Europe's best army and most advanced industrial system, it now included a great navy designed to challenge British domination of the sea.

The second portion of the film flies off in a number of directions.   It considers the era of good times for Europe's upper classes presided over by the "comfortably disreputable" British monarch Edward VII. It takes up the diversity of the British Empire and the dangers to empires made evident by the Boer War. The Day of Empires ends with a survey of Europe's other empires. The horrors of Belgian king Leopold's exploitation of the Congo appear in graphic photographs of mutilated Africans. Another grim aspect of empire is illustrated by Italy's battlefield humiliation at the hands of the Ethiopians in 1896.

The film is notably lucid and informative during the first half. One telling point it makes is the link between the power of the Russian tsar and the reputation of his army.   Another is the disruptive effect of both ascending German strength and declining Turkish power. The segments on Russia and Austria-Hungary are coherent enough to stand alone.   Contemporary scenes including Austrian palaces and the ceremonial parade of Britain's Household Regiments make the film visually impressive.

The film's chief weakness is the potpourri of topics it takes up during most of its second half. Important issues such as the state of Europe's masses (and their likely political response to their problems) are mentioned but left to be explored in other segments of the series.

Students can be asked to consider whether the average European of 1900 would have been more impressed by Europe's stability or its growing problems in terms of assessing his own future.

The Drums Begin to Roll: The Years 1904-1914
(Europe: The Mighty Continent series)

52 minutes   color
1974   BBC

Summary: A lucid, gripping, and informative presentation of European diplomatic relations in the decade prior to the outbreak of war in 1914; the film brings under control the inherent complexity of the topic and presents the sense of foreboding many Europeans felt as World War I approached

Grade: A -

The Drums Begin to Roll employs narrators John Terraine and Peter Ustinov and includes maps, newsfilm, photographs and cartoons, and visits to important historical locales. The basic theme of the film is the formation of dangerously competing power blocs and the further impetus to international tension that came from technological change, massive armaments programs, and the involvement of public opinion.

The film begins with Peter Ustinov noting the pride and confidence of Europe vis-à-vis the rest of the world in 1900. John Terraine adds that, starting in 1904, a chain reaction of events in international relations pointed Europe toward catastrophe. The initial major segment of the film examines the Russian Empire and its seemingly unbeatable military strength. The narration emphasizes how Russia's defeat at the hands of Japan reverberated throughout European empires in Asia.

The film goes on to present a picture of an ambitious Germany under the talented, but undisciplined Kaiser Wilhelm II. Britain and France responded with moves toward diplomatic cooperation, while Holland and Spain sought to escape the growing tensions. The first half of the film concludes with Peter Ustinov's witty discussion of the Austro-Hungarian Empire's ethnic diversity and internal strains. He also describes the growing danger in the Balkans as seen in the 1908 crisis over Bosnia-Herzegovina.

The remainder of the film considers growing armies and navies, the technological revolution symbolized by the first flight across the English Channel in 1909, and the influence of the tabloid press. The fading unity of Europe appears on archival film showing Europe's crowned heads at the funeral of Britain's Edward VII in 1910. There follows a chronological account of the string of connected wars and diplomatic crises starting with Italy's invasion of Tripoli in 1911. These ominous events conclude with the assassination of Grand Duke Franz Ferdinand in 1914, the final crisis that led Europe into World War I.

The Drums Begin to Roll succeeds in paring away the complexities of European diplomatic history to show the main lines of development. The newsfilm is splendid, ranging from views of the Russian army prior to 1904 to the funeral of Franz Ferdinand a decade later. Peter Ustinov brings events alive with on-the-scene accounts of Austro-Hungarian tensions from the front of the Hungarian parliament. His visit to the Imperial War Museum where Franz Ferdinand's bloody uniform jacket and limousine are on display is memorable.

Nonetheless, even this lucid account fails at times. It cannot manage a simultaneously compressed and clear account of a number of complex topics. These include Russia's role in the Bosnian Crisis of 1908 or the origins and policies of the Serbian "Black Hand."

<u>Freud: The Hidden Nature of Man</u>
(<u>Western Civilization: Majesty and Madness</u> series)

29 minutes   color
1970   Learning Corporation of America

Summary: A lively, imaginative presentation of Freud's pioneering ideas about the human mind; marred at the close by a clumsy dramatization of a sexual dilemma faced by a young man in modern society

Grade: B

The film employs a narrator and dramatic sequences, with the actor playing Sigmund Freud addressing the audience directly. Examples of modern art indicate the hidden confusion and anguish of the individual. The basic theme of the film is the way in which Freud uncovered hidden forces of aggression and sexual desire that he believed shaped the human personality.

<u>Freud</u> begins with disturbing views of modern paintings. Meanwhile, the narrator asks the questions that obsessed Freud, such as "How did humans become what they are?" An actor playing the elderly scientist describes his life and professional experiences. This introduces an account of Freud's pioneering work. As a young doctor, Freud found himself unable to cure patients with neurological diseases by treating them for physical ailments. Thus, he was drawn to hypnosis. In a painful episode, one of his early patients describes her recollection of childhood sexual abuse at the hands of her father.

Freud goes on to explore the meaning of dreams, starting with his own. In one he had as a child, a group of gigantic birds approached his mother's bed. This leads him to an understanding of his own illicit sexual desires.

The film loses its dramatic impact during its final third. It lapses into a technical discussion of human personality. This is accompanied by a clumsy dramatization about a young man and his girlfriend. Diverse forces in his conscious and subconscious compete to influence his decision about having sex with her. The closing moments of the film return to a higher level. Freud and the narrator sum up the scientist's achievement in helping man to understand himself.

Most of the acting in the film, with the exception of the final dramatization, is effective. The dream sequence with birds is brilliantly done. The continual display of tormented figures from modern art superbly illustrates human anguish. Only the boy-girl sequence at the close detracts from the overall value of the film. Unfortunately, its location in the film makes it difficult to omit.

Students can be asked to consider how a member of Vienna's high bourgeoisie might have responded to Freud's disturbing message about the forces shaping the human personality. Another discussion can evaluate whether Freud is convincing when he claims the information about human nature he has discovered can help man preserve himself from his worst instincts and those of society.

The Glory of Europe--Hey Day Fever

See <u>Hey Day Fever</u>

Hey Day Fever: The Glory of Europe, 1900
(Europe: The Mighty Continent series)

52 minutes   color
1974   BBC

Summary: A rich, often lighthearted view of European life at the start of the twentieth century stressing the role of France, Britain, and Germany; emphasizing the culture of Europe at this time, the film is resolutely Anglocentric

Grade: B

Hey Day Fever employs two narrators, historian John Terraine and actor-writer Peter Ustinov. Terraine is a specialist in twentieth-century European history; Ustinov's family connections with various European countries provide a link to the key developments of the century. The film combines visits to important historical locales with cartoons of the time and extensive newsfilm footage. One basic theme of the film is the dominant role that Europe played in the world at the optimistic beginning of this century. A second theme is the growing antagonism between Great Britain and the newly united Germany. A third element that runs through the film is the cultural vibrancy of European life, at least for its educated elite.

The film begins with Peter Ustinov introducing the entire series. He presents it as an effort by a professor and an amateur to combine their views of Europe in the first seventy years of the twentieth century. Ustinov concedes at once that others will interpret the era in a vastly different fashion. John Terraine's introduction stresses the optimism many Europeans felt at the start of this century: scientific thinking, the belief in progress, and the absence of wars that had marked the beginning of previous centuries contributed to an increasing sense of well-being.

The first segment of the film examines Paris at the time of its 1900 Exposition. The city, Peter Ustinov notes, glorified itself and France with mechanical wonders like a moving pavement. Other exhibits glamorized the French Empire and emphasized France's resurgent military power. Ustinov's rich discussion of French life ranges from the city's splendid network of boulevards to the glamorous courtesans of the time. Ustinov's great-uncle, the stage designer Alexandre Benois serves to illustrate the glories of the French theater.

Next, John Terraine introduces the components of European power: ships, modern industry, military systems, and rising national rivalries. He describes how European nations joined to crush the Boxer Uprising in China in 1900, but notes this was a unique exception to a pattern of ruthless competition.

The second half of the film examines the Anglo-German rivalry. A complacent Britain found itself challenged by newly united Germany. Newsfilm showing the first flight of Count Zeppelin's airship in 1900 illustrates Germany's position on the cutting edge of technical change. Peter Ustinov in a Heidelberg beer hall discusses German militarism, anti-British feeling, and the cult of duelling. The final segment of the film moves to Vienna, which, like Paris was a center of cultural achievement.   There, according to Ustinov, Freud's exploration of human irrationality and potential for violence, indicated "a fever on Europe's brow."

The film is well-written and sumptuously photographed. Some archive footage, such as the segments on the first Zeppelin, is memorable. The narration achieves an important insight by noting how cultural vibrancy was mixed with signs of uneasiness and pessimism.   Nonetheless, Hey Day Fever ranges so widely that students may find it hard to follow. Important elements of European life, such as the Socialist movement, have been deferred for treatment in subsequent episodes. Thus, the film is only a partial picture of a complex whole. The stress on German militarism ignores the British fixation on naval power. In general, the film looks at the history of European from a British point of views.

Students can be asked to speculate on why and how two countries such as Britain and Germany put aside longstanding friendly relations and began to move toward confrontation. They can also be asked to identify the Anglocentric elements in the film.

Into the 20th Century
(Art of the Western World series)

60 minutes   color
1989   WNET

Summary: A rambling, but sporadically informative examination of Western art from the beginning of the twentieth century to World War II

Grade: C +

The film uses the works of art of the time, interviews with leading art historians, photographs and film clips, and visits to locales where key artistic developments took place. A basic theme is the shift away from the Renaissance tradition of art that showed the beauty of physical reality. In its place came a desire to investigate the inner nature of reality including the brutality and ugliness of the world. A second theme is the way in which rapid changes in art coincided with radical changes in society brought by science and the trauma of World War I. Finally, the film looks at the differing ways in which political radicalism expressed itself in art: the imaginative response of pre-1914 Italian Futurism and the art of the Bolshevik Revolution; the die-hard conservatism of Nazi and Stalinist art.

Into the Twentieth Century uses World War I as a dividing line. The initial portion of the film contrasts the stability and political conservatism of the pre-1914 Austro-Hungarian and German empires with the artistic rebellion to which they gave rise. The works of Gustav Klimt in Vienna expressed a new, sometimes gross sexuality; the German Expressionists, as well as their French colleagues in the Fauve movement, were fascinated with the exoticism and absence of industrialization in the non-Western world.

The film stresses the work of Picasso as he moved away from representational art to Cubism. In these same prewar years, however, the art world gave rise to political activists. The Italian Futurist Marinetti, for example, called for a war to cleanse the stodginess from European civilization. Less optimistic predictions of future carnage came in the work of Kandinsky.

The second portion of the film is even more diffuse, moving from World War I to diverse responses to the war. It considers the bitterness and pessimism of George Grosz in Weimar Germany, the optimistic view of an industrial society seen by Léger in France, the attack on scientific truth launched by the Dadaists. Here the film also considers the alliance between Russian artists and the system that emerged from Bolshevik November Revolution of 1917.

There follows an exploration of modern architecture by Le Corbusier and Frank Lloyd Wright, as well as the surrealism of Salvador Dali. Political themes emerge again in Picasso's response to the horrors of the Spanish Civil War, and the straitjacket the totalitarianism of the 1930s placed on the artistic world.

The film is visually exciting. Its first half can stand alone as an introduction to the ferment and tension in European culture in the decade and a half preceding World War I. The segment in the second half of the film on the Russian artists who supported the Bolshevik Revolution with their work makes an important point well. Nonetheless, Into the Twentieth Century is long and marred by descriptions of artistic techniques. In the second half, it degenerates into little more than a cavalcade of briefly described names and movements.

Joseph Conrad

(The Modern World: Ten Great Writers series)

58 minutes   color
1988   Public Media

Summary: A well-acted but slow paced examination of Conrad's literary work set in London at the start of the twentieth century; while it catches the atmosphere of the era, it contains little of direct historical relevance

Grade: C -

The film employs a narrator, photos and newsfilm, interviews and statements from present-day literary critics, and visits to the settings for Conrad's literary work. The basic element in the film, however, is a dramatized version of Conrad's novel The Secret Agent about spies and anarchists in London around 1900. The theme of the film is Conrad's interest in the hidden tensions of modern society. He saw them exemplified by anarchist bomb plots within the center of a great city.

The Secret Agent begins ambiguously. A man in the dress of the early twentieth century suddenly stumbles, causing an explosion. At that point the narrator discusses Conrad's life and work. He notes that by this time Conrad's interests focused life in metropolitan London. The narration proceeds with dramatic scenes covering the plot of The Secret Agent. Interspersed are several discussions of Conrad's life and literary career. The film also examines historical issues such as popular unrest as seen in the Paris Commune of 1871 and the wave of terrorist bombing in Europe around 1900. Two literary critics, Sir V.S. Pritchett and Keith Carabine, present their views of Conrad's literary technique.

The film is beautifully acted and well-staged. It vividly presents the physical appearance and atmosphere of London in the early twentieth century. The narration raises important issues of popular violence and international tensions, and the cartoons and newsfilm footage are fascinating. Nonetheless, the film is sharply focused on Conrad's literary career and his techniques of plotting and characterization. Given the slow pace and the extent to which scenes from The Secret Agent dominate the action, the yield for someone interested in the history of the period is distressingly low.

The Ruling Houses

See The Day of Empires Has Arrived

The Social Classes, 1900

See A World to Win

A World to Win: The Social Classes, 1900
(Europe: The Mighty Continent series)

52 minutes   color
1974   BBC

Summary: A brilliantly photographed but diffuse and poorly paced examination of Europe's social tensions, radical politics, and artistic rebellion from 1900 to the eve of World War I

Grade: B

A World to Win employs two narrators, John Terraine and Peter Ustinov. There are also photographs, cartoons, maps, newsfilm footage, and visits to important historical locales. In addition, the film includes interviews with present-day descendants of notable aristocratic families, scenes of modern workers' demonstrations, and other views of modern European society. The basic theme of the film is the growing set of class antagonisms that split the European population and their expression in movements like Marxian socialism and anarchism.

The film begins with historian John Terraine noting that the pre-World War I era was only superficially a golden age. Beneath the surface Europe contained an angry and dispossessed majority. He illustrates his statement scenes of present-day demonstrators in the Paris streets.

The first portion of the film focuses on the landed aristocracy, then the middle classes, and finally on the peasant and workers who made up the mass of the European population in 1900. Present-day scenes of aristocratic hunting parties in France and peasants in the Alps give way to gripping photographs showing the urban poverty at the start of the century. The French Commune of 1871, which left a legacy of fear and bitterness appears in the form of photographs, paintings, and a visit to Père Lachaise cemetery where many of the insurgents were executed. Scenes of Leningrad in the 1970s, still decorated with Communist slogans, illustrate the eventual success of the radical movement.

The second half of the film is more diffuse. It begins with a discussion of the artistic rebellion in France exemplified by the Fauvist movement. The narration describes the Revolution of 1905 in Russia, proceeding from there to look at the rising tide of unrest in Britain prior to World War I. The closing moments deal in rapid fashion with labor unrest in France, anarchist upheaval in Spain, and the political and artistic rebellion of Marinetti and the Futurists in Italy.

The photography is lush and engrossing. Portions of the film are lucid and well-constructed. The survey of European society and its tensions and the segment on the Russian Revolution of 1905 are skillfully done. But the film covers a vast range of loosely connected topics in cursory fashion, especially in the second half. Moreover, the extensive treatment of developments in Britain in the decade before 1914 reflects an emphatic Anglocentrism.

Students can be asked to consider how the average middle-class European would have reacted to signs of rapid change such as Fauvist or the Futurist works of art. Would these things likely have promoted a sense of imminent crisis? Likewise, one can ask just how worried a Western European was likely to be that the example of the Russian Revolution of 1905 would spread.

The Years 1904-1914

See The Drums Begin to Roll

WORLD WAR I AND THE AFTERMATH

THE WAR

<u>The Arming of the Earth</u>
(<u>A Walk through the 20th Century with Bill Moyers</u> series)

55 minutes   color
1983   PBS
Summary: A brilliantly constructed and graphic depiction of twentieth-century warfare focusing on the development and use of the machine gun, the submarine, and the bombing plane

Grade: A -

      <u>The Arming of the Earth</u> employs narrator Bill Moyers, interviews with historians and eye-witnesses of the events depicted, and large quantities of newsfilm footage. There is also a segment from the film <u>All Quiet on the Western Front</u>. The basic theme of the film is the widening destructive power of warfare, including the involvement of large numbers of civilian casualties, as a result of the technical developments pictured here.
      The film is divided into three parts, each dealing with one of the weapons under consideration. A prologue shows footage of a classic cavalry charge. There follow scenes of the new machine gun which put an end to such romantic imagery. Bill Moyers then discusses the basic theme of the film, noting that eighteenth-century warfare sought to avoid the involvement of civilians whereas twentieth-century warfare has affected the entire population of warring countries.
      An examination of the machine gun focuses on World War I. Historian John Keegan discusses the weapon and how it was used. A scene from <u>All Quiet on the Western Front</u> gives a sense of the horror of a battlefield dominated by

by machine gun fire. The film uses the Battle of the Somme in 1916 to illustrate how the machine gun decimated entire armies and helped to turn World War I into a seemingly endless slaughter.

The second portion of the film begins with Major John Brimsfield, an American army chaplain and historian at West Point. He discusses the ethics of expending huge numbers of lives for seemingly insignificant results. Next, The Arming of the Earth considers the submarine. The deadly attack on the civilian ocean liner Lusitania in 1915 serves as the center of the discussion. There are striking examples of the human cost of such means of warfare. These include an interview with a woman who lost her infant in the water following the torpedo attack.

The final portion of the film traces the growth of aerial warfare. Starting with reconnaissance flights early in World War I, the story progresses through General Billy Mitchell's visionary plans for wars built around air power through the massive urban destruction of World War II.

The film is lucid, well-organized, and frequently gripping. The sections on the machine gun and the submarine vividly illustrate the carnage of World War I. The historians who appear in the film are sharp and knowledgeable; eye-witnesses interviewed make events come alive.

The film's principal weakness comes in its third section. The history of aerial bombing from World War I to the atomic era is treated in a relatively sketchy way. Moreover, the film is marginally inaccurate in identifying historian A.J.P Taylor as a specialist in military history and in failing to note that Major Brimstead, identified as a military historian, is in fact a chaplain. The narration is dated by predictions at the film's close of the likely use of atomic weapons between the superpowers. Students can be asked to consider whether the increasing scope and brutality of twentieth-century warfare can be explained solely in terms of technical change. What other factors need to be brought into the picture?

Good-bye Billy: America Goes to War, 1917-1918

25 minutes   black\white
1972   Cadre Films

Summary: A brilliant and touching examination of the experience and emotions produced by World War I; it considers American society in the war but the picture it paints can stand for any of the belligerents

Grade: A

The film does not use a narrator. Visually, it consists of newsfilm, photographs, posters, and cartoons. The sound track contains songs, poems, letters, recruiting slogans, speeches, and an extended passage written by John Dos Passos. The theme of the film is the transformation of people's feelings about the war from naive enthusiasm and patriotism to penetrating sadness.

The film begins with a variety of images: President Woodrow Wilson in a parade, troops embarking for Europe, horseplay among the soldiers on the ships bound for the war. A captioned episode shows General John Pershing at the Lafayette Memorial in Paris. With sound in the background, the film establishes a lighthearted tone using music and wartime rhetoric. Bond rallies, including one featuring Charlie Chaplin, stand beside advertisements touting food conservation to show how the war, in a limited way, penetrates the homefront.

Around the halfway point, the tone of the film turns subtly toward more somber themes. Good-bye Billy now presents a mother's poem remembering her lost son, pictures of combat, and a book of faces. The viewer soon realizes these are the visages of the war dead, presented one at a time. The somber note grows stronger with views of ruined cities and barbed wire.

The final portion of the film focuses on the selection of America's unknown soldier. Newsfilm shows the body being prepared and sent back from the front lines. This segment of the film ends with the formal dedication, including a speech by President Warren Harding and a ceremonial blessing by an American Indian chief. Setting off this chronological account are shots of mutilated soldiers being fitted with artificial faces. At times Harding's pompous words are heard, but the sound track is increasingly dominated by John Dos Passos's quietly scathing account of the unknown soldier's selection, transportation, and burial. The last image of the film is a mother kneeling at a gravestone. The camera pulls back to show a cemetery of frightening dimensions.

Good-bye Billy combines brilliant images with a carefully constructed sound track. The quality of the newsfilm is remarkably fresh and clear, more reminiscent of the cinema record of World War II or later conflicts than of 1917 and 1918. The emotional impact of the film is unforgettable. It is a thoroughly convincing depiction of the emotional ups and downs that helped to fuel the war, then made many Americans look back in disgust at the wartime experience.

Students can be asked to consider whether this American view of the war would hold true for the other participants in the conflict.

The Great War

See This Generation Has No Future

This Generation Has No Future: The Great War
(Europe: The Mighty Continent series)

52 minutes   color
1974   BBC

Summary: A vivid, informative, and emotionally gripping depiction of World War I; the film relies partly on a chronological account of the war and partly on a topical presentation of the war's nature

Grade: A -

    This Generation employs narrators John Terraine and Peter Ustinov, newsfilm, photographs and works of art from the period, and visits to historical locales.   The basic theme of the film is the upheaval brought on by the unprecedented scope of the war and the conflict's transforming effect on the old European order.
    The film's first major segment describes the massive nature of the war and the traumatic experiences it visited on its participants. Present-day views of the trenches give an idea of what a soldier's life in them was like. The graves of soldiers drawn from the empires of Britain and France illustrate how the conflict was indeed a world war. Units of the Belgian army are shown still clearing away shells embedded in the Ypres salient six decades after the Armistice. Newsfilm records the enthusiasm of Britain's millions of volunteer soldiers. Peter Ustinov's discussion of Allied air aces like Guynemer and Ball shows the youth and ardor of the individual warrior.
    Next, the film consider the massive slaughter of 1916 at Verdun and the Somme. This is followed by a description of the war on the Russian and Italian fronts and a consideration of propaganda, ranging from Ernst Lissauer's anti-British poetry to a British film ostensibly showing German atrocities.
    The second half of the film turns to other specific events of 1916 and 1917: Emperor Franz Joseph dies after sixty-eight years on the Austrian throne, Eric Ludendorff and David Lloyd George take power committed to fighting the war to a successful conclusion. Peter Ustinov stands before the statue of Lenin at St. Petersburg's Finland Station to discuss the collapse of the imperial Russian government. It was, he notes, only the first of several established governments to fall as a result of the war's strains. The Americans enter the war, the French and Italian armies nearly collapse, and the British army meets catastrophe in the bloody 1917 offensive at Ypres.
    The film concludes with combat footage from the 1918 German offensive on the western front. Paintings show the lunaresque landscape left by the war's last great military encounters. A final image is an aerial view of a devastated city.
    This Generation balances the chronology of the war with a discussion of key topics. The narration by Terraine and Ustinov is eloquent, but the film gets its emotional force from well-chosen images: paintings of depersonalized

hordes of men moving up toward the front, photographs of the dead, the immense military cemetery on Vimy Ridge.

The kaleidoscopic treatment of the war makes the film most suitable for students already familiar with the conflict. The narration is highly successful in accompanying the film's images, but there are some gaps. In scenes of the Russian turmoil, for example, central figures like Alexander Kerensky and General Lavr Kornilov appear without being identified.

Lenin and the Great Ungluing

See review under THE DICTATORSHIPS

Verdun
(Legacy series)

black\white   30 minutes
1965   WNET

Summary: A brilliant examination of the greatest battle of World War I and the longest battle in history; it stresses the suffering of the average soldier on the French side

Grade: A

The film employs a narrator, visits to important historical locales, excerpts from diaries and other historical documents, and views of both German and French veterans of the battle who have survived to the 1960s. The most important technique used in the film is a collection of dramatic and compelling photographs taken during World War I. The basic theme of the film is the hellish experience of participants in the new kind of battle epitomized by Verdun. A secondary theme is the way in which the ultimate French success drained the country of talent and vitality for decades thereafter.

Verdun begins with pictures of veterans and tourists visiting the battlefield. The narrator reads from the German chief of staff General Erich von Falkenhayn's memo setting down the reasons to attack at Verdun. The Germans did not intend to break through the French line. Rather, as the entire film makes clear, they hoped to inflict intolerable manpower losses on the French army. Views of the grave of the French unknown soldier in Paris, identified as a casualty at Verdun, suggest how successfully the plan worked. The narrator reads the total figures of the losses for both sides.

The centerpiece of the film is a description of the German attack and the French defense at Verdun shown in still photographs. Verdun traces the battle from the extensive German preparations, through the first devastating assault, and on to the endless fighting that occupied most of 1916.

Quotations from one French soldier's diary describe the massive artillery bombardments that characterized the entire battle. Quotations from another paint the expressions on a platoon of men about to go up to the front to meet certain death. Eerie present-day photographs show the torn earth and trenches. One can still see the erect bayonets of soldiers buried alive in 1916. The narrator characterizes the horror of Verdun by noting that of every ten Frenchmen sent to the battle, three would be buried alive. Present-day scenes of French cemeteries show endless rows of graves. An examination of individual headstones lets the viewer think of lost Frenchmen as one individual tragedy after another.

In its closing moments, the film returns to the center of Paris. At the Arch of Triumph, the French people continue to visit their unknown soldier, who was chosen from a group of unidentified dead at Verdun. Verdun closes by jumping to 1940, when Adolf Hitler's invading army smashed through this part of France almost effortlessly. The film suggests that the explanation for this World War II defeat comes from France's longstanding exhaustion, a legacy of Verdun.

The film is crisp, clear, and almost unbearably effective in showing the human cost of World War I. The high quality of the narration and the skillfully chosen documents are memorable. Its greatest strength, however, is in the extraordinary still photographs employed in conjunction with present-day views of the landmarks of Verdun.

It should be noted that the film does not clearly identify the documents it quotes. Moreover, it loses some of its impact in its closing minutes when lingers on scenes from present-day Paris. These minor failings scarcely detracts from Verdun's exemplary quality.

Students can be asked to consider why Germany, which also suffered catastrophic losses at Verdun, did not find itself as weakened as France two decades later.

THE POST-WAR PERIOD

Are We Making a Good Peace? The Results of War
(Europe: The Mighty Continent series)

52 minutes   color
1976   BBC

Summary: A lucid, well-paced examination of the Versailles Peace Conference

Grade: A

The film employs narrators John Terraine and Peter Ustinov, maps, photographs, newsfilm, and visits to important historical locales. The basic theme of the film is the way in which elements of idealism, cynicism, and fear mingled at the global peace conference to produce a flawed settlement. It penalized Germany excessively and left an unstable Europe to find its way into the future.

Are We Making a Good Peace? begins with brief statements by Ustinov and Terraine. They stress the conflicting motives of the peacemakers and the novel phenomenon of a peace conference with delegates from all over the globe. They also note the impossibility of predicting at the start what kind of settlement would be produced.

The first half of the film shows President Woodrow Wilson's triumphal reception in Europe and the damage left behind by the war's campaigns. It also discusses the aims of the European governments on the victorious side. Narrator Peter Ustinov quotes British diplomat Harold Nicolson to show the idealism with which some representatives to the Conference approached their task. After the rival claims of the participants had begun to change the atmosphere, Nicolson's views appear again. This time he expresses his disappointment and poses the despairing question, "Are we making a good peace?"

The second half of the film touches briefly upon the Russian Revolution and the founding of the Communist International. This shows how non-European powers, Soviet Russia along with the United States, now influenced the fate of Europe's major countries. Peter Ustinov uses a map of Europe in the form of a jigsaw puzzle to illustrate the momentous changes the Conference made in Europe's borders.

The centerpiece of the second half of the film is the description of the harsh settlement levied on Germany. One scene shows the pair of second-rank German officials who were forced to accept the peace treaty. Another shows their two signatures on the official document itself. The film concludes with a leap to the mid-1920s and the Locarno Conference. Only at this point, it notes, did European leaders begin a process of genuine reconciliation.

Are We Making a Good Peace? succeeds in the difficult task of presenting an event in diplomatic history on film. The wit and insight of the narrators combine with such effective images as pictures of the devastated Belgian city of Ypres to draw the viewer into the story.

Students can be asked to consider if the victorious governments could have adopted an alternative policy toward a defeated Germany. How, for example, could they have made such a policy acceptable to their voting publics?

<u>From Kaiser to Fuehrer</u>
(<u>The Twentieth Century</u> series)

26 minutes   black\white
1960   CBS

Summary: A complex, diffuse, but engrossing view of Germany from the revolution at the close to 1918 to Hitler's assumption of power in 1933

Grade: B +

The film employs a narrator and copious newsfilm, including speeches of the young Adolf Hitler. The paintings of the time along with a segment of the film <u>Metropolis</u> illustrate cultural developments. The basic theme of the film is the stress of change Germany endured in the era after World War I. Change came first in the form of the chaos of the immediate postwar period through 1923, then in a brief era of stability and seeming prosperity under the Weimar Republic, and finally in the economic and political catastrophe of the Depression.

<u>From Kaiser to Fuehrer</u> begins with scenes of German crowds milling in the nation's streets. The former Emperor William II sits in exile in Holland, and a youthful Adolf Hitler cries out to his audience: "<u>They</u> are the ones responsible for this." The narrator then describes a Germany in despair, having been defeated in World War I and stripped of its overseas empire.

Following the titles, the film shows the street fighting that erupted in late 1918 as the war was lost and the monarchy fell. Delegates arrive at Weimar to found a new state, and right-wing forces try unsuccessfully to take power in the 1920 Kapp Putsch. The extraordinary inflation that devastated Germany's middle classes is illustrated by spinning printing presses grinding out new currency while workers carry off their day's wages in a wheelbarrow. Meanwhile, the poor pick through garbage dumps, and the newly rich enjoy the era's cafe society. The film shows the Nazis appearing as bands of marchers, apparently only one of many groups of extremists on the scene.

The second major segment of the film shows a recovering Germany. It regains its position as the economic and technological powerhouse of Europe and develops a moderate political system with Field Marshal Paul von Hindenburg, the hero of World War I, as the nation's president. In striking counterpoint, the work of artists like Georg Grosz and Käthe Kollwitz reveals the grim underside of Germany in the 1920s. Twin images of prosperous Germans enjoying their tea dances while Hitler's storm troopers eat in soup kitchens show a system with no apparent prospects for extremists of the right.

In its final third, <u>From Kaiser to Fuehrer</u> describes the economic catastrophe following the American stock market crash in late 1929. A key sequence shows a confident Hitler delivering a speech mocking the weak, multiparty political system of the time. In short order Hitler assumes power. He and his coalition cabinet, made up mostly of non-Nazis, appear in conventional business suits. Thereupon, an ominous torchlight victory parade of Hitler's followers suggests the emotional force the Nazis would bring to the new government.

The film shows compellingly the atmosphere of change that characterized German affairs over this relatively brief period. The views of Hitler emphasize his youth and energy and give generous samples of his speaking ability. Other vivid scenes show the false prosperity of the years from 1924 to 1929. Technical achievements like early bullet trains, for example, indicate a stable, progressive Germany.

One must note, however, that the first ten minutes of the film show events in kaleidoscopic fashion. Scenes of one crowd or another, some representing Communist insurgents, some representing right-wing vigilantes are hard to sort out. Moreover, the picture of German political life at the start of the 1930s is sanitized. There are vivid scenes showing mass poverty but no suggestion of the bloody street violence and collapsing public order that tormented the society.

The Hope of Mankind: The League of Nations
(Europe: The Mighty Continent series)

52 minutes   color
1976   BBC

Summary: An informative but somewhat diffuse examination of the role of the League of Nations in European affairs from 1919 to the end of the 1930s

Grade: B

The film employs narrators John Terraine and Peter Ustinov, newsfilm, works of art and architecture from the time, and visits to historic locales. The basic theme of the film is the disintegration of the vast hopes placed in the great international organization established at the close of World War I. The second theme is the continuing national rivalries and domestic tensions that made any European stability unlikely during this period.

The Hope of Mankind begins with statements by both narrators. Peter Ustinov disparages the high-flown rhetoric of the preamble to the Covenant of the League of Nations. John Terraine notes the new shape of postwar Europe, similar to today's map, and he remarks on the need for an international organization with the authority to keep order.

The film then considers the new tools of communication such as the radio that seemed to produce a more informed public in many countries. According to Terraine, this gave credence to the argument that an international organization could act to discipline international wrongdoing. Much of the first half of the film shows why such hopes were baseless. The narration examines the flaws in the League's membership. It shows that key countries like the United States and Soviet Russia refused to participate. An extended examination of Fascist Italy shows the kind of unbridled nationalism unlikely to submit to external discipline. There follows a grim view of the other states of Europe. Small countries like Hungary were tempted by Italy's example. Germany, the largest of the discontented countries, was destabilized by inflation and infuriated at the penalties the Peace Conference had placed on it.

The Hope of Mankind notes that there was a brief point in the mid-1920s when leaders managed to rise above their difficulties to become good Europeans. Peter Ustinov visits the restaurant in Geneva where conciliatory figures like Gustav Stresemann of Germany and Aristide Briand often met. There is newsfilm of Briand, a distinguished orator, welcoming the Germans into the League in 1926.

The second half of the film shows Europe in the 1930s. Great buildings constituting the League's permanent home were arising near Lake Geneva. Meanwhile, international stability crumbled. Germany became a Nazi state, other dictatorships thrived throughout Eastern Europe, and the League proved helpless when Japan, then Italy went to war against member states. The film closes with a striking image of the League's completed buildings. Ironically, they were ready in 1939 as the Continent was plunging into World War II.

The merits of the film include a strong central theme, namely the fortunes of the League. The extended treatment of Fascist Italy can stand by itself. It combines vivid newsfilm and a clear description of the complex, contradictory political system. All this is topped off with striking present-day views of the grandiose architecture of Mussolini's state. John Terraine puts the basic issue of the film clearly by asking whether Europe would follow the tenets of Fascist Italy or the international ideals of the League.

Unfortunately, the film's pace is slow. Much of the narration is verbose. The Hope of Mankind considers a profusion of Anglocentric topics, some of which roam far from the basic theme. Viewers are likely to be perplexed, for example, by the significance of British society's renewed interest in cricket, for example.

The League of Nations

See The Hope of Mankind

The Results of War

See Are We Making a Good Peace?

THE DICTATORSHIPS

FASCISM AND NAZISM

The Democrat and the Dictator
(A Walk Through the 20th Century With Bill Moyers series)

55 minutes   color
1984   PBS

Summary: A strikingly effective comparison of the lives and political careers of Franklin Roosevelt and Adolf Hitler

Grade: A

The Democrat and the Dictator employs narrator Bill Moyers, photographs and works of art, newsfilm, and an interview with Fritz Hippler, one of Hitler's subordinates. Its basic theme is how Roosevelt and Hitler stood as representatives of their respective nations and political cultures, notably during the economic and diplomatic crises of the 1930s and through the events of World War II.

The film first shows the two taking power in 1933. Next, it explores their early political careers following World War I, then reaches back to compare their childhoods. This thematic approach continues by considering their personalities and speaking skills. It then shows some of the symbolic institutions of America and Germany in the 1930s: Roosevelt's fireside chats, the Civilian Conservation Corps and the paintings of WPA artists; Hitler's speeches at the Nuremberg Party Congress of 1934, his SS, the heroic art of Nazi election posters.

The highpoint of the film comes during the second half with a series of excerpts placed side by side from the speeches of each figure. These illustrate their contrasting ideas--Hitler's "The future belongs to us," Roosevelt's "I hate war"--while encouraging the viewer to consider how such ideas fared in the later stages of each one's career.

The eloquent narration by Bill Moyers links the diverse elements contained in the film. The Democrat and the Dictator succeeds admirably in capturing the personalities and ideas of its two protagonists. It is equally successful in illustrating the political "feel" of America and Germany in the 1930s. Moyers has drawn a number of extraordinary, rarely displayed scenes from the era's film records. These include: a surprisingly young Hitler campaigning by means of air travel in the 1920s; Roosevelt reviewing a tiny parade of disheveled American soldiers in the 1930s; the American president, only weeks before his death, giving a final report on the war to Congress. The narration also insists on recalling uncomfortable facts from the historical record: Hitler's widespread popularity in Germany in the late 1930s; the American alliance with a tyrannical Joseph Stalin in order to defeat Nazi Germany. The statements from Hippler, an unrepentant follower of the Nazi dictator, provide a striking contrast to Moyers's outrage at Hitler's crimes.

One weakness of the film is the absence of a clear chronological framework. The first portion, for example, jumps from 1933 back to the aftermath of World War I and then to the last years of the nineteenth century. Moreover, the dramatic speeches by Hitler and Roosevelt appear without an indication of the time and circumstances surrounding these utterances. These are minor failings.

The Democrat and the Dictator offers a treasure trove of material for class discussion. Likely topics include the contrasting political cultures of Germany and the United States, the techniques by which Hitler and Roosevelt appealed to their respective audiences; factors that would incline a German in the 1930s to accept or reject Hitler as a national leader. Equally intriguing issues are the psychology of Fritz Hippler, and Hitler's use of modern technology (the radio, the airplane, film) in his political career.

Form! Riflemen, Form!: Rise of the Dictators
(Europe: The Mighty Continent series)

52 minutes   color
1976   BBC

Summary: A well-structured and lucid examination of growing international tensions in the 1930s; it stresses the Spanish Civil War as the point where the spread of Fascism was directly challenged

Grade: A

The film uses narrators John Terraine and Peter Ustinov, newsfilm, works of art, excerpts from the literature and music of the time, and visits to important historical locales. The main theme is the inability of the Western democracies to block the threat Hitler and Mussolini posed to the existing international order.

Form! Riflemen, Form! begins with a discussion of the sour political environment in Europe following World War I. Using the works of artists like Salvador Dali, the film shows a pessimistic intellectual temper in which patriotism and other traditional ideals seemed irrelevant. A discussion of unemployment shows how more tangible developments threatened the European majority. The remainder of the first half of the narration discusses Hitler's new dictatorship and its apparent success in dealing with unemployment. It follows by showing the spread of the Nazi example. The ominous trend even reached Britain in the form of Oswald Mosley's British Union of Fascists. Italy shook the international order by attacking Ethiopia, while the Soviet Union developed its own form of ugly dictatorship exemplified by the purges of the late 1930s.

The second half of the film focuses on the Spanish Civil War. Visits to the sites of battlefields show ruins that have come down to the present. The film presents the war as a complex struggle combining tensions within Spain with divisions in Europe as a whole. Nonetheless, the narration depicts the Spanish Civil War in large part as the moment when part of European society finally took up arms against the Fascist dictators.

The film closes with an account of the Munich Crisis of 1938 and its aftermath. It makes clear how Hitler's continuing aggression, notably the seizure of all of Czechoslovakia in the spring of 1939, changed the international environment. Even spokesmen for appeasement like Neville Chamberlain determined to stand fast, and World War II began in short order. The final image of the film is a massive World War I graveyard that had been filled with the dead only twenty-one years earlier.

The merits of Form! Riflemen, Form! include a clearly stated theme and dramatic newsfilm. The narration indicates precisely the way in which an exhausted and discouraged Europe found it easier to acquiesce to Hitler and Mussolini than to stand firm against them. The film distinguishes itself in capturing the mood of ideological fervor that drove Europeans of the political left to fight in Spain.

The Last Nazi: Albert Speer

72 minutes   color
1976   Learning Corporation of America

Summary: An overly long but interesting examination of the personality and career of one of Hitler's most important subordinates

Grade: B +

The film employs newsfilm, home movies of Hitler's household taken by Speer, and visits to historical locales. The centerpiece of the film is a narration by Patrick Watson, along with Watson's face to face conversations with Speer. The basic theme of the film is Speer's relationship with Hitler and his key role in maintaining Germany's industrial production during World War II. A secondary theme is Speer's effort to rehabilitate his reputation and to show he was not associated with the worst crimes of the Nazi era.

The first half of the film provides an account of Speer's early life. Speaking in English, he describes his memories of World War I, his childhood friendship with a Jewish student, and his education as an architect. Speer goes on to discuss his attraction to the Nazi movement, his first meeting with Hitler, and his role in staging the annual Nazi rally at Nuremberg. A highpoint of the first portion of The Last Nazi is Speer's discussion of Hitler's personality. A visually striking sequence comes in scenes from the home movies Speer took of Hitler, the dictator's entourage, and Speer's own family at Berchtesgaden.

The second half of the film moves chronologically from the Blood Purge of 1934, through the foreign policy crises of the 1930s, and into World War II. Speer describes his role as the organizer of German industry from 1942 until the close of the war. He insists that others were responsible for the hideous conditions under which forced laborers lived and worked. Speer justifies his industrial leadership, even though he knew the war was lost, as a means of keeping the Russians from moving quickly into Central Europe. He stresses his role in preventing the implementation of Hitler's orders for a "scorched earth" policy of total destruction of Germany in the face of the Allied invasion in the spring of 1945.

The film constitutes an intriguing character study of the only top Nazi leader to admit his guilt at the Nuremberg War Crimes Trials. Moreover, The Last Nazi presents a lucid introduction to Nazism accompanied by vivid film footage. Speer's home movies of Hitler in the dictator's mountain retreat are memorable. The film's main weakness is its excessive length. It is, however, already divided into two discrete segments that can be shown separately. It is also possible to drop the final quarter of the film entirely without seriously diminishing its impact.

Students can be asked to consider the veracity of Speer's account of his career as a Nazi. In particular, they can seek the points in the film where he seems to be notably vague, evasive, or apologetic concerning his role in the years from 1933 to 1945.

Minister of Hate
(The Twentieth Century series)

25 minutes   black\white
1960   CBS

Summary: A crisp, authoritative, and engrossing examination of one of Hitler's key subordinates, Joseph Goebbels, the Nazi minister of propaganda from January 1933 to the close of World War II; it provides numerous insights into the operations of the Nazi system

Grade: A -

Minister of Hate uses a narrator, interviews, newsfilm, and excerpts from feature films. There are generous samples of Goebbels's oratory. Its main themes are the power of the Nazi system over the individual German, the image of Hitler presented to the German population, and the role of propaganda in manufacturing and maintaining popular enthusiasm. Another theme is the way in which Goebbels supplanted Hitler during the last years of World War II as the spokesman for the Nazi regime.

The film is divided into two sections. It deals first with the 1930s and the character of Nazi society. This section features a chilling interview with film maker Fritz Lang. He recalls being harassed by Goebbels for The Crime of Dr. Mabuse, a movie that appeared to be critical of Hitler and the Nazis. Scenes from the concentration camp at Dachau, the burning of books of which the Nazis disapproved, and torchlight parades demonstrate the brutality of the system along with the dramatic spectacles designed to solidify popular support.

Minister of Hate shows Hitler amidst adoring crowds. It makes it clear, however, how Goebbels's propaganda arts--film, radio, and staged public appearances--were used to shape the image of an adored, charismatic leader.

The second portion of the film focuses on the World War II years. It includes rare scenes of the anti-British propaganda film, Oom Kruger. Set during the Boer War, that story portrayed Anglican ministers braying their prayers as they pass out Bibles and rifles to black Africans. As the war turned against Germany, Hitler faded from public view. Goebbels became the government's voice for an intensified national effort. The film shows his dramatic speeches calling for vengeance against the Allies. Meanwhile, there are bizarre scenes of well-dressed Germans marching through the rubble of their bombed cities, a testimony to the success of Goebbels's messages to the pubic.

The film features a lucid, dramatic narration and splendid newsfilm. It makes clear how consent was manufactured in the Nazi dictatorship, and it shows how Hitler's role changed during the course of the war. An interview with historian Hugh Trevor-Roper helps to provide a picture of Goebbels's historical role.

There are some minor problems in the film. Minister of Hate contains a number of scenes out of chronological order. Placards and speeches that are presented only in German. These are minor blemishes.

Mussolini
(The Twentieth Century series)

27 minutes   black\white
1959   CBS

Summary: A brisk, superficial, but useful sketch of the career of the Italian dictator

Grade: B -

The film employs a narrator and extensive newsfilm. The basic theme of the film is the way in which the Italian leader created a notable place for himself on the European stage of the 1920s and 1930s, only to plunge into catastrophe in the events of World War II.

Mussolini begins with a brief statement from the dictator's son, Romano, and a description of the unrest in Italy after World War I. Thereupon, the film traces Mussolini's career with an emphasis on his years as Italy's dictator. A number of scenes display Mussolini's Italy in the 1920s: the grandiose buildings constructed, Mussolini as horseman, skier, and family man; Italian children in military uniforms replete with gas masks to make their war games more realistic; the dictator addressing his crowds. There follows a treatment of the 1930s which stresses Mussolini's foreign adventures: the invasion of Ethiopia, intervention in Spain, the growing tie to Nazi Germany including Mussolini's sponsorship of the Munich Pact of 1938.

The final portion of the film deals with the Italian role in World War II. It focuses on the series of failures starting with Italy's invasion of Greece in 1940. It closes with Mussolini's execution at the hands of Italian anti-Fascist guerrillas in the last days of the war.

Mussolini features well-edited, but rarely seen footage on many aspects of Mussolini's career. It captures much of the grandiose atmosphere of Fascist Italy and of the brutal international environment of the 1930s. On the other hand, the film has little to say about the doctrines of Fascism. Nor does it describe Mussolini's career prior to becoming Italy's leader in 1922. It also presents a misleading picture of the speed with which Mussolini consolidated his dictatorship. It suggests, in particular, that the process was completed within a short time after the March on Rome in 1922. A key flaw in the film is the absence of a sample of Mussolini's oratory in front of a massive crowd. This was a crucial tool in his political success.

A New Germany, 1933-1939
(World at War series)

52 minutes   color
1973   HBO\Thames Television

Summary: A vivid, well-paced, and engrossing examination of Nazi Germany from 1993 to 1939; it stresses the changes in German life and society as the new system became entrenched

Grade: A -

A New Germany combines extensive and rare newsfilm, interviews with eyewitnesses, and a lucid narration sketching the era's principal political events. The basic theme is the popularity that Nazism developed in Germany as a result of the measures the new regime took to meet the nation's needs. A parallel theme is the reshaping of a traditional society, separated by barriers of class and region, into a population of devoted followers of a charismatic and ruthless leader.

The film begins with a brief prologue for the entire series: a visit to the French village at Oradour-sur-Glane, devastated by German S.S. units in 1944. The first two-thirds of A New Germany traces the internal history of Nazi Germany from Hitler's rise to power to the reoccupation of the Rhineland in March 1936. Familiar events like the first Nazi victory parades and the burning of subversive books appear in the form of fresh and dramatic footage. The extension of Nazism appears in telling instances: a child at a wedding dressed up as a miniature Storm trooper, the Christmas trees of 1933 decked out with swastikas.

The film gives a strong sample of Hitler's oratory. It also shows Nazi leaders like Goebbels and Goring trying to construct national solidarity by collecting funds for charity in the street. A telling sequence shows the entire military establishment taking a personal oath to Hitler in 1934. The narrator makes clear the political and emotional significance of such a pledge for German military leaders.

This portion of the film includes a description of Hitler's annual meeting with a vast assemblage of peasant farmers. Meanwhile, the military bid for popularity with open houses in which grandmothers and young boys are encouraged to sample its weaponry. An extended sequence shows Hitler at his favorite retreat, Berchtesgaden, in the Bavarian Alps.

Next, the film departs from domestic affairs to describe the expansion into Austria, the Czech Sudetenland (in September 1938), and the remainder of Czechoslovakia in the spring of 1939. But it returns to its central point with a chilling discussion of the intensifying persecution of the Jews in late 1938.

Scenes of Hitler's birthday celebration in Berlin in April 1939 show a loyal population and a powerful military, the fruits of six years of dictatorship. A final segment on the summer crisis of 1939 returns to the area of foreign affairs.

A New Germany demonstrates successfully the impact of the Nazi movement. The film offers a fine balance between the presentation of significant events such as the Blood Purge of 1934 and the response of eyewitnesses to such happenings. The music of the Nazi party and the army plays a significant part in the film's background, and the interviews show Germans from numerous social levels, responding to Nazism's appeal, sometimes against their own will. Hitler, shown in home movies made by his mistress, Eva Braun, appears at Berchtesgaden against a background of kitschy, popular music devoted to him.

The film raises the issues of how difficult is was to resist this pervasive dictatorship. On this question, interviews show the perspective of a German army officer, a student opposed to Hitler, and an Englishwoman married to a German.

The only serious failing is the way the film shifts its focus repeatedly to consider Nazi foreign policy. Moreover, there is no effort to introduce the individuals interviewed in more than cursory fashion. Finally, the film says little about the institutions of the Nazi state, e.g., the secret police. Nor does it seriously consider the daily life, as opposed the grand ceremonial occasions, of the average citizen.

Students can be asked to consider why some Germans continued to resist Nazism or at least to harbor doubts about it in the face of its visible successes. One can also discuss the relative importance of the economic revival as opposed to the theatrical side of Nazism in building loyalty. Finally, it is worth pondering the origins of the psychology of mass hysteria that accompanied Hitler's ceremonial appearances and speeches.

Rise of the Dictators

See Form! Riflemen, Form!

The Twisted Cross
(Project 20 series)

55 minutes   black\white
1958   NBC

Summary: An unimaginative, poorly paced account of Adolf Hitler's rise to power and the period of the Nazi dictatorship

Grade: C

The film employs a narrator, newsfilm, and dramatizations of important events. The basic themes of the film are how Hitler became Germany's dictator in 1933, the barbaric system the Nazis imposed on German life, and Hitler's betrayal of the German people in leading them into the catastrophe of World War II.

The film begins with scenes of German poverty and unemployment after the country's defeat in World War I. It shows the emergence of Hitler as leader of the small Nazi party and as a popular orator and rising politician. The Nazis are presented in the person of marching bands of Storm Troopers and as seen in their election placards. The film introduces the main personalities of the circle surrounding Hitler: Joseph Goebbels, Hermann Goering, and Heinrich Himmler.

The Twisted Cross concentrates on the period following Hitler's appointment as Germany's prime minister in January 1933. For the 1930s, it presents scenes to illustrate the revival of the country's economy, the suppression of political opponents and their ideas (e.g., book burning), national rearmament, and anti-Semitism. Scenes of Hitler in private at his retreat in the Bavarian Alps, where he made world shaking decisions, lead to an account of his aggressive diplomacy in the late 1930s. The film's account of World War II emphasizes how the dictator virtually disappeared from public view following the 1941 invasion of the Soviet Union and the ensuing march of events that led to military disaster and the invasion of the German homeland

The Twisted Cross is unable to deal effectively with the vast topics is raises. The chronology of events is frequently muddled. Key background developments that influenced the Nazi movement, e.g., the political and economic stabilization of Germany between 1924 and 1929, are left out entirely. Moreover, the course of events is grossly oversimplified. For example, the Nazi movement is presented as the only such organization of the radical right in Germany in the post-1918 period.

The most obvious flaw in the film is the virtual absence of samples of Hitler's mesmerizing oratory. With one minor exception--a brief excerpt from a speech Hitler gave to the Reichstag in early 1939--the Nazi dictator is never heard at all. In addition, the treatment of major events is flat and unimaginative. The growth of the Nazi Party is illustrated by innumerable scenes of S.A. marchers. A scene of Hermann Goering going to the polls illustrates the often bloody elections of the early 1930s that brought Nazism to the brink of power. The brief dramatizations are poorly filmed and distracting.

A superior film in dealing with the rise of Nazi is <u>From Kaiser to Fuehrer</u> (q.v.). The period after Hitler came to power can be examined more effectively in <u>A New Germany</u> <u>(q.v.)</u>.

RUSSIAN REVOLUTION AND COMMUNISM

<u>The Birth of the Soviet Cinema</u>

49 minutes   black\white
1972   Films for the Humanities

Summary: An examination of the work of the Soviet movie industry after the Bolshevik Revolution focused on the feature films of three outstanding directors; it presents a brilliant picture of the ideological fervor that accompanied the Revolution

Grade: B +

The film employs a narrator, photos and newsfilm, as well as excerpts from films made before and after the Revolution. The major part of <u>The Birth of the Soviet Cinema</u> consists of a detailed examination of eight major films by the three great Soviet directors of the 1920s, Sergei Eisenstein, Vsevolod Pudovkin, and Alexander Dovzhenko. The basic theme of the film is the way in which the Bolshevik Revolution gave rise to a cadre of brilliant directors, each of whom set out to glorify the Revolution's origins, course, and results.

A brief prologue shows scenes from the earliest Russian movies. These were adaptations taken from the stage in the first part of the twentieth century. The film moves on to show how the Bolsheviks used movies for propaganda during the Russian Civil War (1918-1921). It also examines an early adventure story, <u>Mr. West in the Country of the Bolsheviks,</u> and the work of pioneers of documentary film in Soviet Russia like Dziga Vertov. Both examples of early film making have left us intriguing street scenes from Moscow in the early 1920s.

The major portion of the film starts with the work of Sergei Eisenstein. Assuming the viewer is familiar with Russian history in the first decades of the twentieth century, the narration analyzes <u>Strike</u>, <u>Battleship Potemkin</u>, and <u>Ten Days That Shook the World</u> in terms of the cinematic techniques Eisenstein employed in each. It notes, for example, the way in which he favored using a collective hero such as the mutinous crew of the <u>Potemkin</u> over a story focused on a single individual.

Next, the film takes up the more conventional plots and characterizations used by Pudovkin in <u>Mother</u>, <u>The End of St. Petersburg</u>, and <u>Storm over Asia</u>. The narration illustrates how both of Eisenstein and Pudovkin, in their different ways, glorified the men and women whose work created and secured the triumph of the Revolution.

The remainder of the film examines Arsenal and Earth, two productions set in the Ukraine and directed by Alexander Dovzhenko. The first dramatically presents the proletarian defender of a besieged arsenal as impervious to the bullets of his reactionary foes. The second is a lyrical account of agricultural collectivization. Here the spread of the Revolution into the countryside is presented as an inevitable process akin to the coming of spring.

The Birth of the Soviet Cinema draws brilliantly on the eight films it analyzes, presenting the essence of each work through a number of crucial scenes. The plots used by both Eisenstein and Pudovkin appear clearly in this abbreviated form. Meanwhile the excerpts capture the cinematic novelty and ideological elan the films contain. Similarly, Pudovkin's emotional support for the Revolution emerges vividly from the scenes selected from his films.

The flaws in this account center on the absence of any significant historical introduction to the films shown. Students who lack an understanding of the growth of the Bolshevik Party, the revolutions of 1905 and 1917, as well as the course of the Civil War, will find the details, although not the tone, of the films difficult to grasp. The lack of a coherent historical introduction is particularly burdensome with the films of Dovzhenko. Arsenal, for example, deals with relatively obscure events in the Ukraine during the Civil War. It displays its cinematic power to everyone, but the historical topics it treats are conspicuously murky.

The Birth of the Soviet Cinema cries for an extensive introduction to each of the directors shown. Nonetheless, its considerable virtues rest in capturing successfully the atmosphere, the appearance, and the elan of the Russian revolutionary movement and early Soviet Russia.

Lenin and the Great Ungluing
(Age of Uncertainty series)

57 minutes   color
1977   BBC

Summary: A rambling, but informative parallel examination of the course of World I and Lenin's career as he approaches the triumph of the Bolshevik Revolution

Grade: B

The film employs narrator John K. Galbraith, cartoons and skits, maps, newsfilm, and visits to important historical locales. An actress reads important passages from the recollections of Lenin's wife concerning this period. One basic theme of the film is the way in which the war undermined the old, apparently unshakable European order. The second theme is the way in which the exiled Russian revolutionary leader Vladimir I. Lenin prepared to use the opportunities created by the war to take power.

The film begins with a discussion of pre-war Europe against the background of the beautiful Polish city of Cracow. Here, narrator Galbraith reminds the viewer, was where Lenin lived up to the outbreak of fighting in August 1914. Using skits and cartoons, the film shows the countries of Europe in conflict with one another. Next, Galbraith analyzes the reasons for the war. He notes that the emergence of a general conflict from the Balkan Crisis of 1914 was a "rogue reaction," a chain of events whose results no one could foresee. The European working class movement, which had expected to halt international conflict by calling a general strike, was caught up in the war fever itself.

The Great Ungluing then alternates between an account of Lenin's life between 1914 and 1917 and a description of the escalating slaughter of the war. The Russian leader traveled, developed his ideas, and tried to persuade his fellow Marxists to use the war as the occasion for revolution. The film shows the locales in which Lenin lived and called his colleagues together for conferences. The cost of the war appears in scenes showing the operation of the machine gun and battlefields like the Somme where the young men of Europe were being cut down. In the final major segment of the film, Galbraith recounts how Lenin, now in Zurich, received word of the collapse of the imperial Russian government. He describes how Lenin returned to Russia via Germany in the famous "sealed train."

In its last five minutes, however, the film jumps abruptly to Italy in the 1970s. It shows the Fiat factory in Turin from which Italian experts were helping the Soviet Union develop its automobile production. Galbraith uses this setting to consider issues like the declining dynamism of Communism and the similar, large-scale bureaucracies that could be found in both capitalist and communist countries at that time.

The film is visually striking, and Galbraith's witty narration enlivens the entire account. A number of scenes, including Lenin's favorite coffeehouse in Cracow and the portion of the 1916 Somme battlefield where a Canadian regiment suffered 91 percent casualties in forty minutes, are memorable.

Unfortunately, The Great Ungluing often moves very slowly, with topics like Lenin's daily activities described in excessive detail. The skits Galbraith uses to explain the August Crisis of 1914 are childish and confusing. The final segment dealing with the Turin car plant and its implications seems totally out of place.

Leon Trotsky

See Leon Trotsky: Revolution and Leon Trotsky: Exile

Leon Trotsky: Exile

61 minutes   color
1990   Films for the Humanities

Summary: Also presented under the general title Leon Trotsky, this is the second of a two-part biography of the important Russian revolutionary leader; it deals with Trotsky's life from 1929 to his assassination in 1940

Grade: B -

The film uses several narrators, an extensive set of interviews with scholars and eyewitnesses, news film, and visits to important historical locales. The basic theme of the film is how Trotsky tried to preserve his reputation and to maintain some influence over the development of various revolutionary movements. The second theme is the personal tragedy of the former Soviet leader, driven from one place of exile to another and racked by family misfortunes.

Leon Trotsky: Exile starts by showing how Soviet authorities now erased Trotsky's image from films and photographs of an earlier era. Recollections of eyewitnesses help to show Trotsky's life in exile in Turkey and Western Europe. Several of them were young radicals who gathered from Europe and the United States to stand by their hero and mentor. Events in the Russian leader's personal life appear alongside the larger scene: the rise of Hitler to power, Stalin's program of agricultural collectivization and planned industrialization, and the Moscow Purge Trials.

The final half of the film focuses on Trotsky's last years, from 1937 to 1940, which he spent in Mexico. During this period, Trotsky defended his reputation in front of the specially constituted commission led by philosopher John Dewey. He hoped thereby to counter Stalin's attacks on his lifetime of political activity. This segment features a rare appearance by Trotsky in which speaks at length in English.

The closing ten minutes of the film show how Trotsky's entourage was infiltrated by a Soviet agent. Rámon Mercader assassinated the aged Russian leader at his Mexico City home. The film ends with recollections of the event by Trotsky's grandson, scenes from the funeral, and a reprise of Trotsky's moments of triumph in the era of 1917 and the Russian Civil War.

The film is an engrossing personal story showing a key historical figure in circumstances where he was unable to exercise power. It can serve to show "history in miniature" to students who have been grounded on the big picture presented in texts. Regrettably, most of those interviewed for the film are left unidentified, and key terms such as OGPU are not defined. Moreover, the film suffers from a weak narration. Viewers are expected to have a background in the complexities of Europe's political development in the 1930s. In general the events shown here form a fascinating story on the margin of European history.

Leon Trotsky: Revolution

61 minutes   color
1990   Films for the Humanities

Summary: Also presented under the general title Leon Trotsky, this is the first of a two-segment biography of the important Russian revolutionary leader; it deals with Trotsky's life from his childhood to his expulsion from the Soviet Union in 1929

Grade: B +

Leon Trotsky: Revolution uses several narrators, an extensive set of still photographs and newsfilm, and segments from Soviet dramatic films dealing with the Revolution. There are as well posters, prints, and cartoons from the period, visits to historic locales, and numerous interviews with eyewitnesses to crucial events in Trotsky's life. A number of scholars also discuss Trotsky. The basic theme of the film is the rise and fall of Trotsky's career. He went from an amateur revolutionary in the Ukraine to a stellar figure in Russian Marxism, a leader in the Bolshevik revolution of November 1917 and the ensuing Civil War, then failed in the power struggle of the 1920s.
      The film begins with a mixture of images: soldiers in the historic uniforms of the Civil War parading in Red Square in 1987; views of Mexican locales where Trotsky spent his last years. Here, Mikhail Gorbachev refers to Trotsky in a speech before the Communist Central Committee, the first time a Soviet leader had made such a public reference in more than half a century.
      The first half of the film focuses on Trotsky's years up to the November Revolution, including his personal and family life. One of the scholars who speaks during this segment notes how Trotsky undermined his later political ambitions by joining Lenin's Bolshevik Party only in 1917.
      The second half of the film deals with Trotsky's triumph in the Civil War when he formed and energized the Red Army. It also reassesses his repression of the Kronstadt Rebellion of 1921 against the Communist government, Joseph Stalin's rise to power, and Trotsky's defeat by his once obscure rival. One eyewitness explains why Stalin made the important error of exiling Trotsky to Turkey in 1929 rather than executing him.

The film is clear and direct. Many of those interviewed for the film have valuable and vivid recollections of their encounters with Trotsky. The newsfilm, much of its rarely shown, is first-rate. Unfortunately, the film's narrators are uncertain in their pronunciation of Russian names and terms. More important, the narration failed to identify most of the individuals who appear to present their recollections or analyses. Students who are not familiar with the course of Russian history in the first part of the century will find the level of detail unmanageable. There are some inaccuracies in the film as well: the government formed by Lenin and Trotsky in November 1917 did not, as the film states, consist only of members of the Bolshevik party.

Students can be asked to consider what personal characteristics and talents (and fortunate breaks) led Trotsky from obscurity to approach the pinnacle of power in Russia, and what factors brought him down.

The Life and Times of Joseph Stalin

90 minutes	black\white
1990	Films for the Humanities and Sciences

Summary: A rich, detailed, and informative account of the life of the Soviet dictator; it is particularly strong on the period up to 1945

Grade: A -

The film uses a narrator, photographs and newsfilm, maps, and segments from Soviet dramatic films. The basic theme of the film is how Stalin rose to national power by 1929 and global power by 1945.

The Life and Times begins with archival film showing the Russian Empire, notably Stalin's Georgia, at the close of the nineteenth century. There follows an account of Stalin's youth and early career in the Bolshevik movement culminating with his prominence by the time of Lenin's death in 1924. Scenes illustrate the 1920s, with society increasingly coming under Communist influence, by striking images of boxers and soccer players parading through Red Square.

Propaganda films accompany the forced industrialization and agricultural collection imposed on the Soviet people by a victorious Stalin in the 1930s. They show happy, marching children with Stalin as a national father-figure. At the same time, the film takes up the set of changes Stalin imposed on Soviet society. Scenes presenting the Purge Trials of the 1930s are accompanied by views of the great industrial achievements of the time and the visits of sympathetic foreign intellectuals like André Gide and George Bernard Shaw.

The second half of the film deals with a variety of topics. It is most coherent in describing the Soviet triumph in World War II. Thereafter it speeds up to survey Soviet control in Eastern Europe, the success of Chinese Communism, the Cold War, and Stalin's death.

The Life and Times is lucid and accessible in depicting Stalin's career up to 1945. It features rarely shown archival footage. The views of Soviet society shown in propaganda images of happy progress are invaluable for illustrating the totalitarian controls of the 1930s. Despite the film's substantial length, the pacing through the first two-thirds is brisk.

The film loses much of its shape, however, during the final third. Here it touches on a variety of loosely connected issues dealing with Stalin in the post-1945 era. Even in treating the 1920s, the narration is sometimes too rapid for a novice in Russian history to follow. The excessive length of the film makes it difficult to present in a single sitting. It can be split neatly, however, after the treatment of the Purge Trials.

Students can be asked to consider the various ways in which the person of the dictator was popularized through film and other means in Soviet Russia.

WORLD WAR II AND THE HOLOCAUST

THE WAR

The Allies--The End of the War

See Human Rights, Fundamental Freedoms

Alone, May 1940-May 1941
(The World at War series)

52 minutes   color
1973   HBO\Thames Television

Summary: A vivid, emotionally engaging examination of the armed conflict between Britain and Germany from the Dunkirk evacuation in the spring of 1940 over the following year; it shows how the war profoundly involved the British civilian population

Grade: A -

The film uses a narrator, extensive combat footage, newsfilm and maps, as well as interviews with military participants at all levels and Londoners who faced the German bombing campaigns. One theme of the film is the ability of the British government and armed forces to fend off an attack from Hitler's heretofore unbeatable military machine. A second theme is the extraordinary resiliency and resourcefulness of Britain's civilians once they faced direct German attack.

Alone begins with an examination of the situation at Dunkirk. There, the bulk of the British army in France, pinned against the sea by the Germans, managed to escape destruction.The months following Dunkirk show the mobilization of British resources:a Home Guard forming, beaches mined, factories producing at breakneck speed. Civil servants energized by Churchill's example even sprinted down the corridors of government buildings. The view from the top appears with famous figures like War Minister Anthony Eden, Minister of Aircraft Production Lord Beaverbrook, and BBC commentator Joseph Priestley. Interviews with them reflect an awareness of Britain's plight and a determination to resist at all costs.   British movie newsfilms, with their lighthearted commentary and sports event rhetoric, show the attitudes, or at least the psychological facades, of the time.

Next, the scene shifts to the German side. Berlin crowds greet Hitler's return from the western front while the invasion fleet assembles in Northwestern Europe. An interview with Luftwaffe fighter pilot Adolf Galland adds a crucial element to the film. He remembers his pessimism. There had been no serious preparation for an attack on Britain.

The second half of the film stresses the air battle over Britain in August and September of 1940. It indicates the three stages of the campaign. First came the assaults on Channel shipping and seaports, then on the RAF airfields, and, finally, on the city of London. Gripping combat film combines with interviews from pilots on both sides. The discussion of the air assault on London includes interviews with a circle of Londoners. They recall their experiences and emotional reactions during the seventy-six nights of continuous bombing. There are striking scenes of life going on as usual: an executive and his secretary work outdoors on a business letter in the open air, shopkeepers invite customers into wrecked stores. The final portion of the film shows the war spreading to the Mediterranean. The British launch an attack on the Italians in Libya in late 1940. The German assaults on Greece and Crete follow in the first months of 1941.

Alone has been made with loving care by British film makers anxious to present a picture of their nation's most crucial experience in the war. The interviews are especially vivid in humanizing the major events of the time. On the other hand, the film loses its focus at the close as it shifts from events in Britain. Moreover, it lacks any interviews from the upper levels of the German government or the military system. There is a brief reference to Londoners embittered at Winston Churchill for exposing them to such wartime horrors. This important issue goes unexamined.

One can ask students to consider the relative significance of different elements that contributed to the outcome of the Battle of Britain: technology, leadership, morale, the errors and miscalculations on both sides. The contrast between this film and France Falls (q.v.) is rich with possibilities for considering how the two nations met crisis. Finally, one can ask if the picture painted here is not too cheery. To what extent was there discontent with the war and unwillingness on the part of some elements of the population to join in the defense effort?

Barbarossa, June-December, 1941
(The World at War series)

52 minutes   color
1973   HBO\Thames Television

Summary: A lucid and visually compelling account of the German campaign against the Soviet Union in 1941; it present the conflict primarily from the German point of view

Grade: A

The film uses a narrator, newsfilm and combat footage, maps, and the martial music of both sides. There are extensive interviews from the German side from common soldiers to senior military and government leaders, although only one interviewee from the Russian side. The basic theme of the film is how the immense power and confidence of the German military system was stymied by the opposition it faced in the Soviet Union in 1941. A secondary theme is the terrible price the Soviet Union paid for confusion and poor planning prior to the German attack and in its first phases of the fighting, and the way in which these failings were remedied.

Barbarossa's first third shows a victorious Germany following its defeat of France in 1940. In contrast, Soviet Russia appears powerful but uncertain. Early scenes show the welcome Hitler received upon his return to Germany from the western front in the summer of 1940. Next, the film discusses Hitler's reasons for turning his forces eastward: interviews with General Walter Warlimont and Albert Speer indicate that he was ready to launch his attack as early in 1940. The Russians are shown frantically reforming their military system. Meanwhile, German diplomatic pressure combined with the invasions of Yugoslavia and Greece to bring most of Eastern Europe under Hitler's domination. German military parades, gleeful crowds, and the martial music of the victorious soldiers provide an insight into the popular mood in Germany as the Russian war approached.

The remainder of the film deals with the 1941 campaign. There are the predictable scenes of German forces sweeping eastward. These are combined, however, with a remarkable series of interviews with German war veterans. Each recalls a sense he came to have in 1941 of Russia's measureless spaces. Scenes of Russians, women as well as men, digging vast tank traps outside Moscow also provide a somber counterpoint to the German advance.

The final portion of the film examines the mounting German difficulties. The mud, the increasingly effective Russian resistance under General Georgi Zhukov, and, most vividly, the snow and the cold tormented them. Frozen German bodies, immobilized vehicles, and unusable artillery pieces contrast with crack Soviet winter troops of the Siberian armies concentrating to defend Moscow. German propaganda films for the home front shows the country's troops laughing off the cold and bathing nude in icy water. Barbarossa ends with the successful advance of the Siberians. Its results were lines of German prisoners, Hitler's forces in retreat, and frozen German corpses.

The film presents memorable shots of German vehicles struggling in the mud and German troops crippled by the cold. These give a vivid sense of what the war must have been like. Similarly, scenes of Hitler's welcome home in 1940 illustrate the mental attitude that let numerous Germans enter the conflict with unrestrained enthusiasm.

There are only minor flaws in the film. The discussion of the diplomatic maneuvering that Germany pursued in Eastern Europe in late 1940 and early 1941 slows the early part of the story. Several of the interviewees are not identified when their comments are heard as voice-overs. The lone Russian interviewed is left unidentified. Moreover, the German viewpoint is emphasized at the expense of the Soviet.

Students can be asked to consider these events from the standpoint of the average German or Soviet citizen. Was it the force of the dictatorship or patriotic considerations that tied such individuals to their participation in these bloody events?

The Bomb, February-September, 1945
(The World at War series)

52 minutes   color
1973   HBO\Thames Television

Summary: A verbose, confused account of the American decision to use the atomic bomb against Japan and the close of the war in the Pacific

Grade: C

The film centers on a series of interviews with American and Japanese figures involved in the diplomatic and military decisions made in 1945. There are a few interviews as well with victims of the atomic bomb attack on Hiroshima. The film also employs a narrator, maps, photographs, and newspaper headlines. The basic theme is the way in which the atomic bomb was used to tilt the balance in American-Soviet relations. A second theme suggests that, given the damage done by conventional warfare to Japan, the use of the bomb may not have been necessary.

The Bomb begins with the death of President Franklin Roosevelt and scenes from his funeral. It then considers the agreements he made with Winston Churchill and Joseph Stalin at Yalta in February 1945 and the subsequent friction that developed among the allies. Interviews with American diplomats Averell Harriman and Alger Hiss stress the conflict with Russia over Eastern Europe and the way American officials may have seen the atomic bomb as a means of pressuring the Russians.

The film then jumps to the Pacific war, focusing on the bombing campaign against Japan. Air force General Curtis LeMay claims that conventional bombing would have crushed the Japanese capacity to resist by September 1945. Interviews with officials from the Japanese foreign office and cabinet stress the possibility of a negotiated settlement.

Against the background of the bloody fighting at Okinawa, the film presents an extensive interview with Assistant Secretary of War John McCloy. He recalls urging that the American government back away from its call for unconditional surrender in order to bring the war to a halt without using the atomic bomb.

In its final third, the film ends its discussion of diplomatic maneuvering to record the attack on Hiroshima. The epochal event appears in films of the attack, in an interview Colonel Paul Tibbetts, the pilot of the plane that dropped the bomb, and in the memories of survivors of the blast.

The Bomb concludes with a tangled account of political maneuvering within the Japanese government. Moderates hoping to end the war clash with fanatics determined to fight to the bitter end. The theme that has dominated most of the film now shifts in a confusing manner. Here, interviews with Averell Harriman and, paradoxically, Curtis LeMay, defend the use of the bomb as essential in bringing the Japanese to surrender.

The film raises issues that historians have continued to debate in recent decades over the need to use the bomb and the range of possible motives for doing so. Unfortunately the conflicting opinions and the shifts in diplomacy described add up to an impenetrable muddle. The film is dominated by "talking heads" and is almost totally devoid of cinematic value.

The English, D-Day and the Holocaust

See With Hardship Their Garment

France Falls, May-June 1940
(The World at War series)

52 minutes   color
1973   HBO\Thames Television

Summary: A vivid, dramatic examination of the German penetration of the Maginot line and the defeat of France in 1940; it emphasizes the French side of the story

Grade: B +

France Falls uses a narrator, newsfilm, maps, contemporary music, and visits to important historical locales. There are also interviews with British war correspondents and with military officials from several countries. A basic theme of the film is the contrast between France and Germany. The former's political divisions, military lassitude, and uncertainty confront the latter's ferocious energy and determination. The film also shows how industrial technology was employed in preparing for World War II: the French build a defensive wonderland in the Maginot line; the Germans develop the tanks and aircraft that would render those defenses useless.

The film's prologue shows the remnants of the Maginot line today. It notes that the line's purpose of stopping a direct German onslaught depended upon Germany's attacking according to French expectations. The first portion of the film examines the France of the 1930s, stressing the country's internal divisions. It shows how France had adopted a defensive military system designed to avoid the hideous casualties of World War I. The Maginot line appears as a modern marvel of industrial planning, but the French army also relies on cavalry units and flimsy looking machine guns. France's uncertain response to war in 1939 can be seen in overblown reports of the weak French offensive into the Saarland. It can be heard in the music of the time proclaiming "Paris Will Always Be Paris." A crucial witness throughout the film is General André Beaufre, who describes the attitudes and ideas prevailing at French Supreme Headquarters.

The view from the other side of the battlefront comes from German generals like Hasso von Manteuffel and Walther Warlimont who describe the plan to penetrate the French defenses at their weak point in the Ardennes forest. A visit to the densely wooded terrain in that region shows why the French believed no German attack could take place there.

The second portion of the film begins with the German assault on Belgium and Holland. That was a prelude to the German breakthrough in the Ardennes that followed immediately. Scenes of the devastating advance alternate with views of panic-stricken French refugees and long lines of French prisoners of war. Thereafter, the film describes the German push into the French heartland and the collapse of French resistance. France's military humiliation appears in various forms: the formal surrender at Compiègne in the same spot where the Armistice was signed in 1918; Hitler's visit to Paris; the German army's victory parade into the French capital.

The film effectively captures the changing atmosphere in France: from the 1930s through the "Phoney War" of late 1939 and early 1940 into the six devastating weeks when the country fell to German attack. German military power and leadership appear in vivid contrast to the ineptitude, unrealistic expectations, and finally emotional collapse on the French side. On the other hand, the film's interviews concentrate on high ranking military figures and British journalists to the exclusion of the average French citizen. Moreover, the treatment of the French political scene both during the 1930s and in the climactic months of May and June 1940 is compressed to the point of being opaque.

Students can be asked to consider the impression the Fall of France made throughout Europe. How could someone defend parliamentary systems against the Nazi claim to superiority after the fall of France? One could also discuss he differing ways in which France and Germany applied their industrial resources as well as their respective experiences in World War I to plans for a future war.

Home Fires, Britain 1940--1944

52 minutes   color
1973   HBO\Thames Television

Summary: A wide-ranging, lucid, and informative examination of a democratic society responding to the strains of total war between 1940 and 1944

Grade: B +

Home Fires employs a narrator, newsfilm, posters and newspapers, and interviews with participants at all levels of British society. There are also selections from the propaganda films of the time. The basic theme is the way in which the British people and their government responded to the challenge of World War II. They reshaped but did not abolish the country's traditions of civil liberties and parliamentary government. The film also illustrates the close tie between Britain and the Soviet Union during the war, and the ability of some British leaders, although not Prime Minister Winston Churchill, to plan for major domestic changes after the war had been won.

The film begins with dramatic scenes of bombed cities like Coventry and Plymouth. The strain caused by these events appears in the accounts recalled by local and national political leaders, One interview takes place with a woman who lost most of her family in a single attack. There are excerpts from Churchill's stirring speeches, semi-comic scenes of the Home Guard being organized, and an examination of how enemy aliens were rounded up and interned.

Next, the film considers the role of two of Churchill's most important cabinet minister: Ernest Bevin, who directed the civilian work force and Lord Beaverbrook, who directed weapons production. It notes Bevin's decision to compel women to participate in the war effort, choosing between work in the armed forces or armaments factories. Both Beaverbrook and Britain's ambassador to Moscow, Sir Stafford Cripps, speak out in favor of close cooperation with the Soviet Union. The strains and resiliency of democratic life during wartime appear in several episodes. Churchill fails to shut down a critical newspaper. Parliamentary elections continue. The prime minister's political foes try unsuccessfully to vote him out of office.

The second half of the film takes up other facets of civilian life such as rationing and the humorous film campaign to promote it. Wartime popular culture appears in the songs of Gracie Fields and the BBC show "Hi Gang." The strains on the labor force can be seen in wildcat strikes in the coal mines; meanwhile, young men are drafted to serve in the mines. The film concludes with Beveridge's plan for postwar social reforms and the D-Day landings. Meanwhile, a new threat to the civilian population arises with attacks by the V-1 flying bomb.

Home Fires explains crucial aspects of British life during the war. Some of the most dramatic sequences come at the start as the film looks at the carnage brought by German bombing. There are other striking segments, however, such as the account of women being incorporated into the work force and the military. Editor Michael Foot's tirade against government censorship is likewise memorable. The film's cinematic qualities reach a peak, however, in showing the frightening novelty of the V-1.

On the other hand, the film loses focus due to the number of topics considered. There are overly detailed accounts of relatively specialized issues such the work force in the mines and the political conflict between Bevin and Beaverbrook. The importance of Beveridge's proposals, the basis for the future welfare state, is not made clear. Non-British audiences will find it hard to grasp the significance of the BBC program "Hi Gang" to its wartime listeners. To Britons of the time, it was a part of their weekly routine, happily something that even the bombing could not interrupt. This account assumes a knowledge of the nature of Britain's wartime coalition government and the pre-war structure of the society.

The film can be used in conjunction with the parallel films in the World at War series on the German and Russian homefronts. Topics for consideration include the wartime role of women, the nature of political life, the tone considered effective in propaganda.

Human Rights, Fundamental Freedoms: The Allies--The End of the War
(Europe: The Mighty Continent)

52 minutes   color
1974   BBC

Summary: A complex but sporadically useful examination of the close of World War II and the conflict's aftermath; its most coherent part deals with the establishment of Soviet control in Eastern Europe

Grade: B

The film uses narrators John Terraine and Peter Ustinov, newsfilm, maps, and visits to important historical locales. The major theme of the film is how the closing campaigns of the war put the Soviet Union in a commanding position in Eastern Europe. A secondary theme is the paradox of several liberated countries of Europe trying to maintain control over their restless imperial populations.

The film begins by tracing Polish history from 1939 to 1944. It notes the savage way in which Poland was partitioned in 1939, and the brutal regime imposed here by Nazi Germany. Vivid newsfilm shows the rising of the Polish Home Army in the summer of 1944. When Soviet forces failed to come to their rescue, the revolt failed and Warsaw was destroyed. Soviet power, marked by the military victories of the Red Army, now spread across Eastern Europe. Standing in present-day Budapest, Peter Ustinov discusses the brutal battle fought there in the waning months of the war. An account of the Yalta Conference stresses the strains in the wartime alliance.

Human Rights, Fundamental Freedoms loses its cohesion in the second half. Vivid newsfilm shows the celebrations in London that accompanied V-E Day, and both narrators eloquently discuss the exhausted mood of the British people when the European war ended. In rapid fashion, the film takes up the restlessness of the populations in imperial possessions like India, postwar austerity, and the tightening Soviet hold in Eastern Europe. There are memorable scenes of French collaborators being tormented by their fellow citizens. The film closes with the French withdrawal from Indo-China while Charles de Gaulle, now out of power, follows events from his country home.

The film's first half presents a memorable picture of the Soviet advance into Eastern Europe. Thereafter the profusion events covered seriously diminishes its value.

Inside the Reich, Germany 1940-1944
(The World at War series)

52 minutes   color
1973   HBO\Thames Television

Summary: A lucid, informative, and gripping view of the German homefront from 1940 to the spring of 1945; it stresses the resiliency and substantial unity of the population as the war turned from a parade of victories to imminent catastrophe

Grade: A -

Inside the Reich uses a narrator, newsfilm, and interviews drawn from a range of eye-witnesses. One key theme is the Nazi government's effort to shield the German population from any concerns about the war, even as the strains of fighting the conflict became increasingly painful. A second theme is the changing balance at the top of the Nazi hierarchy: Hitler became increasingly isolated while Joseph Goebbels became the public symbol for total war and fortitude in the face of repeated military setbacks.

Inside the Reich begins with the return of the victorious German army to Berlin in the summer of 1940 after its triumph over France. It illustrates how the government promoted feelings of confidence and well-being in a population that was still nervous about how the war might end: the availability of luxurious clothes and beach vacations, the promotion of a baby boom, and movies with bands of happy typists singing in unison as they worked for the war effort. This facade is balanced with an interview with Hans Kehrl. A ranking Nazi economics official, Kehrl grew concerned about the failure to keep up war production as the government told the population to believe the conflict was as good as over.

Rounding out the first third of the film is a survey of the government's control devices. It shows the system's reliance on the radio (and barring listening to foreign broadcasts) and newspapers. There is a chilling excerpt from a film designed to promote euthanasia for the mentally defective.

The following third of the film focuses on the consequences of widening the war to include an assault on the Soviet Union in June 1941. It is particularly gripping in showing the funeral of Minister of Armaments Fritz Todt following an airplane crash during a visit to the Russian front. Todt was the first of Hitler's close associates to die in the war, and there are somber scenes of a shaken Hitler. Todt was replaced as armaments minister by Albert Speer, and Speer's activities are shown as economic wonders. But the film indicates they were a departure from Nazi ideals: foreign laborers now flooded into Germany, and the average German became more than ever a cog in the machinery of the big businessmen the Nazis had once denounced.

The final portion of the film starts with the defeat at Stalingrad and the increasing aerial bombardment of German cities. There are engrossing scenes taken from the mass meeting of Nazi followers in early 1943 where Goebbels proclaimed total war. Interviews with Traudl Junge give a picture of Hitler's lassitude and isolation. Christabel Bielenberg, an Englishwoman married to a German, recalls the painful unity of a population caught together under the bombs. She is even more shaken encountering the murder of Jewish neighbors. Albert Speer gives a carefully qualified denial of any direct responsibility for such events.

The emotional pitch of the film grows with an account of the July 1944 plot to kill Hitler, and the chilling trial and execution of the plotters. Meanwhile the German people, in wrecked cities, fly flags on the ruins, and continue to produce war materials. The most memorable segment of the film comes at the close. Middle-aged men of Berlin's Volkssturm (home guard) take an oath in the center of the city. Then, they march out, automatic weapons carried over their civilian overcoats, to confront the approaching divisions of the Red Army.

The film is vivid and affecting in almost every segment. Its narration is lucid and accessible. The interviews are memorable, including one with Otto Demers, the officer who played a crucial role in foiling the July Plot of 1944. The account of the shift to total war under Goebbels's leadership is another strong segment. The numerous musical excerpts show the emotional appeal the government tried to maintain.

The film's only weak point is the vast variety of topics it undertakes. Despite its clear basic structure, it sometimes lapses into a fascinating potpourri of the German homefront.

Students can consider the chief strengths and failings of the Nazi system in wartime. If the system had depended upon a charismatic leader prior to 1939, what took the place of that asset once the war began? To what extent did the population's resolution during the war depend upon the coercive power of the police state as opposed to the fortitude of a population under siege?

Morning, June-August 1944
(The World at War series)

52 minutes   color
1973   HBO\Thames Television

Summary: An informative but uninspired account of the Normandy invasion and the campaign in France through August 1944

Grade: B

The film uses a narrator, animated maps, newsfilm from both the Allied and the German sides, and interviews with American and British participants from all levels. A basic theme of the film is the enormous set of preparations required for success at Normandy, including the concentration of troops in southern England and then on the ships taking them to France. A second theme is the tension and uncertainty both for Dwight Eisenhower, the Allied commander-in-chief, and the average soldier as poor weather delayed the final order for the landings to take place. Thirdly, the film shows the human cost of the landings and the advance inland: bodies on the beaches, the destruction by carpet bombing of the city of Caen.

Morning begins with scenes from the unsuccessful experimental landing at Dieppe in 1942. That event showed how difficult it would be to capture an existing port. As a result, plans centered on invading France by securing a series of northern beaches on the Normandy peninsula. In preliminaries to the landing, General Bernard Montgomery encourages British war workers, Allied troops rehearse their landings, and the Germans under Rommel strengthen their defenses. Interviews with individuals close to the key decision makers-- Eisenhower's driver and companion, Kay Summersby, Dr. Stagg, the chief Allied weather forecaster--show the growing tension at Allied headquarters.

The middle portion of the film slows to show troops aboard ships docked at English ports waiting for the signal to leave for France. It then shows the final stages of preparation--Eisenhower visiting paratroopers about to assault the Continent, the vast armada crossing the continent--and the landings. There are dramatic scenes showing the landing craft bobbing at sea with their seasick human cargo. They move toward the shore, and finally place Allied troops on French soil. The following newsfilm shows the ensuing combat from the viewpoint of both sides.

The remainder of the film becomes diffuse. It examines the advances on Cherbourg and Caen, the Allied breakout from Normandy, and the partial entrapment of German forces at Falaise, as well as the rising of the Parisian population against the Germans. Accounts of Falaise present a contrast between the aggressive American advance under leaders like Patton and the more cautious British attack under Montgomery

The film is lucid and informative in showing the scope of the Normandy invasion and its human cost. Individual reminiscences presented in voice-overs while the film shows the wreckage on the beaches, the dead and the wounded, are memorable. Nonetheless, the overall pace of the film is slow, and its tone is deliberately undramatic, almost elegiac. The interviews show events only from the Allied side, and they focus on secondary figures or individual soldiers. Most damaging is the film's excessive scope, which takes it far beyond D-Day into the subsequent campaign in France.

Nemesis, Germany February-May, 1945
(The World at War series)

52 minutes   color
1973   HBO\Thames Television

Summary: A wide-ranging, detailed, but informative look at the collapse of Nazi Germany; it captures the atmosphere of a crumbling totalitarian system

Grade: B

Nemesis employs a narrator, extensive newsfilm, and interviews with participants from all the major countries involved. The basic theme is the contrast between the bizarre unreality of life in Hitler's bunker and the momentous collapse of Nazism as the Allies advance into the heart of Germany.

The film's prologue shows the fire bombing of Dresden in February 1945, described by the narrator as "another monument to total war." The first fifteen-minute segment of Nemesis focuses on the British and American advance from the west and the growing desperation of Germany's position. Allied forces push rapidly through wrecked cities encountering only irregular resistance; Hitler depends increasingly on teenage recruits. American GIs have their first meetings with German civilians in occupied areas. The Allied forces liberate the first concentration camps, and German townspeople are forced to witness the horrors that took place in these nearby institutions. Outraged prisoners attack their former guards.

The following portion of the film emphasizes the Soviet army's offensive on Berlin. The attack began symbolically with a huge artillery barrage on Lenin's birthday, April 21. Meanwhile, desperate German soldiers streamed westward to surrender to the Americans. The film calls in witnesses like Hitler's valet and his private secretary. They describe an eerie atmosphere in Hitler's Berlin bunker: a birthday party for the Fuhrer, political jockeying among the Nazi leaders, and the wedding of Hitler and Eva Braun.

As the Soviet noose tightens around Berlin, the film relies increasingly on interviews from participants at all levels. A German woman recounts being raped by Soviet soldiers. An anti-Nazi German talks about being released from a Gestapo prison. Soviet officers describe the climactic offensive, and, once again, the eyewitnesses in the bunker speak about the last hours of Hitler's life. The film concludes with British forces linking up with their Soviet allies. Meanwhile, Germans wander through the wreckage of their cities.

The film captures the grim atmosphere of a collapsing Germany. Its looting and fleeing refugees make an extraordinary contrast with the unreality of life in Hitler's inner circle. The film shows how even the most momentous events such as the end of the Nazi era arrive in a confusing, day by day manner. The range of interviewees is particularly impressive.

On the other hand the film shifts its focus repeatedly. It follows numerous developments on both sides of the battle line, and it is often overly detailed. Scenes of the liberation of Allied prisoners of war and concentration camp inmates are restrained. They give an unreal picture of the horrors and violence that accompanied these events. A more vivid picture of what the Allies found can be seen in With Hardship Their Garment (q.v.).

Occupation, Holland 1940-1944
(The World at War series)

52 minutes   color
1973   HBO\Thames Television

Summary: A lucid account of Holland under German occupation; it offers a panoramic picture of collaborators, resisters, and victims

Grade: B +

Occupation employs a narrator, extensive newsfilm, and interviews with Dutch eyewitnesses. One basic theme is the changing nature of the occupation. It began as a relatively mild set of policies, even toward the Jewish population, and reached increasing harshness and repression. A second theme is the diversity of the Dutch responses. They ranged from participation in anti-Nazi resistance activities to joining the Dutch Fascist Party or enlisting in an SS unit.

The first major portion of the film shows the overwhelming German invasion of Holland, including the terror bombing of the port of Rotterdam. Interviews reflect the Dutch sense of shock at being involved in war for the first time since 1815. The initial era of goodwill between the conquerors and conquered is illustrated by an early speech from Seyss Inquart, the Nazi official in charge of the occupation, in which he denies any German imperial designs for Holland and calls for cooperation between "two Germanic peoples." Goodwill gestures include a speedy return of Dutch war prisoners, Austrian holidays for Dutch school children, and a massive rally of Dutch Nazis under the leadership of Anton Mussert.

The occupation takes on more ominous overtones with a universal program of fingerprints, identity cards, and personal questionnaires. The questionnaires serve to identify Jewish members of the population. Within the first year, anti-Jewish actions lead to a strike by Dutch workers in support of their fellow citizens. On the other hand, the scope of collaboration widens. It is exemplified by the son of a leading German sympathizer who is sent to an SS school in Germany.

By the middle of the film, the entire atmosphere of occupation has changed. Hitler's invasion of the USSR leads Mussert to call for direct aid to Germany. Meanwhile, resistance groups and the Dutch broadcasts of the BBC keep the spark of independence alive. As the tide of war turns, the Germans conscript labor and start an elaborate system of coastal defenses.

The second half of the film is dominated by the deepening persecution of Dutch Jews, the growth of resistance, and the increasing hardships of occupation on the entire Dutch population. A film clip from the German propaganda film The Eternal Jew illustrates the invaders' campaign to stereotype and isolate Holland's Jewish population. Some of those interviewed recall what it was like being a member of an imperiled Jewish family or a bystander witnessing deportations one was unable to stop. Others interviewed describe the life of Jews in hiding and of resisters trying to maintain underground newspapers, to destroy German vehicles, and to strike out at Dutch collaborators. The film ends as the Allies liberate the extreme southern part of Holland at the close of 1944. The rest of the country is shown freezing and starving in the final winter of the conflict. Liberation remained months away.

The film lucidly traces the shifts in German occupation policy. Much of the newsfilm, such as the scene of young Dutchmen marching off to war as a newly formed SS unit, is rare and striking. The useful interviews cover a broad segment of the Dutch population. On the other hand, the film does not tie shifts in occupation policy clearly to changes in the overall course of the war. Also, there are no interviews that show events from the standpoint of the German occupiers.

Students can be asked to consider how occupation policies, and the experience of living under German occupation, varied between favored countries like Holland and more brutalized countries like Poland. The prominent role played by Dutch Nazis can be used as a basis for discussing the way in which many nations in the 1930s had produced extreme rightwing movements.

Reckoning, 1945 and After
(The World at War series)

52 minutes   color
1973   HBO\Thames Television

Summary: A lucid but episodic account of the participants in World War II, including the peoples in Europe's imperial possessions in Asia, at the close of the war and during the remaining months of 1945; it treats most issues briefly and lacks a sense of the emotional currents of the time

Grade: B -

Reckoning employs a narrator, newsfilm, maps, and interviews with eyewitnesses from a variety of backgrounds. The most significant theme in the film is the rising tension between the Western allies, led by the United States, and the Soviet Union. A second theme is Europe's postwar devastation and the initial efforts to rebuild the Continent. Finally, the film focuses on the collapse of European control in the non-Western world, and the ascendancy of the United States and the Soviet Union to the status of world powers.

The film begins by showing the surrender of masses of German troops to the Western allies, and the arrival of German refugees from Eastern Europe.

Meanwhile, American and Soviet forces meet at the center of the Continent. Interviews with an American veteran and Kay Summersby, General Eisenhower's aide, give diverse recollections of the Russians. Some recall their friendliness; others remember their basic hatred of Britain and the United States.

The film describes the growing mood of official tension between Moscow and Washington. It then shifts for a brief treatment of Japan's surrender, Douglas MacArthur's arrival as head of the occupying forces, and the liberation of American prisoners of war. The story shifts back to Europe for a discussion of the Nuremberg War Crimes Tribunal featuring an interview with the Lord Shawcross, a leading British prosecutors at the trials.

The second half of the film jumps back to Asia. It shows the Japanese surrender in this vast area and the difficulty of restoring European control. An interview with Lord Louis Mountbatten, the Allied commander in Southeast Asia, includes a consideration of the French determination to come back to Indo-China predominantly through the use of military power. As the narration notes, this set the stage for future tragedy. The remainder of Reckoning focuses on Europe and the United States. It presents the German population under military occupation, the great victory parades in the United States and the Soviet Union, and the demobilization and homecoming of British servicemen.

The film considers a wide range of significant developments. Despite its episodic character, it tells the story with clarity, and its interviews are informative. Interviewees include both significant participants in these events such as American diplomats Averell Harriman and Charles Bohlen as well as noted historians like Stephen Ambrose and Noble Frankland.

Unfortunately, the film proceeds slowly and its muted tone disguises the emotional turmoil of the time. Scenes of freed war prisoners and concentration camp inmates implausibly show only well-fed and well-clothed individuals. The scenes of devastated German cities and their supposedly impoverished citizens also seem deliberately sanitized. The medium of film is not suited to show the most crucial political development of the time: the growing rift between Moscow and Washington.

Red Star, The Soviet Union 1941-1943
(The World at War series)

52 minutes   color
1973   HBO\Thames Television

Summary: A gripping but diffuse examination of the Soviet experience in World War II; it focuses on the siege of Leningrad (1941-1944), the role of the civilian population, and the Battle of Kursk (1943)

Grade: B +

Red Star traces the Soviet wartime experience from the disasters and retreats of 1941 to the liberation of the motherland by the victorious Red Army. The film uses a narrator, maps, as well as Soviet and German newsfilm. There are also interviews with Soviet participants in the war: a Leningrad housewife, a partisan, a factory worker, and two high ranking army commanders at the Battle of Kursk. The basic themes are the harshness of the German occupation and the resilience and fortitude of the Soviet system in a time of crisis. The emotions of the time appear in gripping fashion in clips from feature films, wartime poetry, and the music of wartime Russia.

After a brief prologue showing Leningrad in the 1970s, the film presents a panoramic picture of the German invasion of 1941 and the responses it stimulated. These varied from a warm welcome to Hitler's forces by the minority populations of the Baltic states and the Ukraine to the scorched earth tactics of the Soviet government. The latter left industrial showpieces like the great Dnieper Dam in ruins.

The first half of the film concentrates on the Siege of Leningrad, in which millions of Soviet civilians were cut off in the nation's second city. Red Star stresses the hardships of the siege. Supplies could be brought in only over Lake Ladoga: they came by ship in warm weather, over an ice road in winter. Millions died of starvation and disease. Nonetheless, despite hunger and massive bombardment, the city held out, its population remaining disciplined and determined.

The second half of the film begins with the new German victories of 1942 such as the Battle of Kharkov. It follows with the Soviet and Allied efforts in that year: convoys of supplies sent to Murmansk through the German blockade; a Soviet government policy of identifying the regime with the Church and traditional Russian heroes like Alexander Nevsky, the medieval prince; the adoption by Soviet forces of the trappings of the pre-1917 army such as gold braid and guards regiments. Stirring renditions of wartime music accompany vivid scenes showing the devotion of the population to wartime arms production.

The final segments of the film shift to the last great German offensive on the eastern front: the failed tank attack at Kursk in July 1943. From there, Red Star traces the experience of liberation: cities welcoming the victorious Red Army, funerals for the battle dead, the destruction of Soviet resources by the retreating German army.

This account is consistently interesting and emotionally stirring. Two poems are quoted at length. "Wait" conveys the emotional strain of hoping for the return of a loved one from the front. "Farewell," recited at the close of the film, describes the acceptance of death in battle. Much of the newsfilm, including examples of the harsh treatment meted out to collaborators is vivid. On the other hand, the film touches on a large number of issues. It shifts its focus repeatedly from the homefront to purely military events such as the Battle of Kursk. The chronology of the early part the film is muddled. It moves in a confusing manner in one instance from the occupation as seen in 1942 back to scenes of the Germans arriving and establishing control in 1941. The narration touches on the harshness to which the government resorted, e.g., in deporting suspect ethnic groups like the Crimean Tartars. Nonetheless, it drops that theme, and its explanation for the Soviet success is the spontaneous outpouring of energy and anti-German feeling of the population.

Students can consider some of the neglected issues in the film. What was the role of Stalin's leadership and his wartime image? What was the relative importance of popular enthusiasm and the dictatorial control of the government in producing the Soviet victory?

Stalingrad, June 1942-February 1943
(World at War series)

52 minutes   color
1973   HBO\Thames Television

Summary: A lucid, harrowing, and well-balanced account of the epic battle of late 1942 and early 1943 that became the turning point of World War II in Europe; in presenting the battle from sides, the film captures the destructiveness and ferocity of Stalingrad for winner and loser alike

Grade: A

Stalingrad employs a narrator and animated maps. It quotes a diary kept by one soldier to indicate the changing mood of the imperiled German Sixth Army. Most of the film consists of combat footage of extremely high quality from both German and Russian sources.

After a brief prologue, the film begins with a map illustrating Hitler's offensive strategy on the eastern front. In 1942, he called for a massive strike eastward to the Volga. A subsequent map sequence shows Hitler shifting direction. He now ordered armies to throw their weight toward the Caucasus oil fields. This jeopardized the overly extended Sixth Army still advancing on Stalingrad. The first major segment of the film presents scenes of peacetime Stalingrad. A mobilization of its population takes place as the Germans approach, and combat newsfilm shows the initial German assaults on the city. At this stage, the diary of German soldier Wilhelm Hoffmann contains a hope the war will be over by Christmas.

Next, the film shows the increasingly effective Russian resistance within Stalingrad that the Germans encountered. Meanwhile, Hitler shakes up his high command as doubts about the Stalingrad campaign began to infect Germany's leading generals. At this stage, Hoffmann writes of fighting "fanatics" and "devils" employing "gangster methods. Grim scenes of street fighting combine with animated maps to show the precarious German position.

At the midway point in the film, the focus shifts to the Russian side. It shows the growing effectiveness of the military system, civilian workers supporting the fighting men, and the vast build-up of reserves threatening the German flanks. Scenes of the decisive Soviet attack in November 1942 include a staged reenactment of the linkup of the armies surrounding Stalingrad. The actual joining of the Soviet pincers came too fast to be recorded. There is a good sampling of the Soviet martial music of the time.

The final portion of <u>Stalingrad</u> shows the growing desperation of the German Sixth Army. Frozen and starving, they were assailed by Soviet armies as obsessed with obliterating them as Hitler was obsessed with taking the city. The closing sequences of the film show the debris of defeat: hordes of wretched German prisoners, mass cemeteries, tons of shattered equipment. Scenes of joyful Soviet citizens include a brief shot of a youthful Nikita Khrushchev, at that time a lieutenant general in the Soviet army.

The film is dramatic, gripping, and even harrowing to watch. The newsfilm and the narration emphasize the German point of view, but the Soviet side of the conflict comes across well. The excerpts from Hoffmann's diary are memorable in showing the disintegration of German hopes. Some scenes, such as Field Marshal von Paulus meeting with Soviet leaders to surrender his army are memorable.

The flaws of the film are minor. The strategic thinking of Hitler and his high command looms large in this account, but there is no comparable discussion of high level planning on the Soviet side. Some of the strategy of the campaign is left unclear: viewers are not told, for example, that the counterattacking Soviets failed to take Rostov. Thus, the Germans in the Caucasus were able to withdraw without suffering the fate of the army at Stalingrad.

Students can be asked to consider this account in comparison with the one in <u>France Falls</u> (q.v.). What made the difference between countries that fell to the Nazi onslaught and those that did not? In the same category, students can be asked how the film shows the difficulties of Hitler's army in the novel circumstances of urban warfare. Hitler's lack of military realism and successful demand for fanatic sacrifices from his army can launch a discussion of the strengths and weaknesses of the Nazi system and the German army.

<u>Whirlwind, Bombing Germany September 1939-April 1944</u>
(<u>The World at War</u> series)

52 minutes   color
1973   HBO\Thames Television

Summary: A graphic, harrowing, and informative examination of the Allied bombing campaign against Germany from 1939 to the spring of 1944; it presents the campaign from both sides and shows the reactions from participants at all levels

Grade: A

Whirlwind uses a narrator and features extensive footage of combat air operations and the life of air crews. There are interviews with pilots, air force leaders, and civilians in bombed cities, as well as selections from the music and the propaganda films of the period. The basic theme is the escalation of the Allied air campaign over the course of the war. It went from attacks on precise targets at the start of the war to assaults on entire German cities and their civilian populations.   Another theme is the thrust and counterthrust of tactics and technology as each side sought ways to gain an advantage. Finally, the film investigates the stress of war on the individual, both combatant and non-combatant.

A prologue indicates several facets of the air war: the view of the individual flyer toward bombing civilians, the optimism of RAF Air Marshall Sir Arthur Harris that strategic bombing can win the war for the Allies, and an aerial view of the damage being done by incendiary bombs. The film sketches the pre-war history of the RAF. Although the basic purpose of the British air force was strategic bombing, the Battle of Britain in 1940 showed how well a country could defend itself against such attacks.

Whirlwind goes on to recount the early efforts at precision bombing. Failures and heavy losses accompanied these attacks. In early 1942, when Harris took over RAF Bomber Command, he began a campaign of attacks against entire German cities. That pattern dominated the air war for the next three years. The remainder of the first half of the film shows the escalation of the air campaign on both sides. The British launched huge raids starting with one against Cologne in May 1942 involving a thousand bombers. They employed radio transmissions to guide their forces to German targets. The Germans countered with radar guided fighter defenses. Meanwhile, the American air force, with its strategy of daylight bombing, joins the air campaign. A German and British pilot both recount their experiences. American actor Jimmy Stewart, then a colonel in the air force, describes American aerial tactics. Albert Speer explains how German industry was able to keep going even under air attacks.

The second half of the film emphasizes the human cost of the air war. There are scenes of Allied bombers being shot down and mutilated American flyers being removed from smashed planes. In an interview, a British pilot describes being hit by anti-aircraft fire. Dramatic film from Hamburg, which was the target of devastating air attacks in the summer of 1943, shows part of the German side of the story. Interviews with Allied leaders like American generals Curtis LeMay and Ira Eaker show the optimism and determination that pushed the attacks on. A British newsreel account stresses the effectiveness of the bombing. There follow scenes from a musical production in Berlin emphasizing the resilience of the German population.

The film ends abruptly by introducing two new elements. American long-range fighters now escorted bombers all the way to their targets. Thus, Germany was increasingly helpless against air assault. Meanwhile, the Allies shifted air resources away from Germany to Northwestern Europe in preparation for the Normandy invasion.

Whirlwind is brilliantly written and edited. It offers intriguing contrasts. For example, it presents both the viewpoint of individual pilots and the senior strategists directing their efforts. It places the experience of air crews in combat side by side with their hours on leave in London shortly thereafter. Albert Speer speaks about the limited effectiveness of the bombing; then, a Hamburg journalist describes the decimation of the civilian population in his city.

Students can consider the gap between pre-war planning and the reality that appeared after 1939. Another topic to consider is the psychological and organizational strengths that permitted civilians and airmen to survive this experience. Finally, one can explore the way in which technology developed in the response to the course of the conflict.

With Hardship Their Garment: The English, D-Day and the Holocaust
(Europe: The Mighty Continent series)

52 minutes   color
1974   BBC

Summary: A skillfully constructed and eloquent account of World War II in Europe

Grade: A -

The film employs narrators John Terraine and Peter Ustinov, newsfilm, works of art, maps, and visits to important historical locales. There are excerpts from Winston Churchill's speeches and present-day views of the aircraft that won the Battle of Britain. The main theme of the film is the vast scope of the war and the enormous wounds it inflicted on European civilization.

With Hardship begins with the narrators noting how Eruopeans were horrified in 1939 to find the recent experience of World War I being repeated. The conflict now beginning would come close to destroying European civilization, and it would inflict hardships that continued long after the fighting ended.

The first images of the film show the success of Hitler's attack on Poland. They emphasize the damage done to Warsaw and the rest of the conquered country. It was a harbinger of what was to befall most of the Continent. Following an account of Hitler's victory in the West in 1940, Peter Ustinov introduces a lighter note by talking about his experiences in a poorly equipped army unit assigned to defend Dover. The remainder of the first half of the film traces the war through the German invasion of the Soviet Union. Most scenes show a victorious Germany. Nonetheless, the successful defense of cities like Leningrad marked a turning point in the conflict. The narration makes the important point that the German attack on the Soviet Union vastly expanded the scope and the consequent cost of the war to both sides.

The second half of the film shows America's growing role in the conflict. A central event the narration considers is the Allied dilemma in Italy involving the Monastery at Monte Cassino. It was one of the great monuments of Western civilization, but it also appeared to be a key German stronghold. John Terraine uses the destruction of the monastery by aerial attack to exemplify the horrible cost to European culture the war was exacting. Then, Peter Ustinov visits the German bunkers at Normandy. He uses them as an example of how the course of the conflict had changed. In 1940, the French had huddled behind the Maginot line leaving the initiative to a more powerful enemy. In 1944, on the French coast, the Germans took on the same passive role.

The film closes on a note of undiluted horror. Both narrators discuss the liberation of the concentration camps. The accompanying pictures of broken bodies and mass graves appear in uncensored and graphic form.

With Hardship successfully presents the most significant themes and events of the European war. It integrates the military course of the conflict, major diplomatic meetings, and personal recollections. At times the account pace speeds up notably, but, on the whole, it remains accessible even to someone unfamiliar with the course of the war.

Students can be asked to consider how the future must have looked to an average European from the winning and the losing side of the war.

HOLOCAUST

Genocide, 1941-1945
(The World at War series)

52 minutes   color
1973   HBO \Thames Television

Summary: A carefully organized, vivid, and harrowing depiction of the murder of European Jewry by Nazi Germany; it extends from the roots of genocide in pre-war Nazi thought to the liberation of the death camps in the first months of 1945

Grade: A -

The film employs a narrator, maps, still photographs, newsfilm, and interviews with participants ranging from Anthony Eden, the British Minister of War, to SS officers and death camp survivors. The basic theme of the film is how Heinrich Himmler's vision of a purely Aryan society was translated into a horrific reality. It became a substantially successful, step by step campaign to exterminate the Jews of Europe.

Unlike other episodes in the series, Genocide begins with the narrator, Sir Laurence Olivier, cautioning the audience about the film's graphic horrors. The first portion of the film focuses on the ideas of Heinrich Himmler. He dreamed of restoring an allegedly pure, ancient German culture. In practice this meant trying to breed Aryan supermen out of the youth of contemporary Germany. His most important instrument was the SS, modeled on the Jesuit order. He is shown personally administering its "oath unto death" to new recruits.

Implementing Himmler's racial dreams also meant waging war against Germany's Jews.   The film demonstrates their escalating persecution. Propaganda films libel them. The Nazis burn their synagogues on Crystal Night in November 1938. Hitler raises the specter of extermination in a threatening speech in January 1939. The outbreak of the war and the rapid conquest of Poland brought a new Jewish population under German control. Genocide shows the deliberately catastrophic conditions created in new Polish ghettoes. The German attack on the Soviet Union in the summer of 1941 leads to direct execution of masses of Jews by the "inefficient" device of firing squads.

The second half of the film begins with the Wannsee Conference of January, 1942. There plans took shape for murder factories designed to kill with poison gas. The victims' bodies would be disposed of in crematoria.   The remainder of this account uses the viewpoint of victims to explain how the extermination camps operated. It also shows that leaders and even average newspaper readers in Allied countries were aware of what was happening. A brief interview with Anthony Eden indicates the ineffectual response. Rare footage, such as the scenes showing the conditions within the Warsaw Ghetto, indicates the atrocities that preceded the extermination camps. The essence of the film, however, comes in the statements by camp survivors: from Poland, Czechoslovakia, Hungary, and Holland.   For example, speaking with eerie composure, Dov Paisikowic, a Hungarian Jew, recounts his experiences as a forced worker at Auschwitz. In all, the film vividly ties the fantasy of a racially pure society to the entire enterprise of the Holocaust

The film's dramatic impact is unforgettable, but there are some minor flaws. The focus on Himmler (and his subordinate Adolf Eichmann) encourages the viewer to forget the essential role of Adolf Hitler in the course of this crime.

The important postwar debate over what the Allies could have done to hinder the operation of the death camps gets little attention.

Students can be asked to consider how Europeans, came to grips with the fact that their civilization had produced such an ultimate horror. What did this meant for one's expectations for the future of European society?

Night and Fog

32 minutes   color
1955   McGraw-Hill

Summary: A vivid and horrifying examination of the German concentration camps and death factories of World War II

Grade: B +

Night and Fog employs a French-speaking narrator (with English subtitles) along with present-day views and archival film footage of the camps. There are also a number of still photographs. One theme of the film is the contrast between the shabby, deserted camp sites of today and the multifaceted horror they embodied in the 1940s. A second theme is the way in which the perpetrators of these atrocities were not intrinsically different from humanity in general.

The film is impressionistic rather than rigidly chronological. It begins with color scenes of a concentration camp today, a "peaceful landscape" filled with weeds, deserted buildings, and crumbling walls. A memorable scene at the beginning shows how the entrance to the camp appeared to a World prisoner arriving by train. With a minimum of narration or chronology, the first two-thirds of the film moves from the Nazis' early moments in power to roundups throughout Europe, and the horrors of camp life. Interspersed with grisly scenes from the 1940s are more shots of the camps today. They appear shabby relics of a bygone era.

The final portion of the film stresses the camps as scenes of mass, industrialized execution. Himmler arrives in 1942 to redirect the purpose of the camps. The crematoria go from architectural drawings to operating reality. The horrors of mass extermination are recorded in a variety of ways: fingernail scratches on the concrete ceilings of the gas chambers, half burned bodies in funeral pyres, baskets filled with the heads of the victims. A memorable aerial shot of a camp in 1945 gives an eerie sense of the vastness of the entire enterprise.

The film concludes with scenes of the camps being liberated, and their officials being placed on trial. At the close, the narrator reminds the viewer that such monstrous urges remain alive. We must wonder, he asks, who the next executioner will be.

The film combines a restrained narration with unforgettable visual images. Shifting from historical footage to the present-day reality of these sites of horror is notably effective. But, despite its strengths, Night and Fog presents some difficulties. Following the narration in the original French requires a very high competence in the language. The subtitles are often illegible against the background of the film's images. The overall ideology that led to the death camps is not explored. Thus, Genocide (q.v.) provides a more systematic, but not more moving, consideration of this topic.

Students can be asked to consider the contrast between the superhuman effort required to organize this enterprise and the subhuman morality that its operation exhibited. Do the camps provide a view of the boundaries of human qualities?

Out of the Ashes
(Heritage: Civilization and the Jews series)

60 minutes   color
1984   WNET

Summary: A lucid, harrowing, and incisive survey of the fate of European Jews in the first half of the twentieth century; it stresses the origins and impact of the Holocaust

Grade: A

The film employs narrator Abba Eban, newsfilm, photographs, interviews with eyewitnesses, visits to scenes of historical significance, as well as actors reading from documents of the time. The basic theme of the film is how the Jews became the chief victims of a disrupted and unstable era in European history in which the norms of civilization no longer commanded a consensus. A secondary theme is how the apparent success of Jews in fully entering European life at the start of the century proved illusory.

Out of the Ashes begins with a striking sequence in which an actor's voice reads a passage from Franz Kafka's The Trial. It reflects the psychology of an uncomprehending victim of the modern state. The reading is accompanied by film images taken from Germany in the Nazi era.

The first segment of the film, approximately ten minutes in length, presents images from the 1920s. They show positive elements like the cultural freedom of the Jazz age and the success enjoyed by prominent Jews like Albert Einstein. The images then change to reflect social tensions as seen in tormented paintings of Georg Grosz and scenes from the fascist state Mussolini was forming in Italy. Thus, narrator Abba Eban introduces the key theme that European society had splintered; compromise among Europeans was increasingly out of reach. In this age without consensus, he notes, the Jews would be the chief victims of the time. This extended introduction ends with a sampling of the thriving Yiddish culture to be found in films, newspapers, and in the masses of East European Jewry. Another perspective on Jewish life appears in images of Zionist settlers in Palestine.

The remainder of the film focuses on Germany and Europe in the Nazi era. Using contemporary views of Dachau and other German locales and gripping archive footage, the film examines the rising tide of persecution. Nazi propaganda chief Joseph Goebbels directs and gloats over the burning of Jewish books. In contrast, Mayor Fiorello La Guardia protests Nazi persecution of the Jews in a Madison Avenue Square Garden rally of the 1930s.

The second half of the film deals with the war years. Scenes of the German army invading Poland give way to heartbreaking views of families, apparently from rural Jewish villages, being separated by the victorious Germans. Eban makes the important point that it was the series of German military successes, especially in Eastern Europe, that brought very large numbers of Jews under German control. This set the stage for the Holocaust. Out of the Ashes shows the horror of life in crowded ghettoes like the one in Cracow, where the bodies of victims of illness and starvation are gathered from the street. This gives way to eyewitness accounts of death camps like Auschwitz.

The film gives some attention to important accompanying themes of the Holocaust years. It discusses armed resistance by Jews in the Warsaw Ghetto and in partisan bands in the forests of Eastern Europe as well as the successful efforts of the Danes and other nationalities to shield their Jews from extermination. It also raises the issue of the failure of Allied governments to block operation of the Holocaust machine. Scenes from Oradour-sur-Glane, the French village whose entire population was murdered in June 1944, remind the viewer that the Jews were not the only victims of Nazi inhumanity.

The last minutes of the film show the masses of displaced persons in Europe in the summer of 1945. They included 100,000 Jewish survivors of the death camps. There are contemporary views of Cracow where a synagogue and cemetery survive although the huge Jewish population has virtually disappeared. In a final moment, Elie Wiesel speaks eloquently about the significance of the Holocaust.

The film is lucid, vivid, and emotionally striking. Its composition around the central event of the Holocaust is impeccable. The interviews with individual Jews who recount their experiences as refugees, death camp inmates, and resistance fighters are particularly valuable. It compares favorably with Genocide, although the latter gives more attention to such topics as Nazi ideology.

POST-WORLD WAR II ERA

The Aftermath

See How Are the Mighty Fallen

A Certain Amount of Violence: The New Europe
(Europe: The Mighty Continent series)

52 minutes   color
1976   BBC

Summary: An uninspired presentation of key events in European history from the Hungarian and Suez crises of 1956 to the close of the 1960s; despite the numerous dramatic topics its considers, it is flat and unexciting

Grade: C +

     A Certain Amount of Violence uses narrators John Terraine and Peter Ustinov, newsfilm, and visits to important historical locales. The main theme of the film is the trauma that struck Europe in late 1956 and the depressed political atmosphere that followed. A second theme is the shrinking of Europe's global role, as seen in the wave of decolonization and the pivotal, if evolving Soviet-American relationship.
     The film begins by showing a Polish audience for an outdoor playing of Chopin. This emphasizes the continuing force of nationalism in Eastern Europe. Next, it presents the twin crises of late 1956. The Russians crush the Hungarian Uprising while the French and British engage in a futile colonial expedition against the Egyptians in Suez. Both events, the narration notes, illustrate the futility and weakness of European role in the NATO alliance.

When President Dwight Eisenhower condemned the move at Suez and forced an Anglo-French withdrawal, the film claims, relations between the United Sates and its key European allies were permanently impaired. Moving in a different direction, the film examines the existentialism of the Parisian intellectual community and the personality of Jean Paul Sartre. These supposedly show Europe mired in pessimism as it faces its impotence.

The second half of the film ranges even more widely. It considers the European departure from empires in Asia and especially Africa, the movement toward European union, and the evolution of Soviet control in Eastern Europe. Other topics include the Cuban Missile Crisis, the space race, and the emergence of an affluent society. The latter is shown giving rise to a youth culture distinguished by bizarre dress and behavior.

This account places a host of developments before the camera. Virtually no major event from the mid-1950s to the late 1960s fails to appear here. The very inclusiveness of the film, however, becomes a failing. All events are offered with equal emphasis. There is no effort to capture the drama in developments like the Hungarian Uprising, the hasty Belgian departure from the Congo, or Charles de Gaulle's visit to Algeria after returning to power in 1958. Viewers are likely to smother in a heap of undifferentiated detail.

A European Idea: The Search for Unity
(Europe: The Mighty Continent series)

52 minutes   color
1976   BBC

Summary: A verbose and confused episode that concludes a distinguished series on twentieth century Europe; it combines a view of the century to date with an effort to glimpse the future

Grade: D

The film employs narrators John Terraine and Peter Ustinov, newsfilm, maps, works of art, and visits to sites of historic significance. There is no coherent theme in the film. John Terraine attempts to identify the basic trends of the first seven decades of the century, but the film delves into a potpourri of topics ranging from student unrest and the growth of the European Common Market.

The film begins with statements by both narrators. Peter Ustinov stresses the unrest that has marked the twentieth century, making it "an action-packed story." John Terraine, speaking from the ruins of the Roman Forum, ponders the possibility for European unity. From that point, A European Idea moves forward without a discernible structure. There is a long segment on university unrest in the 1960s culminating in the events of 1968 in Paris that nearly overthrew Charles de Gaulle. The film considers the Czech crisis of that same year, then moves into a detailed, Anglocentric account of the Common Market. Peter Ustinov details his work with the United Nations Childrens Fund.

In the second half of the film, John Terraine discusses the wars of the twentieth century and the development of repressive forms of government. He claims that the conflicts of the future are likely to take place within existing states, such as Britain's territory in Northern Ireland and Yugoslavia. He also remarks on the growing role of technology in modern life.

The film's lack of structure makes virtually impossible to follow. Made in the mid-1970s, its statements about future developments, e.g., in Yugoslavia, have been taken over by reality.

How Are the Mighty Fallen: The Aftermath
(Europe: The Mighty Continent series)

52 minutes   color
1976   BBC

Summary: A poorly paced but inclusive picture of crucial events within Europe from the close of World War II to the death of Stalin

Grade: B -

The film employs narrators John Terraine and Peter Ustinov, newsfilm, and visits to important historical locales. The main theme is the development of postwar Europe into two new hostile alliances of nations as was the case in 1914. A second theme is the Continent's economic revival, and the sense many Europeans had, following Khrushchev's denunciation of Stalin in early 1956, that their continent poised on the brink of momentous change.

How Are the Mighty Fallen begins with a long segment showing millions of displaced persons and shattered cities, the human and material aftermath of the war. Scenes of Polish refugees housed in displaced persons' camps in Wales in the mid 1970s illustrate the persistence of the human disruption. Sparkling urban reconstruction in cities like Warsaw shows how much more easily the physical cost of the war was reversed.

The film examines the founding of the United Nations and its location in New York, noting this was a sign of Europe's declining influence. So too was the massive admission of the new states of Asia and Africa into the international organization. The civil war in Greece and vivid scenes of postwar austerity in Britain complete the picture of a Europe hanging on by its fingertips. A frivolous development serves to break the gloom: the "New Look" fashion revival of Christian Dior.

During the second half of the film, the focus falls on the growing estrangement of the United States and the Soviet Union. It considers Europe's economic recovery via the Marshall plan, the development of nuclear weapons, and Czechoslovakia's forced entry into the Soviet camp. In contrast, Yugoslavia escaped from a Soviet link at the same time. Divided Germany appears as "the epicenter of the Cold War" with the Berlin Blockade and Airlift of 1948-49 as the crucial events. Stalin's death in 1953 and the ensuing power struggle in the Soviet Union opened the way for change that could offer new hope or disaster for Eastern Europeans.

The film encompasses the crucial themes in European history over this period. It uses newsfilm with dramatic effect, e.g., in showing the austerity winter of 1946-47. The recovery sparked by the Marshall Plan appears vividly in present-day scenes of Austria's scenic Limburg Dam. The film makes a useful point in noting the diverse possibilities Europeans saw in early 1956 in the wake of Khrushchev's speech denouncing Stalin. At the same time, the film moves rapidly through numerous issues, and it omits any effort to show the drama inherent in these events. For example, scenes of East European Communist leaders on trial during the waning years of the Stalinist period omit the fantastic confessions the defendants uttered. The cultural revival seen in the English theater is presented with a complete lack of imagination merely by showing copies of playbills.

Students can consider how the film, which strives mightily for objectivity, reflects the Anglocentrism of its narrators and the perspective of the mid-1970s.

Human Rights, Fundamental Freedoms

See review under WORLD WAR II

In Our Own Time
(Art of the Western World series)

60 minutes   color
1989   WNET

Summary: A nearly incoherent discussion of artistic trends in Europe and the United States after World War

Grade: D

The film uses a narrator, the art of the time, photos and film clips, interviews with leading art historians, and visits to the locales where important art has been produced. The basic theme of the film is the lack of direction and coherence in the art world after 1945.

In Our Own Time lacks any perceptible organization. It begins with an atomic bomb test in the Nevada desert. The narrator notes that this ultimate weapon, and the catastrophe for mankind it threatened, cast a shadow over all post-World War II art. The film makes the point that Europeans were inclined to reflect the horror of their World War II experience. On the other hand, American artists stayed apart from politics, developing new movements such as Abstract Expressionism as exemplified in the work of Jackson Pollock. Next, the film introduces a cavalcade of mainly American artists, including De Kooning, Rothko, Warhol, Liechtenstein and the movements to which they belong. The year 1968 is presented as a landmark point following which established traditions of Western art suffered even greater abandonment than before.

The film can serve only to show, in lengthy and unpalatable form, the confusing cross currents that have buffeted Western Civilization since 1945. The basic incoherence of the presentation is exacerbated by lengthy technical analyses of the various works and trends presented.

The New Europe

See A Certain Amount of Violence

The Search for Unity

See A European Idea

SUBJECT INDEX

Welles, Orson, 10
Wesley, John, 129
Whitefield, George, 129
Wiesel, Elie, 216
Wilberforce, William, 141
Wilhelm II of Germany, 157. See also William II of Germany
William II of Germany, 156, 172
William the Conqueror, 52
Wilson, Woodrow, 167, 171
"Witchcraft craze," 105
Wolfe, James, 122
Woodforde, James, 129
Wordsworth, William, 126, 135, 149
Worms, 87
WPA, 175
Wreck of the Medusa, 121

Wren, Christopher, 110
Wright, Frank Lloyd, 161
Wuthering Heights, 149
Wycliffe, John, 76, 83

Yalta Conference, 194, 199
Yiddish, 150, 216
Ypres, 168, 171
Yugoslavia, 193, 219-20

Zanzibar, 145, 153
Zeppelin airships, 160
Zhukov, Georgi, 193
Zionist movement, 150, 216
Zurich, 186
Zwingli, Uldrich, 87

SERIES INDEX

TITLE INDEX

About the Author

NEIL M. HEYMAN is professor of history at San Diego State University. His previous books include the *Biographical Dictionary of World War I* (Greenwood, 1982) and *Russian History* (1993).

ISBN 0-313-28438-5

EAN

9 780313 284380

90000>

HARDCOVER BAR CODE